The 100% Complete Illustrated Guide to Japanese Systems:
Society, Customs, Health Care, Recreation, and Sports

装幀 ● 菊地信義
装画 ● 野村俊夫

翻訳 ● Lucy North
　　　David Thayne

編集協力 ● 株式会社 日本実業出版社

Published by Kodansha International Ltd.,
17-14 Otowa 1-chome, Bunkyo-ku, Tokyo 112-8652

First Edition, 2001
　　03 04 05　10 9 8 7 6 5 4 3 2

ISBN 4-7700-2727-3

全図解
日本のしくみ
［生活文化・社会・医療・娯楽・スポーツ編］
The 100% Complete Illustrated Guide to
Japanese Systems:
Society, Customs, Health Care, Recreation, and Sports

安部直文［著］
テッド・高橋［イラスト］

まえがき

本書は、1月に上梓した講談社バイリンガル・ブックス『全図解日本のしくみ［政治・経済・司法編］』の続編です。2冊合わせると取り上げている項目が190になり、とかく不明瞭とされがちなわが国の社会のしくみの輪郭がほのかに見えてくるはずです。前著ともども、ご愛読いただければ幸いです。

21世紀を迎えた日本は、あらゆる分野で「制度改革」が進行中です。本書でご紹介しているのは、そうした流動的なしくみの一断面であり、その"入り口"に過ぎません。したがって、興味をもたれた項目についての現状をさらに詳しく知りたい方は、自らお調べくださることをおすすめします。また著者には、当然ながら折り折りの改訂の義務があると心得ます。

日本の社会のしくみは国際化・情報化といった時流に合わせて変化していますが、その底流には日本人のオリジナリティーともいうべき精神の不変の流れがあると、私は見ています。それは、若き日に私淑したドイツ文学者の高橋義孝氏の「(人生とは) 精神的身銭を切って初めて、その返報に、その代償に、ものが見えてくる、ものの味がわかってくるしくみなのではあるまいか」という言葉に象徴されます。この"人生のしくみ"へのアプローチこそが、日本を、日本人を深く理解する近道ではないかと思うのです。

バイリンガル・ブックスシリーズに拙著を加えていただくきっかけをつくってくださった講談社インターナショナル編集部の浦晋亮さん、ご協力いただいた日本実業出版社書籍出版部の皆さんに、感謝いたします。

2001年4月

安部　直文

Preface

This book is the continuation of The Complete Illustrated Guide to Japanese Systems: Politics, Economics, Law and Order which was published in the Bilingual Books series in January 2001. Taken together the two volumes cover a total of one hundred and ninety topics. This should be sufficient for readers to start to get a general sense of Japan's various notoriously hard-to-understand systems. I sincerely hope that people will read and enjoy both volumes.

As we enter the twenty-first century, Japan is experiencing 'system revolutions' in almost every field. This book is therefore no more than a way to get to grips with just a part of the ever-evolving systems which it talks about. I strongly recommend that readers take it upon themselves to look deeper into the subjects which interest them and about which they wish to know more. It goes without saying that I, as the author, have a duty to update and revise the book at intervals.

The systems of Japanese society are changing in step with the current trends of globalization and information technology. I do, however, believe that beneath the zeitgeist there flows an unchanging undercurrent-the unique and original spirit of the Japanese people. When I was young I was deeply impressed by the words of Yoshitaka Takahashi, a scholar of German literature whom I admired. "Life" he said, "is a system whereby only those who first dip deep into their funds of spiritual capital will see any return on their investment." This approach of looking at life itself as a 'system' is an excellent shortcut to understanding Japan and the Japanese.

Finally I should like to thank Kuniaki Ura, my editor at Kodansha International who arranged for the inclusion of this book in the Bilingual Books series, as well as everyone at Nippon Jitsugyo Publications Book Division.

Naobumi Abe
April 2001

目次
CONTENTS

まえがき————4
Preface

第1章 家庭の中を見わたせば
意外と知らないことだらけ！

Chapter 1: Even in Your Own Home
There's a Lot You Don't Know

確定申告のしくみ————16
Filing an Income Tax Return

地価のしくみ————18
Land prices

国勢調査のしくみ————20
The National Census

郵便配達のしくみ————22
Postal Delivery Service

宅配サービスのしくみ————26
Delivery Service

クーリング・オフのしくみ————30
"Cooling Off"

ゴミ処理のしくみ————32
Waste Disposal

米の流通のしくみ————34
Rice Distribution

ミネラルウォーター流通のしくみ————38
The Distribution of Mineral Water

牛乳の製品化のしくみ————40
Milk Products

第2章 ゆりかごから墓場まで
ウ〜ン、人生って複雑だ〜！

Chapter 2: From Cradle to Grave
Why Is Everything So Complicated?

戸籍制度のしくみ————44
Family Register System

養子縁組のしくみ————48
Adoption Alliance

結婚のしくみ————50
Marriage

離婚のしくみ————52
Divorce

教科書採用のしくみ————54
Selection of School Textbooks

教育委員会のしくみ————56
Boards of Education

大学入試のしくみ————60
University Entrance Examinations

海外留学のしくみ————62
Study Abroad

公正証書作成のしくみ————64
Drawing Up a Certificate of Seal Registration

叙勲のしくみ————66
Decorations

文化勲章授与のしくみ————70
The Order of Cultural Merit

葬儀社のしくみ————72
Funeral Undertakers

法事のしくみ————76
Memorial Service

遺産相続のしくみ————78
Property Inheritance

第3章　街でなじみのランド・マーク
しくみを知ると、いっそう親しみが湧くぞ！

Chapter 3 : Common City Landmarks
A Little Knowledge Goes a Long Way

宝くじ販売のしくみ————82
Lotteries

共同募金のしくみ————84
Joint Fund-raising

書店のしくみ———— 86
Bookstores

古書店のしくみ———— 90
Second-hand Bookstores

画廊のしくみ————92
Art Galleries

自動販売機のしくみ————94
Automatic Vending Machines

JAのしくみ————98
JA

生協のしくみ———— 100
The Japanese Consumers' Cooperative Union

公衆浴場のしくみ———— 102
Public Baths

駅のしくみ———— 104
Stations

カラオケボックスのしくみ————108
Karaoke Boxes

第4章　どうなってるの？　この仕事
長年の謎が解けるかも!?

Chapter 4 : Who Does What
Questions about Jobs You've Always Wanted to Ask

コンパニオンのしくみ————112
"Companions"

石焼芋屋のしくみ────────── 114
The Stone-Baked Sweet Potato Vendor

落とし物処分のしくみ────────── 116
Treatment of Lost Property

邦人保護のしくみ────────── 118
Protection of Japanese Nationals

高速道路料金のしくみ────────── 120
Highway Tolls

新聞拡張業のしくみ────────── 122
Newspaper Subscription Canvassing

野犬処分のしくみ────────── 124
The Treatment of Stray Dogs

マンガ制作のしくみ────────── 126
The Production of Manga

アニメ制作のしくみ────────── 130
The Production of "Anime"

視聴率のしくみ────────── 134
TV Audience Ratings

天気予報のしくみ────────── 136
Weather Forecasts

有線放送のしくみ────────── 140
Cable Broadcasts

第5章 知っててよかった業界のウラオモテ
これであなたもギョーカイ通!?

Chapter 5 : Behind the Scenes at the Industrial Level
Now You Know It All

コンビニのしくみ────────── 144
Convenience Stores

パチンコ店のしくみ────────── 146
Pachinko Parlors

小売業界のしくみ────────── 148
Retail Trade

観光バスツアーのしくみ────────── 152
Guided Bus Tours

タクシー業界のしくみ———————— 156
The Taxi Industry

ブライダル業界のしくみ———————— 160
The Bridal Industry

生保業界のしくみ———————— 164
The Life Insurance Industry

テレビ放映権のしくみ———————— 168
TV Broadcasting Rights

第6章　規制緩和でここがこうなる
この程度じゃあ、とても満足できないかも!?

Chapter 6： What Will Change with Deregulation
Who'll Be Happy and Who Not

車検制度のしくみ———————— 172
Automobile Safety Inspection

ガソリンスタンドのしくみ———————— 176
Gas Stations

銀行サービスのしくみ———————— 180
Bank Services

食品表示のしくみ———————— 184
Food Labeling

飼犬登録のしくみ———————— 188
Dog Licensing

個人輸入のしくみ———————— 192
Private Purchasing of Foreign Goods

再販売価格維持制度のしくみ———————— 196
The Resale Price Maintenance System

住宅容積率のしくみ———————— 200
Floor-area Ratio Regulations

第**7**章　ちょっと気になる社会現象
知らないとソンするよ！

Chapter 7:　Some Interesting Social Phenomena
The Whys and Wherefores

PL法のしくみ──────── 204
The Product Liability Law

悪徳商法のしくみ──────── 206
Commercial Malpractice

相続税物納のしくみ──────── 210
Inheritance Tax Payment in Kind

自己破産のしくみ──────── 212
Declaration of "Self Bankruptcy"

過労死認定のしくみ──────── 214
Death from Overwork

定期借地権付き住宅のしくみ──────── 216
House Built on Leased Land

廃棄物処理のしくみ──────── 220
Waste Disposal

第**8**章　この違いがわかれば……
世の中は2倍おもしろい！

Chapter 8:　Knowing the Difference Goes a Long Way
A Case of Organizational Look-alikes

幼稚園と保育園の違い──────── 226
Kindergartens and Nursery Schools

育児休業と介護休業の違い──────── 228
Childcare Leave and Care Leave

商品券とギフトカードの違い──────── 230
Gift Certificates and Gift Cards

地震保険と火災保険の違い──────── 232
Earthquake and Fire Insurance

手形と小切手の違い──────── 234
Bank Drafts and Checks

上場株と店頭株の違い——————— 236
Listed Stocks and Over-the-Counter Stocks

信用金庫と信用組合の違い——————— 238
Credit Associations and Credit Unions

本醸造酒と吟醸酒の違い——————— 240
Authentically Brewed Sake and Quality Sake

第9章　医学の進歩は永遠なり
命にかかわる大事なことです！

Chapter 9： Medicine Marches On
It's a Matter of Life and Death

医療費のしくみ——————— 246
Medical Expenses

認定医承認制度のしくみ——————— 248
The Doctor Specialization System

在宅医療のしくみ——————— 250
Home Medical Care

介護保険のしくみ——————— 252
Long-term Care Insurance

脳死判定のしくみ——————— 254
Declaration of Brain Death

臓器移植のしくみ——————— 256
Organ Transplants

骨髄バンクのしくみ——————— 260
Bone Marrow Banks

予防接種のしくみ——————— 262
Vaccinations

医薬分業のしくみ——————— 264
The Separation of Pharmacy and Clinic

新薬許可のしくみ——————— 266
Approval of New Medicine

薬価差益のしくみ——————— 268
Differences in Medicine Prices

第10章　娯楽とスポーツの世界へようこそ
そうそう。これを知りたかったの！

Chapter 10： Sports and Entertainment
Some Facts You Never Knew

祇園のしくみ――――― 272
The Rules of Gion

宝塚歌劇団のしくみ――――― 276
The Takarazuka All Women's Opera Company

歌舞伎界のしくみ――――― 280
The Kabuki World

落語界のしくみ――――― 284
The World of Rakugo (Traditional Comic Monologues)

将棋界のしくみ――――― 288
Shogi

囲碁界のしくみ――――― 292
Go

プロ野球界のしくみ――――― 296
Professional Baseball

ＦＡ制度のしくみ――――― 300
The Free Agent System

ドラフト制度のしくみ――――― 302
The Draft System

Ｊリーグのしくみ――――― 304
The J. League

プロゴルフ界のしくみ――――― 308
Professional Golf

競馬界のしくみ――――― 312
Horseracing

相撲界のしくみ――――― 316
The World of Sumo Wrestling

打ち上げ花火のしくみ――――― 320
Fireworks

第**1**章
家庭の中を見わたせば
意外と知らないことだらけ！

Chapter 1
Even in Your Own Home
There's a Lot
You Don't Know

確定申告のしくみ

個人の所得にかかる所得税は毎年、前年1年分の所得を総合して税額を計算し、申告納付することになっている。収入が会社からの給料・賞与のみという人については、支給されたときに源泉徴収されている税額を、年間を通じて再計算する年末調整で納税手続きは完了する。ただし年収が2000万円を超えた人、不動産などを売却して所得があった人はサラリーマンでも確定申告が必要。ローンで住宅を購入したり、年間10万円を超える医療費を支払った人は、還付申告すれば税金の払い戻しを受けられる。

Filing an income tax return 所得税の確定申告	
Earned income (salary/bonuses) 給与所得（給与・賞与）	Income from interest, dividends, real estate, business, inheritance, etc., or occasional, miscellaneous, etc., income 利子・配当・不動産・事業・譲渡・一時・雑などの各所得

End of year adjustments 年末調整	Withholding tax at source 源泉徴収	Withholding tax at source 源泉徴収

Simplified compensation statement 簡易給与所得表、速算表	Special deduction for necessary expenses and inheritance 必要経費・譲渡の特別控除など

Income tax amount 所得金額

Income tax deductions 所得控除

Personal and basic deductions such as social insurance premiums, life insurance premiums, health insurance premiums, medical expenses, charitable deductions, spouse, and dependents
社会保険料・生命保険料・損害保険料・医療費・寄付金控除、配偶者・扶養などの人的控除および基礎控除

Filing an Income Tax Return

Self-assessment and payment of tax on individual income are calculated based on the total income of the previous year. The payment procedure ends with year-end adjustments for tax withheld from paychecks over the course of the year for people whose income only involves salaries and bonuses from companies. However, those who make over 20 million yen a year and those with income from the sale of real estate must file an income tax return even if they are salaried employees. Individuals who have taken out loans to buy homes or have paid medical expenses over 100,000 yen a year can get a refund on their taxes if they file a return.

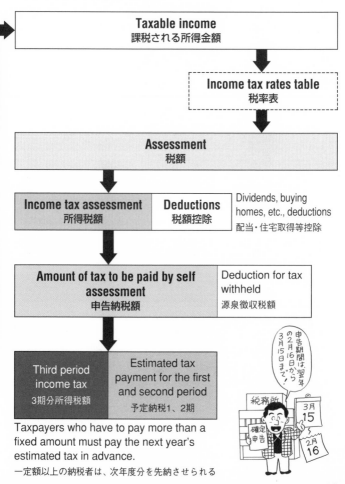

Taxable income
課税される所得金額

Income tax rates table
税率表

Assessment
税額

| **Income tax assessment** 所得税額 | **Deductions** 税額控除 | Dividends, buying homes, etc., deductions 配当・住宅取得等控除 |

| **Amount of tax to be paid by self assessment** 申告納税額 | Deduction for tax withheld 源泉徴収税額 |

| Third period income tax 3期分所得税額 | Estimated tax payment for the first and second period 予定納税1、2期 |

Taxpayers who have to pay more than a fixed amount must pay the next year's estimated tax in advance.
一定額以上の納税者は、次年度分を先納させられる

申告期間は、翌年の2月16日から3月15日まで!

税務所
確定申告
3月15
2月16

地価のしくみ

　地価には取引上の「実務価格」と、法律でその基準を定めたものとがある。地価の基準となるのは地価公示法による「公示価格」で、国土交通省が毎年1月1日現在で調査し、4月1日付で発表。自治体による指導価格の目安とされる地価である。次に、規制区域内の基準価格の凍結や取引許可制を定めた国土利用計画法にもとづく地価を、俗に「基準地価格」という。さらに、国税庁が毎年7月1日現在で調査する「路線価」がある。これは、相続税や贈与税の課税基準になるものだ。一方、地方税の「固定資産税評価額」は、固定資産税等の課税基準で、3年に1度評価替えされる。このように、地価は実勢価格以外に「一物四価」である。

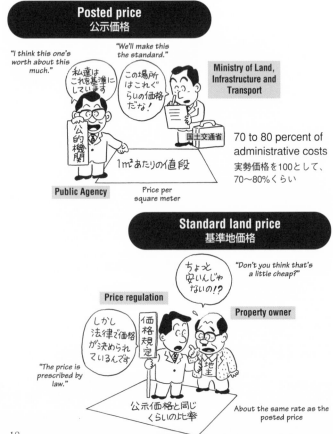

Posted price
公示価格

"I think this one's worth about this much."
私達はこれを基準にしています

"We'll make this the standard."
この場所はこれぐらいの価格だな！

Ministry of Land, Infrastructure and Transport
国土交通省

公的機関

Public Agency

1㎡あたりの値段

Price per square meter

70 to 80 percent of administrative costs
実勢価格を100として、70〜80%くらい

Standard land price
基準地価格

ちょっと安いんじゃないの!?

"Don't you think that's a little cheap?"

Price regulation

しかし法律で価格が決められているんです

価格規定

Property owner
地主

"The price is prescribed by law."

公示価格と同じくらいの比率

About the same rate as the posted price

Land Prices

The price of land involves the "administrative costs" of doing business, and land price standards as prescribed by law. The standard land price is made public by the Land Price Disclosure Act. The Ministry of Land, Infrastructure and Transport carries out a survey every year on January 1, and announces the results on April 1. The land prices are a rough standard of guideline prices by municipality. In addition to this are prices based on the National Land Utilization Planning Act that establish the standard linkage and dealing prices within regulated districts. These are popularly called, "standard land prices." The Bureau of Internal Revenue also conducts a survey every year on July 1 to appraise the value of land facing a thoroughfare. This appraisal becomes the tax base for inheritance and gift taxes. On the other hand, the "assessed value of fixed assets," is a tax base for fixed assets in regional taxes, and is re-evaluated every three years. In this way, there are "four prices for one item" in addition to the administrative cost when dealing with the price of land.

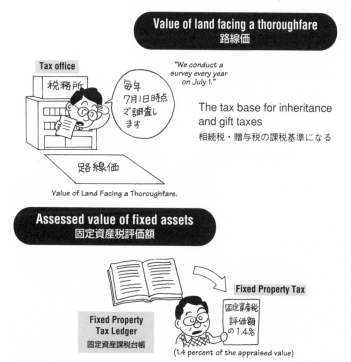

Value of land facing a thoroughfare
路線価

Tax office

税務所

毎年 7月1日時点 で調査します

"We conduct a survey every year on July 1."

The tax base for inheritance and gift taxes
相続税・贈与税の課税基準になる

路線価

Value of Land Facing a Thoroughfare.

Assessed value of fixed assets
固定資産税評価額

Fixed Property Tax Ledger
固定資産課税台帳

Fixed Property Tax

固定資産税 評価額 の1.4%

(1.4 percent of the appraised value)

Re-evaluated once every three years.
3年に1度、評価替えが行われる

国勢調査のしくみ

　国民全体にわたる年齢、職業、配偶者の有無などについての調査である。第1回が1920年で、以来10年ごとに正式調査を、その中間の5年目に簡易調査を行う。最近では、2000年に正式調査が実施された。

　調査は総務省統計局を主管官庁として、総理大臣、知事、市町村長、国勢調査指導員、調査員の系統を通じて実施される。調査員は原則として1調査区（約50世帯）に1名が配置され、受持ち調査区内の世帯調査にあたる。調査済みの調査表は、最終的に統計局に提出され、最新式の大型電子計算機で集計される。近年、プライバシー意識の高まりを背景に、調査票を密封して提出する市民グループ運動もある。

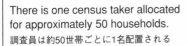

There is one census taker allocated for approximately 50 households.
調査員は約50世帯ごとに1名配置される

Polling
集票

Census taker
国勢調査員

ご協力お願いします。

調　査　票
Survey Card

これ書けばメシでももらえるの？

プライバシーをまもろう！

封

The homeless are also included in the national census.
ホームレスの人も国勢調査の対象となる

There are also citizen organizations to seal the cards in an envelop for submission in order to protect privacy.
プライバシー保護の立場から密封して提出する市民運動もある

The National Census

A survey of the entire population across age, employment, and marital status. The first census was in 1920. Since then, an official survey has been performed every 10 years, and simplified versions at five-year intervals. The most recent census was officially conducted in 2000.

The Statistics Bureau of the Office of the Ministry of Public Management, Home Affairs, Posts and Telecommunications is the main government office responsible for the census, and it is conducted under the leadership of the prime minister, prefectural governors, and mayors of cities, towns and villages. One census taker is assigned per census area (approximately 50 households), to conduct household surveys within the area to which they are assigned. The results of the survey are submitted to the Statistics Bureau, and compiled with state-of-the-art electronic calculating equipment. In recent years, an increasing recognition of privacy has lead to the creation of citizen organizations that seal the survey sheets in envelops for submission.

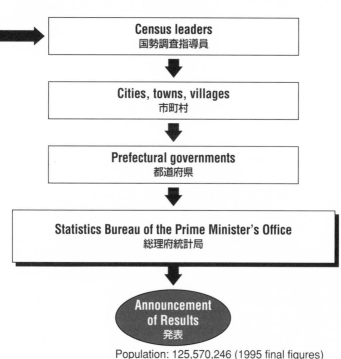

Census leaders
国勢調査指導員

Cities, towns, villages
市町村

Prefectural governments
都道府県

Statistics Bureau of the Prime Minister's Office
総理府統計局

Announcement of Results
発表

Population: 125,570,246 (1995 final figures)
人口・1億2557万246人（95年確定値）

郵便配達のしくみ

郵便局は、全国に約2万4000局以上あるが、このネットワークを有効に生かした新しい郵便配達のしくみが展開されつつある。ファクシミリを利用した電子郵便サービス、ゆうパックでおなじみの郵便宅配便、ビジネス郵便など、従来の郵便配達のイメージを転換させる各種のサービスに努めている。だが、"より速く、より確実に"郵便物を配達するための最終ランナーは、配達人である。そして、この配達人の人手不足が郵便局のアキレス腱になっている。郵便のイメージアップも大事だが、配達人の確保も急務の課題だ。

Pickup times are indicated on mailboxes.

ポストには集めにくる時刻が記されていますよ

Receiving Office
〒 引き受け局

Letters are postmarked here and are put into separate bags according to postal districts.

郵便物に消印を押して、宛先別に区分けして袋に入れる

Overland mail by truck
トラック便

Overland mail by rail
鉄道便

Rail post office
鉄道郵便局

Airmail
航空便

Sea mail
船便

Intermediate office
〒中継局

Central post offices are set up in large cities such as Tokyo and Osaka where mail is concentrated.

東京や大阪など郵便物が集中する大都市には、中央郵便局が設置されている

Postal Delivery Service

There are around 24,000 post offices throughout Japan, forming a network that makes it possible to develop new services that change the image of the post office, such as an electronic mail service using faxes, a package delivery service called U-pack, and a special business mail service. Mail carriers play an important role in making delivery fast and reliable. Currently there's a shortage of mail carriers. Post offices are working to improve their image and also to recruit more mail carriers.

Very fast!

速達
ですよ

Distribution center
〒　配達局

After arriving at the distribution center, mail is sorted according to delivery zone and delivery route. From there, mail carriers deliver letters and parcels.

配達局へ届けられた郵便物は、配達区域ごとに分けられて配達の順路ごとに並べ、配達人の手で配達される

A zip code is assigned to each postal delivery zone which helps to speed up the distribution process. From February 1998, four digits were added to each zip code.

郵便番号は配達局の受け持ち区域ごとにつけられていて、配達のスピードアップに役立っている。98年2月から7ケタ制が導入された

When the zip code frames are black or when the 〒 postal mark is added, the machines are unable to read the codes correctly and so mail may be delayed.

郵便番号枠を黒にしたり、〒記号を書き加えると機械が読み取れずに配達が遅れる場合もある

Change of Address Notice
転居届

After a move, letters are forwarded to the new address for one year.

引っ越しするときは、転居届を提出しておくと、その日から1年間、旧住所あての郵便物を新住所に転送してくれる

Mail holding service
旅先での受け取り

Mail can be held for up to ten days while you're out of town.

旅先で郵便物を受け取りたいときは、宛先を○○局留置とすると、10日間保管してくれる

PO box
私書箱

A free PO box is available for those who would like to receive mail quickly or who expect a large amount of mail.

郵便物を早く受け取りたい場合や、大量の郵便物がくる会社や個人のために、郵便局には私書箱が設置されていて無料で開設してくれる

Super Express Mail
超特急郵便

A service that delivers letters and packages within an hour. This service is available only in Tokyo's 23 wards, Osaka and 11 neighboring cities, and Nagoya.

東京23区、大阪市内および隣接の11市、名古屋市内では至急の郵便物をおおむね1時間以内で配達する郵便システムがある

Special delivery within the day
即日配達郵便

This is available only in the following cases:
Mail that goes between any two of the three major cities—Tokyo, Osaka, or Nagoya—or mail that is addressed to Tokyo coming from Fukuoka or Sapporo.

東京、大阪、名古屋の3大都市相互間と福岡、札幌から東京にあてて出される郵便物には、即日配達の郵便システムがある

Delivered at 10 AM the next day
よくあさ10時郵便

Just call and the mail will be picked up at your home and delivered to the addressee at 10 AM the next day.

電話をすれば郵便局から集荷にやって来て、翌朝10時に配達する郵便システムがある

Make just one call, then I'll pick up your mail.

電話一本で駆けつけます

宅配サービスのしくみ

宅配サービスが盛んである。荷物はもとより、ホームケータリングと呼ばれる料理や食材などの宅配も、定着化してきている。なかでも米国式の宅配ピザの成功にならって、寿司・お好み焼きなどの和食宅配も市場を広げつつある。といっても、そば屋や寿司屋では昔から "出前" という宅配サービスをしている。

これがウケないのは、ひとえに配達のパフォーマンスのせいではないだろうか。派手なコスチュームと屋根付きバイク、それに配達時間厳守という今どきの宅配サービスのノウハウを真似れば、結構いけるかも知れない。

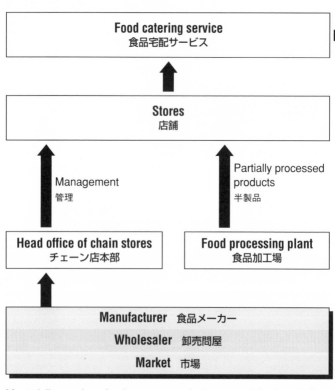

Food catering service
食品宅配サービス

Stores
店舗

Management
管理

Partially processed products
半製品

Head office of chain stores
チェーン店本部

Food processing plant
食品加工場

Manufacturer 食品メーカー

Wholesaler 卸売問屋

Market 市場

Most delivery pizza businesses are chain stores. The head office purchases food in bulk and distributes partially processed products to branch offices.

宅配ピザはチェーン展開をしているところが多く、本部が一括して仕入れて、半製品状態で各店舗に配送するシステムになっている

Delivery Service

Delivery services are flourishing in Japan for not only parcels, but also for groceries and food dishes. After the success of American style pizza, Japanese food such as sushi and okonomi-yaki are considered developing markets. In fact, noodle and sushi restaurants have long provided catering services, known as demae. Such services had been on the decline, probably because the service by such shops was considered old fashioned. By imitating newly developed styles such as gaudy costumes, motorcycles with cabs, and strict punctuality, demae might once gain popularity.

Home
家庭

In cities, over 40 percent of packages are delivered when the recipient is not at home, a rather serious problem for delivery companies.

都市部では配達先の不在率が4割を超え、業者を困らせている

Absence is the biggest problem.

Maximum speed, 30 km/h
最高速度　30km/h

Helmet
ヘルメット着用

Motorcycle license
原付バイク免許

Easily recognizable three-wheeled motorcycles with cabs were legally considered automobiles up until 1991 when they were re-categorized as motorcycles.

宅配サービスでおなじみの屋根付き3輪車は法律上は普通自動車扱いだったが、91年から原動機付き自転車（バイク）扱いになった

Delivery　配達

Delivery service
宅配便

Business office
営業所

Package delivery businesses and the government postal service are rivals. When Yamato Transport expanded its business to include credit card delivery, the former Ministry of Posts and Telecommunications complained, but the delivery industry fought back. Nevertheless Seino Transportation Co., Ltd. tied up with post offices in refrigerated parcel delivery in June 1998. The softening of the ministry's attitude is causing complications in the delivery service industry.

宅配便と郵便小包はライバル関係。ヤマト運輸がクレジットカードの宅配を事業化した時には、かつての郵政省がクレームをつけ、業界側がそれに反発した。だが、98年6月から西濃運輸のクール宅配便が郵便局と提携。郵政省の軟化は、業界に複雑な波紋を投げかけている

Delivery center
集配センター

Packages are sorted out according to each business district.
荷物を営業所ごとに仕分けする

Collection center
集荷センター

Packages are sorted according to regional area.
荷物を地方ごとに仕分けする

Main office
本社

Sales slips are controlled centrally by POS system.

伝票管理は、POSシステムによって集中管理されている

Final report on completion of delivery

配達完了報告

バーコードで入力しています

Bar codes are used for easy input.

Sales report
売上報告

Packages are traceable.
荷物がどこまで行っているのか確認できる

Business office
営業所

Trucks making stops at intermediate offices are becoming larger and larger.

集荷する車は、中継するたびに大型になってゆく

Data entry
伝票入力

Pick up
集荷

クーリング・オフのしくみ

　訪問販売（街頭のキャッチセールスも含む）のセールスマンのしつこさに負けて、商品を買わされてしまった場合、この契約を無条件で解約することができる余裕期間を定めたのが、クーリング・オフ。これは通称「訪問販売法」という法律にもとづいたもので、契約後一定期間は契約者が頭を冷やして考え直したうえで、一方的に解約してもよいという消費者保護の施策である。

　解約の方法は、販売会社にはっきりした意思表示をすること。内容証明付郵便や書留郵便など、解約の通知をしたという証明になる形をとるのが望ましい。電話で解約というのは、なるべく避けた方がよい。申し込み撤回の効果は、書面を発した時に生ずる。

"It's a bargain!"

奥さんこれは安いよ！

Contract
契約

Cooling Off
クーリング・オフ

The cooling off period for door-to-door sales and telephone sales is 8 days after a written contract is signed. For anything involving "pyramid" or "chain" selling, it is possible to withdraw from contracts within 20 days of signing.

訪問販売、通信販売は契約後8日間、マルチ商法およびマルチまがい商法は契約後20日間内なら、書面で無条件に解約できる

The system applies not only to goods, but also to services, and any cash transactions.

物品だけでなく、サービスおよび現金取引も対象になる

どーしよう？？契約しちゃったけど…！

"I wonder whether I should have signed after all…"

"Cooling Off"

In Japan there is a special period of time, known as the "cooling off" time, during which it is possible to withdraw unconditionally from any purchase agreement one may have signed under duress, whether from pesky door-to-door salesman or from so-called "catch-sales" people who try to entice you into "amazing deals" on the street. This period of time was put into effect under the Door-to-Door Sales Act, as a policy of protecting the consumer, and it allows the purchaser a certain amount of time after receiving a written contract to reconsider what may have been a rash decision, and to cancel the agreement unilaterally.

The method of cancellation of the agreement simply involves making a clear indication of one's decision to the distributor firm. Ideally speaking, one should also send notification of cancellation through contents-certified mail or registered delivery, so that one actually has proof that one has cancelled. Cancellation by telephone is probably best avoided. The agreement becomes null and void the minute such written documentation is sent.

Post Office

Notification of one's intention to withdraw from the contract is best done via registered mail or through contents-certified mail.

解約の意思表示は内容証明付郵便、書留を利用するとよい

Withdrawal from contract
解約

Items to make clear in document　解約の文面に明記すべき事項
(1) Date contract was signed.　契約の日付
(2) Specific article/item involved.　品名
(3) Price　価格
(4) Date contract was cancelled.　解約の日付

ゴミ処理のしくみ

　文明はその裏側に、ゴミという難題を抱えこんできた。すでに大都市部では、処分しきれないゴミが山積している状態で、いずれ処分地をめぐってゴミ戦争が勃発するという物騒な予言もあるほどだ。

　消費経済のメッカ・東京では、1日約1万トンを超えるゴミが回収され、清掃工場や埋立地で処分しているが、ゴミの増えるスピードに処理能力が追いつかないのが現状。燃えるゴミ、燃えないゴミの分別収集は今や常識化しているし、粗大ゴミの引取りの有料化も進んでいる。ゴミとして放置されることが多かった家電製品も、販売店に引取り業務（有料）が課せられるようになった。やがて一般ゴミも有料でなければ引き取ってもらえない時代が来るかも。

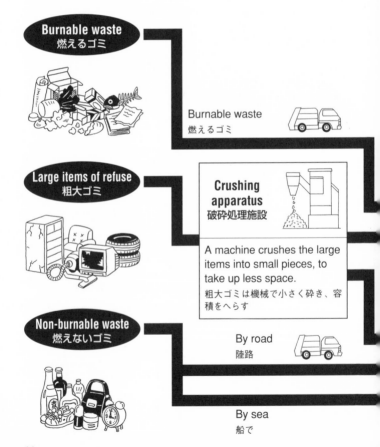

Burnable waste
燃えるゴミ

Burnable waste
燃えるゴミ

Large items of refuse
粗大ゴミ

Crushing apparatus
破砕処理施設

A machine crushes the large items into small pieces, to take up less space.
粗大ゴミは機械で小さく砕き、容積をへらす

By road
陸路

Non-burnable waste
燃えないゴミ

By sea
船で

32

Waste Disposal

Our modern lifestyle of convenience and consumerism has brought as its downside the extremely difficult problem of garbage. Already in large cities and towns, the mountains of refuse accumulated are more than can be dealt with, and predictions have even been made that local areas will soon be having "trash wars" with each other over places reserved to dump waste.

In Tokyo, which is the Mecca of consumerism, every day more than 10,000 tons of refuse are collected. At the moment they are dealt with at waste disposal centers and dumping grounds, but it's a sad fact that the amount of trash is increasing at such a rate that they can't really keep up with it. Nowadays, it goes without saying that waste collection is carried out separately for burnable waste and non-burnable waste, and it's also common to arrange for special services to come and collect large items of refuse (such as furniture or refrigerators) for a fee. In previous times, electrical goods often used to be thrown out with the other trash, but nowadays distributors are obliged, for a fee, to take them back. It's just possible that one day the same thing will apply to other items too.

More and more waste disposal sites are using the heat produced by waste disposal for the generation of electricity. There are also more instances of heated swimming pools being heated by the steam so generated.

ゴミの焼却熱を発電に利用する清掃工場が増えてきた。さらに発電後の蒸気を用いて温水プールなどへの熱供給を行うケースもある

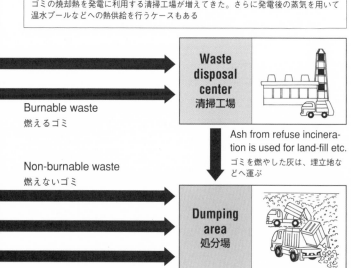

Waste disposal center 清掃工場

Burnable waste
燃えるゴミ

Ash from refuse incineration is used for land-fill etc.
ゴミを燃やした灰は、埋立地などへ運ぶ

Non-burnable waste
燃えないゴミ

Dumping area 処分場

米の流通のしくみ

1995年の「新食糧法」施行で、半世紀にわたった食糧管理法による米行政のしくみが変わった。政府による全量管理、流通規制の枠組みが取り除かれ、米をある程度まで自由に作って売ることが可能になったのだ。とはいえ、需給のバランスをとるための減反強化策は緩められることはなく、生産農家にとって相変わらず冬の時代が続いている。

価格は原則として市場（自主流通米価格形成センター）での入札で決められるが、96年度産米からは小売業者も参加が認められるようになった。

Types of rice from the perspective of distribution
流通からみた米の分類

For reserves 備蓄用

Imported rice 輸入米

Government rice
政府米

Free distribution rice
自主流通米

Other rice
その他

Uncontrolled distribution 計画外流通米

Specially cultivated rice
特別栽培米

Rice given to relatives and others
縁故・贈答用米

Free-market rice (black market)
自由米（ヤミ米）

Rice Distribution

With the enactment in 1995 of the New Staple Food Control Act, the government's 50-year-old "rice policy" underwent a change. Rice had previously been under the complete control of the government, but the law lifted some restrictions on distribution, allowing for more freedom in the harvesting and selling of rice. But since the rice-acreage reduction policy, which helps maintain the supply and demand balance, has not been relaxed, the season of frozen profits continues.

Rice prices are basically decided by auction at the market (price settlement center of free-market rice); but since 1996, retailers have also been able to participate in the auctions.

Rice under government control must pass inspection by the Staple Food Office, and include information about where the rice came from, the type, and when it was harvested. From the 1998 harvest, standards for labels concerning organic and non-chemical fertilizers were standardized.

計画流通米は、食糧事務所の検査を受けることが義務付けられ、産地・品種・収穫年の表示をしなければならない。98年産米からは、有機米や無農薬米の表示が基準化された

Rice distribution under government control 計画流通米として国が把握	
Grade 1	1類
Grade 2	2類
Grade 3	3類
Grade 4	4類
Grade 5	5類
Main entree, nonglutinous rice, rice for sake	主食用 うるち米・酒米
Rice for mochi cake	もち米

Direct delivery

直送

安いわ!!

How cheap!

Formerly illegal, black-market rice is now also included under the Staple Food Control Act. But it is still illegal to display the grade of rice on rice that has not been inspected.

食管法では違法だった自由米（ヤミ米）も「計画外」扱いで追認された。ただし、検査を受けていない米の品質表示をしてはならないことになっている

米の流通のしくみ……2

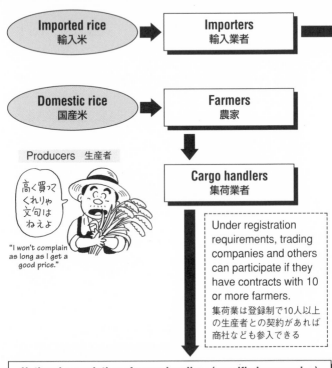

The distribution route for controlled rice
計画流通米の経路

| **Imported rice**
輸入米 | → | **Importers**
輸入業者 |

| **Domestic rice**
国産米 | → | **Farmers**
農家 |

Producers　生産者

高く買って
くれりゃ
文句は
ねえよ

"I won't complain
as long as I get a
good price."

Cargo handlers
集荷業者

Under registration
requirements, trading
companies and others
can participate if they
have contracts with 10
or more farmers.
集荷業は登録制で10人以上
の生産者との契約があれば
商社なども参入できる

National association of cargo handlers (specified companies)
全国集荷団体（指定法人）

Specified by the National Federation of Agricultural Cooperative
Associations and associations of major companies.
全農や大手経済連が指定の対象

From July 1995, a simultaneous-bidding auction was initiated.
95年7月から売買同時入札という方法でスタートした

Government
政府

Under the new laws, wholesalers and
retailers only are registered and new
entry is not limited.
卸・小売業も登録制になり、業者数の制限がな
くなった

Wholesalers
卸売業者

At the wholesale stage, some rice is mixed
together and sent to the market as blend rice.
卸の段階で米のブレンド（混米）がされ、市場に出回る

Retailers
小売業者

"That's why it
takes so long
to get to me!"

私のところへ
来るまでには
やっぱり時間
がかかるわ！

Consumer 消費者

Liberalization of retail and wholesale of
rice was started from June 1996. The
number of rice retailers rose sharply
from 93,000 to 175,000. From 1999,
retailers can sell both government rice
and free-market rice.
96年6月から小売、卸業務の自由化がスタート。
小売店は9万3000店から17万5000店に急増し
た。99年度からは政府米と自主流通米の通販が
できるようになった

ミネラルウォーター流通のしくみ

　安全と水はタダと思っているのが日本人、とはよく言われるセリフ。その日本人が高い水に手を出し始めた。天然の名水をパッケージしたミネラルウォーターである。しかも、水道水の値段にくらべると1000倍もの高い水が、ネーミング通りの名水かどうかという疑問をもつことなしに……。

　少し考えてみれば、天然水なら原価は限りなくタダに近いはず。運賃、手間賃、パッケージ代はかかるにしても、水道水の1000倍とはベラボウ過ぎる。異物が混入した商品も見つかっていて、ちょっと心配。

Obtaining water　採水

The water is drawn by means of wells from underground springs and mineral water supplies. The actual location of such places is apparently kept an industrial secret.

原料となる水は、井戸から汲み上げた地下水や鉱泉水。採水場所は企業秘密だそうだ

Transportation
搬入

Factory
工場

Treatment　処理

This involves balancing the minerals, as well as filtration, sedimentation, and purification.

ろ過、沈澱、殺菌、ミネラル整調など

Bottling　ボトリング

The water is put into labeled bottles before shipment.
ラベルを貼って出荷する

Transportation
搬出

Local stores
小売店

The Distribution of Mineral Water

There's a saying in Japan that water and public safety are free. And now, for some reason, people are now willing to pay for their water—"mineral water," special water that has been taken from natural springs and put into fancy bottles. The curious thing is that this water costs 1000 times as much as tap water, and no one seems to doubt about whether this water really is all that special.

A little reflection should make us realize that the price of bottled spring water should be next to nothing. Even taking into consideration the cost of transportation, handling and packaging, it's absurd for the cost soars to be 1000 times the price of ordinary water. We should be a little more wary in this area, especially after incidents where bottled water was found to contain rather unappetizing amoebae.

> Mineral water is officially defined as "water drawn from such sources as underground wells, and put into bottles for the purpose of drinking."
>
> ミネラルウォーターとは「地下水などのうち、飲用に適した水を容器に詰めたもの」と定義されている

Costs for 2 liter bottle, sold for 300 yen
2ℓ ボトル300円の中味

Transportation costs: 50 yen

輸送費　約50円

Bottling costs: 80 yen

ボトル代など　約80円

名水

Labor, advertising and profit: roughly 170 yen

人件費・宣伝費・利益など　約170円

Many major supermarkets are now coming out with their own special brands of mineral water. Incidentally, a 2-liter bottle of such mineral water costs 198 yen (retail price), 102 yen less than forerunners. When one considers that the cost of the basic ingredient is next to nothing, clearly the mineral water business offers tasty profits. On the other hand, mineral water offered at a cheap price might lose its appeal to consumers.

大手スーパーによるPB商品はミネラルウォーターにも及んできた。ちなみに小売価格は2ℓ198円で、先発商品との差は102円。水の原料費が限りなくタダに近いことを考えると、ミネラルウォーターはかなりうま味のある商売であることが想像できる。もっとも、安過ぎると逆に不安だという消費者心理も問題だ

牛乳の製品化のしくみ

市販の牛乳は、殺菌の手法の違いによって大きく3種類に分類される。従来は保存性が高く、安いことが流通の拡大に直接結びついたが、今は自然に近く美味しい牛乳ということがセールスポイントになっている。それをうたい文句に登場したのが、低温殺菌牛乳。これは大量生産が可能な高温殺菌の牛乳よりも手間暇がかかるが、病原菌がほとんどない安全な牛乳として近年、市場に出回り出した。

もっとも低温殺菌牛乳は、原料の段階で細菌が少ないことが条件とされている。しかし、栄養価という点ではどちらも大差ないという説もある。95年4月から牛乳の製造年月日は任意表示となり、いつまで飲めるかの期限表示が義務づけられた。

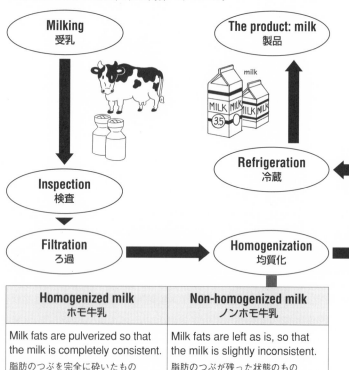

Homogenized milk ホモ牛乳	Non-homogenized milk ノンホモ牛乳
Milk fats are pulverized so that the milk is completely consistent. 脂肪のつぶを完全に砕いたもの	Milk fats are left as is, so that the milk is slightly inconsistent. 脂肪のつぶが残った状態のもの

Nearly all the milk on the market is of the homogenized variety. Homogenization rate is held to be better at higher temperature.

一般に出回っているのはほとんどが脂肪のつぶを砕いて均質化したホモ牛乳である。乳温が高いほど均質化効率が高いとされる

Milk Products

The milk now available on the market can be roughly divided into three kinds, depending on the method of pasteurization used. Previously, it used to be that cheapness and keepability were the keys to whether a particular milk gained a large market or not. Now however, deliciousness and whether the milk is as close to its natural form as possible are the keys to its selling well. And these are the very things that have become possible with low temperature pasteurization. This low-temperature pasteurization requires more effort and time than high-temperature pasteurization, made possible by large-scale production, but in recent years milk produced in this fashion with no pathogenic bacilli has been available on the market.

One of the requirements for milk that is going to be pasteurized at low temperature is of course that it has to be very fresh. As far as the nutritional value is concerned, some people think that little difference exists between these two kinds. From April 1995, it became a legal requirement that both the date of manufacture and the date until which the milk could be safely consumed had to be clearly shown on the milk package.

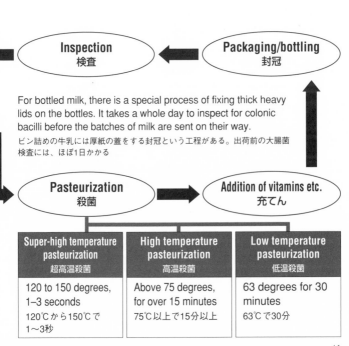

Inspection
検査

Packaging/bottling
封冠

For bottled milk, there is a special process of fixing thick heavy lids on the bottles. It takes a whole day to inspect for colonic bacilli before the batches of milk are sent on their way.
ビン詰めの牛乳には厚紙の蓋をする封冠という工程がある。出荷前の大腸菌検査には、ほぼ1日かかる

Pasteurization
殺菌

Addition of vitamins etc.
充てん

Super-high temperature pasteurization 超高温殺菌	High temperature pasteurization 高温殺菌	Low temperature pasteurization 低温殺菌
120 to 150 degrees, 1–3 seconds 120℃から150℃で1〜3秒	Above 75 degrees, for over 15 minutes 75℃以上で15分以上	63 degrees for 30 minutes 63℃で30分

第**2**章
ゆりかごから墓場まで
ウ～ン、人生って複雑だ～！

Chapter 2
From Cradle to
Grave
Why Is Everything So
Complicated?

戸籍制度のしくみ

わが国の戸籍制度は諸外国にくらべ閉鎖的と言われて久しい。その象徴が、「民法」に定める夫婦同姓の原則。戸籍は夫婦が単位となるが、これは夫を家長とする旧来の"家制度"の名残りという一面もある。話題の夫婦別姓論議は、日本人がようやく"個人"としての生き方を模索し始めたことの現れだ。戸籍は婚姻届で新たに作成されるが、この届出をしない夫婦の子は、戸籍のない子としてパスポートが発給されない、相続分が実子の半分、などの差別を受ける。法務大臣の諮問機関である法制審議会は1995年9月、"夫婦同姓を原則とするが、別姓も可、子の姓は夫婦どちらかと同一姓"との選択的夫婦別姓制度の導入を答申した。

Children born to couples who have not submitted notification of marriage are discriminated against, and treated as illegitimate offspring.

婚姻届を出していない夫婦の間に生まれた子どもは、非嫡出子として区別される

Notification of marriage
婚姻届

One or the other in the couple has a register made in his or her name, and enters his or her spouse's name into it.

夫婦の一方が相手の戸籍に入籍するという形で作成される

A new register is made

新戸籍

When people's names are entered into the records by computer, mistakes in the characters receive automatic correction; however simplified characters are allowed to stand according to usage.

戸籍の事務処理のコンピュータ導入で、誤字は自動的に訂正されるが、俗字は従来のまま使用してよいことになった

Nowadays many women have started to use their husband's family name in the family register, but their maiden name at the workplace. Also increasing is the number of people who take out a family register only upon the birth of a child, after which they then file notification of divorce. It is considered to be a source of shame if a Japanese woman never changed her name; it now seems that such views have undergone a huge change.

戸籍は夫の姓、仕事では旧姓を使う女性が増えている。子どもが生まれた時だけ入籍して、再びペーパー離婚をするという荒ワザを使う人も。苗字が変わらないのを恥としていた日本女性の結婚観は大きく変わった

Family Register System

The family register system in Japan has long been said to be old-fashioned and restricting. The most conspicuous example of this is the rule that married couples must have the same name, decided under Civil Law. In the family register, married couples are treated as one unit, but there are aspects of this system, some people say, that are vestiges of the old patriarchal "ie" (household) system. The discussion surrounding the question of whether husband and wife should be allowed to use separate names is an indication that Japanese citizens have at last started to consider the implications of what it is to live as an "individual." A new family register is drawn up when a couple submits a notification of marriage. Children of couples who do not submit such notification have to face various forms of differential treatment—for example, they will not be able to obtain passports, and they will only receive half the inheritance of children who have family registers, and so on. A legal deliberative assembly, an inquiry body of the Minister of Justice, in September 1995 proposed that a new system should be introduced whereby couples could choose which names they go by; now, though in principle spouses should bear the same name, husbands and wives are free to use their own names if they choose, and their offspring can bear the name of one or the other of the their parents.

Main information entered into family register 戸籍の主な記載事項	
Names 氏名	In principle, couples share the same family name. 氏 (姓) は夫婦同一が原則
Parental Lineage 父母との続き柄	Note is taken of whether the parties are legitimate or illegitimate offspring of their parents. 嫡出子と非嫡出子の区別をする
Adoptions 養親子	Children other than a couple's biological children and special adoptions considered to be of equal status are registered as adopted. 実子と同様の特別養子以外は養子と記載

In the registers, the children of couples who have submitted notification of marriage are noted as "eldest son," "second son," "eldest daughter." Illegitimate children are simply noted as "boy" or "girl." Nowadays this different treatment is regarded as controversial because of its discriminatory implications.

After March 1, 1995, the details in the residents' ledger concerning the relationship of children to the head of each household were changed to make no differentiation between legitimate and illegitimate offspring. Further, offspring are noted simply as "child" regardless of whether they are eldest or youngest, biological or adopted.

戸籍には、婚姻届を出した正式な夫婦の子は「長男、二男…長女、二女…」と記載されるが、非嫡出子の場合は「男、女」とだけ記載される。これが差別につながるとして、問題視されている

1995年3月1日から住民票に記載される世帯主と子の続き柄は、嫡出子・非嫡出子 (ただし認知が前提になる) の区別や長男・二男、養子などの区別なく、すべて「子」と統一された

Original copies of the register and residents' ledger
戸籍原本と住民基本台帳

Notification
届出

Village, Town, Ward or City Office of Place of Permanent Domicile
本籍地の市区町村役所(場)

Original Register
戸籍原本

Record taken using the married couple as basic unit
夫婦を単位にした記録

(Abridged) transcripts of register
戸籍謄(抄)本

Details entered on Original Copy of Family Register 戸籍原本に記録される届出	
Notification of Births	出生届
Notification of Entry into Family Registers	入籍届
Notification of Segregation from Family Register	分籍届
Notification of Transfer of Family Register	転籍届
Notification of Marriage	婚姻届
Notification of Change of Personal or Family Name	名・氏の変更届
Notification of Reversion to Original Family Name	復氏届
Notification of (Special) Adoption	(特別)養子縁組届
Notification of Death	死亡届

Village, Town, Ward or City Office of Place of Residence
住所地の市区町村役所（場）

| Residents' Ledger
住民基本台帳 | Record is made of each individual in a household.
世帯ごとの個人記録 |

| Resident Card
住民票 | Registration of Residence
住民登録 |

Notifications registered on the Residents' Ledger 住民基本台帳に記録される届出	
Notification of Change of Address	転居届
Notification of Moving In	転入届
Notification of Moving Out	転出届
Notification of Change of Head of Household	世帯主変更届
Notification of Change of Household	世帯変更届

Notifications made in the family register of births and deaths are also automatically made on the residents' ledger.

出生届・死亡届は、届出をすると自動的に住民基本台帳に記録されるしくみになっている

養子縁組のしくみ

　生まれながらの親子でない者どうしが、法律上の親子関係を結ぶことを養子縁組というが、この制度は「民法」や「戸籍法」に定められている。その手続きは、養親と養子が合意し、本籍地または住所地にある市区町村の役所に「養子縁組届」を提出することが通例となっている。この場合、養子は成年・未成年を問わないが、養親については制約がある。

　たとえば、成年者であること（ただし婚姻している未成年者は法的に成年とみなされる）、養子より年下であってはならない、尊属にあたる人を養子にできない等である。さらに婚姻中の夫婦は、養子・養親になる際には揃ってなる必要がある。どちらか一方だけが、養子・養親というわけにはいかないのだ。

The adopted child must not be older than the adoptive parent.

養子は養親より年上ではいけない

Adoptive Child
養子

Adoptive Parent
養親
A person over 20
成年者

Alliance through adoption of a child under 15 years of age can be accepted by a legal proxy (the child's legal gurdian).

15歳未満の子供を養子に迎える場合は、法定代理人（親権者）が縁組の承諾をすることができる

Legal proxy
法定代理人

Alliance through adoption of minors

未成年者の養子縁組

Notification　届出

City/ward/town/village administration, either of the place of residence, or where they keep the original copy of their family register

本籍地または住所地の市区町村役所

Adoption Alliance

It is possible for individuals who are not related by blood to agree to become parent and child in the eyes of the law—by means of adoption, referred to as "adoption alliance." This system is one that is recognized by both the Civil Law and the Family Register Law. The procedure for such adoption usually takes the form of the person/people who is/are doing the adopting and the person being adopted (the adoptee) first deciding on the arrangement, and then submitting a Notification of Adoption at the local government office, whether at the city, ward, town or village level.

There are no restrictions regarding the qualifications of a potential adoptee. Restrictions do apply, however, regarding the person who makes the adoption. These include the requirement that the adoptive parent be over 20 years of age (the legal age of adulthood—though people under 20 who are married are legally considered adults); that he or she must be older than the person he or she is adopting; and that he or she may not adopt anybody who stands in the relation of a lineal ancestor. One further stipulation is that married couples have both to become adopted parents of children—that is to say, it is not possible for one party in a married couple to become a single adoptive parent.

Notification　届出

Application for permission to adopt　許可申立

Family Court
家庭裁判所

The rights and duties of an adopted child
養子の権利と義務

When an alliance through adoption is established, legally speaking, relations between the adopted parents and child become the equivalent of those of blood-related kith and kin. At the same time, however, this does not effect the consanguinity between the adopted child and his or her actual parents. For this reason, the adoptee has the right to inherit from both sets of parents, and the obligation to care for both sets too.

養子縁組が成立すると、養子と、養親の血族との間には法律上の血族関係が生じる。また、養子の実の親との血族関係も残る。そのため養子は、養親と実の親の遺産相続の権利と扶養の義務がある。

結婚のしくみ

結婚は、当事者同士の意思で決まるものだが、法律上は婚姻届を提出することによって初めて正式な夫婦関係とされる。届出のないものは、内縁関係と呼ばれる。婚姻届は、当事者と証人が所定用紙に署名・押印して、市区町村の役所に提出すればよく、それが受理されれば成立する。ただし、男性は18歳以上、女性は16歳以上の年齢制限があるほか、重婚や近親婚は禁止されている。

最近は、再婚というケースも結構多いのだが、女性の場合は離婚届を提出してから6ヵ月経たないと婚姻届は受理されない。これは妊娠の可能性があるからだ。同じ相手とならば、離婚と結婚の届出は一日の間に何度でも繰り返してよいが、他人迷惑なだけである。

A marriage comes into being legally with the submission of a Notice of Marriage
結婚は、婚姻届の提出によって、法的に成立する

Offices of local government authorities
市区町村の役所

Submission
届出
This is possible even on holidays and at night.
休日、夜間も受け付けてくれる

People who are under 20 years of age, the official age of adulthood, have to obtain written consent to the marriage from both sets of parents.
20歳未満の未成年者は、両親の結婚同意書が必要

Written Consent

There are very rare cases in which parents attempt to register a marriage even though one or both the parties in question have no intention of marrying. In such cases, if the unwilling party (or parties) submit in advance a petition of non-acceptance, the marriage registration will not be recognized for a period of six months.
本人にその意思がないのに、まれに親などが一方的に婚姻手続きを進めてしまうケースがある。そんな場合は、事前に婚姻届不受理申立書を提出しておくと、6ヵ月間は受理しないことになっている

Marriage

Marriage is something that is decided upon by the two parties involved, but legally it is only when they submit a Notification of Marriage that a man and a women formally become husband and wife. Without this notification, even people who have gone through the ceremony are treated as "common-law" spouses. The Notification of Marriage is a form that has to be signed and stamped with the seal of both parties and a witness, and all they have to do is submit it at local government offices. With official acceptance, the marriage. Comes into being. Some restrictions apply: men have to be at least 18 years of age, and women 16; and polygamous marriages and marriages with close relatives are against the law.

In recent years, more and more people are going in for remarriage after divorce or a spouse's death. A woman has to wait at least 6 months after she has submitted Notification of Divorce before submitting a Notification of Marriage; the reasoning behind this is that she might be pregnant by her former husband. If, however, the person she remarries is the one and the same person as the man she divorced, multiple submissions of both papers is acceptable, even within the space of one day, though the officials dealing with the paperwork involved may be none too pleased.

Marriage between Japanese and non-Japanese people
国際結婚のしくみ

When a Japanese person marries a non-Japanese person, the general rule is that the Japanese must abide by Japanese law, and the non-Japanese must abide by the law of his or her country. Notice of marriage should be carried out in accordance with the laws of the country in which marriage takes place.

日本人が外国人と結婚する場合は、日本人は日本の法律、外国人はその国の法律に従うことが原則。婚姻の届出は、結婚する国の法律にもとづいて行う

The non-Japanese person must fill in the forms for Certificate of Marriage available at the representative organ of his country's government stationed in Japan.

外国人の場合、その国の駐在政府機関が発行する婚姻証明書が必要になる

In the case of marriages between Japanese and non-Japanese, certain procedures have to be taken before the couple take out a new family register: the non-Japanese person has to become a naturalized Japanese citizen to be able to enter his or her name in a family register in Japan. The offspring born to the couple, however, can choose which nationality of their parents they would prefer.

日本人が外国人と結婚しても、新しい戸籍はつくられない。外国人も帰化しない限り、日本の戸籍には入れない。ただし、生まれた子供はいずれかの国籍が選べる

離婚のしくみ

　近頃は"成田離婚"や"関空離婚"が流行語になっている。結婚式を挙げ、海外への新婚旅行からの帰途でもう夫婦喧嘩。空港で別れたまま離婚というケースが目立つそうだ。

　もっとも、夫婦の合意があればその理由にかかわらず、離婚届を役所に提出すれば離婚は成立する。だが、この夫婦の合意というのが問題で、結婚はたやすく離婚は難しいとされるゆえんである。離婚を前提とする当事者間での話し合いで結論が出ない場合は、家庭裁判所に調停を依頼する。この場合も、夫婦の一方が反対ならば、離婚はできない。それでも強引に離婚を進めようとする場合、地方裁判所へ提訴するが、相当の理由がなければ請求を棄却されてしまう。

Consensual divorce
協議離婚

Notification of Divorce

離婚届

All that is needed is the consent of the couple.
夫婦の合意があればよい

Submission
届出

Appropriate government office at city, ward, town or village level
市区町村の役所

If one spouse suspects that his or her partner is going to go expressly against his or her own wishes and to unilaterally issue a Notification of Divorce, it is possible to file a Petition for Non-acceptance of the Notice of Divorce.
離婚の意思がないのに離婚届を一方的に出されそうになった場合は市区町村の役所に「離婚届不受理申出」を行う

When one party of the marriage refuses to consent to divorce
夫婦の一方が同意しない場合は

Petition for Arbitration
調停申立

The person seeking the divorce requests arbitration at the family court in the area of domicile of his or her spouse.
相手の居住地のある家庭裁判所へ調停を依頼する

Divorce

In recent years, "Narita Airport divorce" and "Kansai Airport divorce" have become well-known expressions. After the wedding, a couple goes abroad all smiles for the honeymoon trip, but when they return they are refusing to speak to each other. At the airport they go their separate ways, and the next thing is an official divorce—such is the scenario, which is apparently becoming more and more common.

If both parties are agreed, a marriage is dissolved regardless of the reasons, providing a Notification of Divorce is filed with the appropriate government office. However, this mutual agreement is precisely the difficulty—and one reason behind the saying that "Marriages might be easy, but divorces are hard." In cases where both parties want a divorce but are unable to come to an agreement on the terms, they request arbitration from the family court. Even with such recourse, one party may still refuse to agree to the divorce, which will make it impossible. If the other party is still determined and refuses to give up, the matter goes to the district court. However, there then has to be an overwhelming and undeniable reason for a decision to be approved.

"I hate to think about how much compensation I'll pay!"

慰謝料が心配だ…!!

ドキドキ

Family Court 家庭裁判所		**District Court** 地方裁判所
The proceedings do not actually take the form of a court case, but rather discussions with members of an arbitration committee. 裁判ではなく、調停委員を交えた話し合い	Divorce not approved 不成立	Court Case 裁判 This involves considerable time and money. 費用と時間がかかる
Divorce approved 成立		Judgement 判決
Arbitrated Divorce 調停離婚		Adjudicated Divorce 裁判離婚

教科書採用のしくみ

わが国では1949年以来、教科書検定制度が採用され、教科書は教育課程の国の基準を示す学習指導要領にもとづいて作成され、文部大臣の検定を受けることになっている。しかし、検定制度の違憲性などをめぐる論議も多く、臨教審の答申をふまえて89年には従来の3段階審査から、検定をより簡略化し、2段階にすることで、検定制度の改善が図られた。

教科書の採用に関しては、小・中学校は各市町村の、公立高校は各都道府県の教育委員会の権限内である。ただし、高校では、事実上は各学校に一任している。義務教育の小・中学校の教科書は無償配布になっているが、このことも検定制度に少なからず影響を与えている点が指摘されている。

Ministry of Education, Culture, Sports, Science and Technology
文部科学省

Course of study
学習指導要領

The proposed textbook has a blank cover, and neither the names of publishers nor the project editors are shown.

申請本は出版社名や監修者名のない白表紙

Proposed textbook
申請本

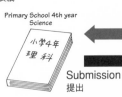

Primary School 4th year Science

小学4年 理科

Submission
提出

Submission
提出

School Textbook Publishers
教科書会社

Petition
申立

Revisions in the textbooks are made every 10 years in order to keep up with changes in the current curriculum. These companies also carry out editing and planning.

10年おきに改訂されるのが慣例の学習指導要領にもとづいて、企画・編集を行なう

Manuscript　原稿

Scholars and academics are asked to write, or at least oversee the writing of, a textbook.

学者・教師などに執筆・監修を依頼

Selection of School Textbooks

Ever since 1949, a system of government authorization of textbooks has been in effect in Japan. School textbooks, put together to meet certain nationally standardized requirements for instruction in schools, must receive official approval and authorization from the Minister of Education, Culture, Sports, Science and Technology. Much contention exists about the constitutionality of this system of authorization, and in 1989, in accordance with a report by a Special Educational Hearing, the process was simplified to involve a two-stage system of inspection instead of the previous three-stage system.

Issues surrounding the selection of which textbooks to use fall under the jurisdiction of the metropolitan and district educational boards in the case of public high schools, and the municipal educational boards in the case of primary and middle schools. The truth is, though, that for high schools the choice of which textbooks to use is left up to each school itself. The textbooks for primary and middle schools, attendance at which is compulsory, are given out free of charge, and it has been pointed out that this must give the system of authorization an unduly large amount of influence.

Textbook Inspection and Authorization Board
教科用図書検定調査審議会

Authorization of textbooks is carried out with inspection at two stages, at the proposed textbook level, and at the revised proofs level. Opinions of the inspectors have compelling force.

検定は申請本と修正表による二段階審査で行なわれ、検定意見は強制力をもつ

Board of inspection's opinions
検定意見

↓

List of required corrections
修正表

↓

Approval and authorization
合格

The period allowed for the raising of objections to the opinions of inspectors is 20 days.

検定意見に対する教科書会社の異議申立期間は20日間である

After 1999, all textbooks used at primary, and high school levels were produced with recycled paper.

99年から小中高の教科書が全面再生紙を使用

4th year primary school. Science.

There are 6 places nationwide where the results of the textbook authorization committees are made public. A list of the places which received opinions from the inspectors and a statement of reasons regarding the textbooks that failed to gain approval are also published.

検定結果の公開場所は全国に6か所あり、検定意見のついた箇所の一覧表や不合格になった教科書の理由書も公開される

教育委員会のしくみ

　教育委員会は、地方公共団体の教育行政機関であり、本来的には文部科学省と同等の立場に立って教育行政にあたることになっている。教育委員会が設置されるのは、都道府県、市（特別区）町村ごとであるが、市町村が合同して一つの教育委員会を置くケースもある。

　教育委員の数は5名ないし3名（町村の場合）で、任期は4年間。委員の任命は地方公共団体の長が行う。ただし、同一の政党に所属する委員が過半数を超えてはならない定めがある。

Prefectural boards of education
都道府県の教育委員会

Boards of education
Five members

教育委員
5名

The members are chosen by the prefectural governor and approved by the assembly. The chairperson of the board of education is chosen by the members.

教育委員は、知事が議会の承認を経て任命する。委員長は、委員が互選する

Chairperson of the board of education
委員長

Member
委員

Member
委員

Board of education
教育委員会

Member
委員

Member
委員

Education chairperson
教育長

Secretariat office
事務局

The education chairperson is the head of the secretariat office, and is assigned by the Ministry of Education, Culture, Sports, Science and Technology for the prefectures and cities designated by ordinance.

教育長は事務局の長で、都道府県および政令指定都市は文部科学大臣が任命

Boards of Education

Boards of education are the governmental education bodies under the direction of regional government bodies. These boards have the same authority as the Ministry of Education, Culture, Sports, Science and Technology. Boards of education are established under each prefecture, city (special ward), town, and village, but some cities, towns, and villages have just one board of education under them.

The number of people on each board is three (for towns and villages), and five for other areas, each serving a period of four years. The members are selected by the head of the local government with the limitation that people from the same political party cannot make up a majority of the board.

"This is what I oversee."

こちらは
わしの担当
だよ

Governor
知事

Universities
大学

Private schools
私立学校

The prefectural board of education has authority over personnel issues such as employment and transfer of teachers, and assignment of principals and vice-principals.

都道府県の教育委員会は、教員の採用・異動や校長・教頭の任免などの人事権をもっている

"You're the next principal!"

校長に
任命します。

教育委員会のしくみ……2

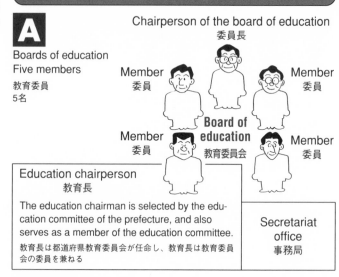

Boards of education of cities, towns, and villages
市町村の教育委員会

A

Boards of education
Five members
教育委員
5名

Chairperson of the board of education
委員長

Member 委員

Member 委員

Member 委員

Board of education
教育委員会

Member 委員

Education chairperson
教育長

The education chairman is selected by the education committee of the prefecture, and also serves as a member of the education committee.

教育長は都道府県教育委員会が任命し、教育長は教育委員会の委員を兼ねる

Secretariat office
事務局

The chairperson of the board of education for cities, towns, and villages has responsibility for each school, and decisions must be made with a majority of the committee members in attendance.

市町村の教育委員長は、各学校の校務に関する問題についての権限をもち、教育委員会の会議は出席委員の過半数で決定する

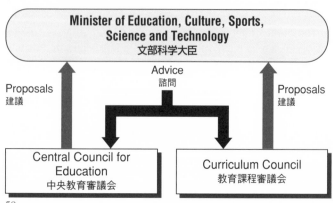

Minister of Education, Culture, Sports, Science and Technology
文部科学大臣

Advice
諮問

Proposals
建議

Proposals
建議

Central Council for Education
中央教育審議会

Curriculum Council
教育課程審議会

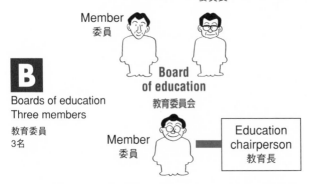

Chairperson of the board of education
委員長

Member
委員

B

Boards of education
Three members

教育委員
3名

Board
of education
教育委員会

Member
委員

Education chairperson
教育長

The members of the board of education are chosen by the heads of the city, town, and village and are approved by the local government assembly.

教育委員は議会の承認を経て市町村長が任命する

School administrator system　学校主任制

The board of education can at its discretion assign various administrators for each school. For elementary schools, administrators for education, for each school year, and for research, lifestyle guidance, health, and office work are assigned. And for junior high schools, these same administrators, in addition to career guidance and student instruction administrators, are assigned. Other administrators can also be assigned as necessary.

教育委員会は、校務分掌の一環として各学校に「主任」を置くことができる。小学校では教務主任、学年主任、研究主任、生活指導主任、保健主事、事務主任、中学校ではこれに進路指導主事、生徒指導主事が加わるが、必要に応じてその他の主任を置くこともできる

Five-day school week　学校週5日制

From April 1995, a policy was introduced to change the six-day school week to five days a week, except for the second and fourth weeks. The five-day school week will be fully implemented in 2003. However, since private schools do not necessarily adhere to this policy, it is likely that the five-day school week will exist for quite some time in name only.

公立学校での週5日制は、95年4月から第2、第4土曜日の月2回実施されているが、完全実施は2003年度をめどにしている。しかし、私立学校が必ずしもこれに同調しようとしていない以上、有名無実化のおそれもある

大学入試のしくみ

ゆりかごから墓場まで

　大学入試の制度が目まぐるしく変わっている。従来は、大学ごとに試験を行っていたのを、大学入試センター試験という統一試験が登場し、受験生たちは新たな受験対策を迫られている。この試験は、国公立大学の一次試験であるとともに、私立大学も自由に参加できる。国公立大学では独自に行う第二次試験の試験日を、連続方式か分離分割方式のいずれかで実施していたが、1999年度から分離分割方式に原則一本化された。

　98年の入試では、国立千葉大が"飛び入学制度"を実施し、3人の高校2年修了生が入学して話題を呼んだ。だが、2003年には定員と受験者数が同数になる見込みで、大学入試は様変わりせざるを得ない。

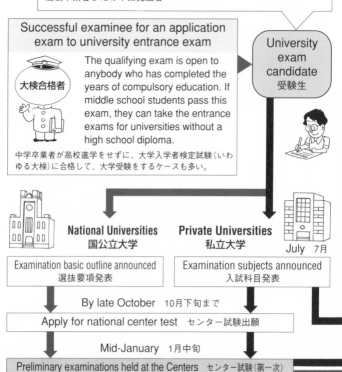

High school graduate or prospective high school graduate
高校卒業者または卒業見込者

Successful examinee for an application exam to university entrance exam

大検合格者

The qualifying exam is open to anybody who has completed the years of compulsory education. If middle school students pass this exam, they can take the entrance exams for universities without a high school diploma.

中学卒業者が高校進学をせずに、大学入学者検定試験（いわゆる大検）に合格して、大学受験をするケースも多い。

University exam candidate
受験生

National Universities
国公立大学

Private Universities
私立大学

July　7月

Examination basic outline announced
選抜要項発表

Examination subjects announced
入試科目発表

By late October　10月下旬まで

Apply for national center test　センター試験出願

Mid-January　1月中旬

Preliminary examinations held at the Centers　センター試験（第一次）

In 2000, there were roughly 530,000 candidates.
2000年は約53万人が受験

University Entrance Examinations

The university entrance examination system in Japan has been changing at a bewildering pace. In previous years exams were held at each university, but now a unified exam has come on the scene, held at National Centers of University Entrance Examinations—all of which poses yet another challenge for prospective examination students to have to handle. These National Center exams are the preliminary round of examinations for public universities, but private universities may also make use of them if they so choose. The dates for the secondary round of examinations, which are held independently at national public universities, used to be held either according to a continuous system, or the separate installment system. As of 1999, however, exams have been standardized according to the separate installment system.

Chiba National University provoked some discussion in the examinations of 1998 when it instituted an "early admission entrance system," and allowed 3 high-school students who had only completed 2 years of high-school education to enter. By the year 2003, the number of candidates is predicted to equal the number of the positions available, so yet more changes in the examination system will be inevitable.

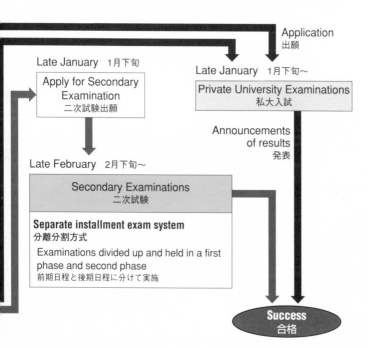

Application
出願

Late January　1月下旬

Apply for Secondary
Examination
二次試験出願

Late January　1月下旬〜

Private University Examinations
私大入試

Announcements
of results
発表

Late February　2月下旬〜

Secondary Examinations
二次試験

Separate installment exam system
分離分割方式

Examinations divided up and held in a first
phase and second phase
前期日程と後期日程に分けて実施

Success
合格

海外留学のしくみ

　各国政府から奨学金が受けられる公費留学生の資格は国ごとに異なるが、英語・仏語等の語学が堪能で30歳から40歳未満の大学卒業（見込）者に限られる。詳細は、各国駐日大使館や（財）日本国際教育協会等への問い合わせが必要である。また、高校生を対象とした各種基金による留学制度（都道府県教育委員会で募集）もある。

　公式の留学制度を受けない私費留学は、自分の目的をはっきりさせ、周到な準備が大事である。大学を選ぶ際の資料は各大学等で用意されている。アメリカ留学を希望する場合は、フルブライト委員会（東京）があり、入学要領や願書を取り寄せなければならない。大学によっては英語標準テスト（TOEFL）の受験が必要となる。

Collect application materials
入学願書を取り寄せる

"You'll stand a much better chance if you can speak English!"

留学スルニハ英語力が大切デス

Decide on which schools to apply to
　　　志望校決定

Required documents: 〈必要書類〉

(1) Application	① 願書
(2) Transcripts	② 成績証明書
(3) Graduation certificate	③ 卒業証明書
(4) Recommendations	④ 推薦状
(5) Proof regarding financial status	⑤ 財務能力証明書
(6) Health certificate	⑥ 身体検査証
(7) Documents pertaining to sponsorship, etc.	⑦ 身元引受人の証書など

English proficiency test 英語標準テスト	For consultation about studying abroad 留学の相談は
This is known as the TOEFL test, and the paper-and-pencil test is held once a month. The computer based test (CBT) began in October 2000. TOEFLといい、毎月1回、ペーパーテストが行われている。2000年10月からは、コンピュータによる受験（CBT）も可能になった	The American Center in Sapporo, Tokyo, Nagoya, Kyoto, Osaka and Fukuoka アメリカンセンター　札幌・東京・名古屋・京都・大阪・福岡
	The Fulbright Committee in Tokyo フルブライト委員会　東京
	The International Education Center in Osaka 国際教育センター　大阪

Study Abroad

The requirements that students have to fulfill in order to receive government grants to study abroad vary according to the country, but such grants tend to be given to people who have graduated (or are about to graduate) from a university, who are between 30 to 40 years of age, and who are proficient in languages such as English or French. For detailed information, requests should be made at the embassies of the particular countries involved, as well as from such public corporations as the Japan International Education Association. There are also various organizations at the local government level that provide funding to enable high school students to study abroad. Local educational boards are responsible for choosing such students.

Those students who go abroad to study using their own personal funds should make sure that they have a clear objective, and that they are thoroughly prepared. The materials necessary to make applications to universities are available on request at each university. If students wish to go abroad to study in the United States, the Fulbright Committee in Tokyo is one place to ask, and they should gather all the information about university entry requirements application forms. Depending on the university, prospective students may be required to take the TOEFL English proficiency test.

Proof of acceptance
入学許可通知

↓

Remittance of university fees
Health insurance
入学金送金／保険加入

↓

Application for university housing/dorm
寮の申込み

↓

Application for visa to study abroad
Application for passport
留学ビザ申請／旅券申請

↓

Entry into university
入学

公正証書作成のしくみ

公正証書は公文書であるため、その証明力は絶大なものがある。土地・家屋の売買や貸借、財産分与、遺言書の作成、金銭貸借等々、公正証書を作成すべき事柄も多いが、後のトラブルを未然に防止するうえで公正証書を作成することはきわめて有効だ。

たとえば、金銭貸借に関しては、強制執行認諾条項をつけた公正証書を作成しておくと、契約不履行という事態が生じた場合に、裁判上の手続きなしで差押えなどの強硬手段をとることができる。また、遺言書は公正証書にしておくことが最良の方法である。

公正証書遺言では、公証人に口頭で遺言内容を伝えるだけで、法律にもとづいた遺言書ができあがる。

Registered Contract of Financial Loan
公正証書金銭貸借契約書

"Just to make sure, let's draw up a Certificate of Seal Registration."

念のため公正証書をつくっておきましょう。

Notary's Office
公証人役場

The procurement of a Certificate of Seal Registration of course requires a fee.

証書作成の手数料が必要になる

Notary
公証人

Default
不履行

Forced execution of payment
強制執行

Drawing Up a Certificate of Seal Registration

A certificate of seal registration (the equivalent of a notarized document) is an official document, so its probative force is absolute. There are many situations when the procurement of a certificate of seal registration becomes necessary—for example, in the purchase and sale of land and buildings, as well as in lending and borrowing of money, in the allotment of land, and in the preparation of wills and bequests. In such cases, drawing up a seal registration is an effective way of preventing any untoward friction or problems occurring after the transaction has taken place.

For instance, when one is making a loan, if one draws up an Article of Permission to Enforce Execution attached with certificate of seal registration, this gives one the right, in the case of failure to abide by conditions of contract, to resort to such tough measures as seizing a person's property in order to compel payment. Wills and bequests should also ideally be attached with a certificate of seal registration.

Once a seal registration certificate is attached to the will, the person making the bequest (testator) merely has to make a verbal request to the notary about the contents for this to have legal validity.

If for reasons of ill health or due to other circumstances, the testator cannot go in person to visit the notary, the notary may pay an official visit to him or her at home.

遺言者が病気などで出頭できないときは、公証人が出張してくれる

How to make a registered will
公正証書遺言

The person who wants to make a will (testator) goes to the notary's office with at least two witnesses.

遺言者は証人2名以上を同行して公証人役場へ

▼

The testator informs the notary of the contents.

遺言者は公証人に遺言内容を話す

▼

The notary commits the wishes of the testator to writing.

公証人は遺言を書面にする

▼

The testator, witness and notary all sign and add their seal to the documents.

遺言者、証人、公証人が書面に署名捺印をする

叙勲のしくみ

　現在わが国の勲章は、大勲位に2階級、旭日章に8階級、宝冠章に8階級、瑞宝章に8階級、それに文化勲章の合計5種類、27階級の勲章がある。

　大勲位は皇室・皇族と外国国家元首が対象となるが、例外的に吉田茂、佐藤栄作、中曽根康弘の3人の元首相が受章。勲二等以上と文化勲章は宮中で親授式が行われるが、勲三等以下の勲章、賜杯、褒章などについては、内閣総理大臣の命を受けた賞勲局長が所管大臣に伝達し、所管大臣から各受章者に伝達する。

Types of decorations
叙勲の種類

Spring and autumn awards
春秋叙勲

Awarded to distinguished persons over the age of 70. Non-Japanese are also awarded.

70歳以上の功労者が対象。外国人叙勲も行う

Posthumous awards
死亡叙勲

Presented after a distinguished person passes away.

功労者が死亡した場合に行う

National guest awards
国賓叙勲

Awards presented when a foreign guest of state visits Japan.

外国から国賓が来日した時に儀礼的に行う

Others
その他

Awards given to those older than 88, commemorative awards, etc.

88歳以上を対象にした高齢者叙勲や記念叙勲など

Decorations

There are five types of official decorations made in Japan: The Supreme Order of the Chrysanthemum (2 levels), the Order of the Rising Sun (8 levels), the Order of the Precious Crown (8 levels), the Order of the Sacred Treasure (8 levels), and the Order of Culture, awarded in varying degrees at 27 levels.

The Supreme Order of the Chrysanthemum is awarded to members of the Imperial Household and family, and overseas heads of state, with exceptions being made for three former Japanese prime ministers: Shigeru Yoshida, Eisaku Sato, and Yasuhiro Nakasone. Award ceremonies for decorations of the first and second levels, and also the Order of Culture awards, are held at the Imperial Palace. Other awards include medals, trophies, and prizes, presented to the recipients by the appropriate minister upon orders from the cabinet relayed to the Decorations Bureau.

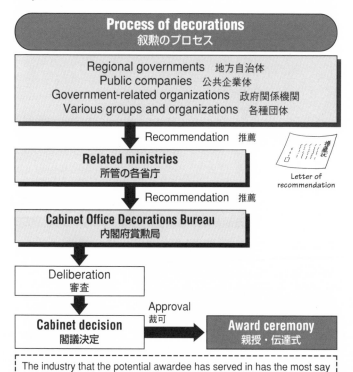

Process of decorations
叙勲のプロセス

Regional governments　地方自治体
Public companies　公共企業体
Government-related organizations　政府関係機関
Various groups and organizations　各種団体

Recommendation　推薦

Letter of recommendation

Related ministries
所管の各省庁

Recommendation　推薦

Cabinet Office Decorations Bureau
内閣府賞勲局

Deliberation
審査

Approval
裁可

Cabinet decision
閣議決定

Award ceremony
親授・伝達式

The industry that the potential awardee has served in has the most say in who will be given an award. The work needed to submit a proposal is quite cumbersome.
叙勲の申請は業界の推薦がものをいう。そのための提出資料づくりは、労力がかかる

叙勲のしくみ……2

Types of awards 勲章の種類		
Supreme Order of the Chrysanthemum 菊花章	Collar of the Supreme Order of the Chrysanthemum 大勲位菊花章頸飾	
	Grand Cordon or Supreme Order of the Chrysanthemum 大勲位菊花大綬章	
Order of the Rising Sun 旭日章	From levels one to eight 勲一等から勲八等まで	
Order of the Precious Crown 宝冠章	From levels one to eight 勲一等から勲八等まで	
Order of the Sacred Treasure 瑞宝章	From levels one to eight 勲一等から勲八等まで	
Order of Culture 文化勲章	Refer to P. 71 70ページ参照	
Ribbons 褒章	Trophy 賜杯	
	There is also the Silver Cup and the Wood Cup. 銀杯、木杯がある	

Personal investiture notification
親授伝達

First level awards and the Order of Culture are presented at the Imperial Palace by the Emperor.

勲一等以上および文化勲章は、宮中で天皇から直接授与される

Second level awards are presented by the Prime Minister with the Emperor in attendance.

勲二等は、天皇臨席のもと総理大臣から授与される

Other awards are presented by the affiliated ministry.

勲三等以下は、所管の大臣から伝達される

Decorations……2

Highest decoration
最高位の勲章

The First Order of the Precious
Crown to be presented to women
女性に与えられる勲一等宝冠章の正章

A sub-award to the Order
of the Sacred Treasure
勲一等瑞宝章の副章

Levels seven and eight were abolished in
principle from March 2001.
2001年3月から、勲七等・勲八等は原則廃止

Medal with Red Ribbon…for saving life
紅綬褒章……人命救助

Medal with Yellow Ribbon…for business and industry
黄綬褒章……業務精励

Medal with Purple Ribbon…for social welfare
紫綬褒章……学術・芸術上の事績

Medal with Blue Ribbon…for public service
藍綬褒章……公共事務

Medal with Dark Blue Ribbon
　　　…for contributing more than 5 million yen to the public
紺綬褒章……公益のために500万円以上の私財を寄付

Medal with Green Ribbon…superior virtue
緑綬褒章……徳行がひときわすぐれた人

For some reason, the Green
Ribbon is currently not presented.
緑綬褒章は、なぜか現在授与なし

69

文化勲章授与のしくみ

　文化勲章は、科学技術や芸術など文化の発展に特に貢献のあった人に授与されるもので、1937年文化勲章令により定められた。49年度以降は11月3日の文化の日に授与が行われている。勲章は橘の花をかたどった清楚な様式である。受賞者は、すでに文化功労者になっている人の中から、文部科学省が委嘱した選考委員会によって選考され、閣議で決定する。

　文化勲章には、他の勲章のような等級はないが、文化・学術界においては最高の栄誉である。さらに文化功労者年金（年額350万円）が終身、国から支給される。

　ちなみに1969年には、人類最初の月着陸に成功したアメリカのアポロ11号の乗組員3名に、外国人として初めて授与された。

Candidate
候補者

Distinguished contributors to culture

文化功労者

Candidates are typically selected by a committee of distinguished contributors to culture, with seniority usually being a factor.

文化勲章は文化功労者から選ばれるのが恒例になっていて、年功序列的な人選がされるケースがほとんど

Artistic Committee　Scholastic Committee

芸術院会員　学士院会員

The members of the scholastic and artistic committees are considered reserve troops for the committee of distinguished contributors.

文化功労者の予備軍とされるのが、学術分野の学士院会員、芸術分野の芸術院会員である

The Order of Cultural Merit is designed in the motif of a mandarin blossom.

文化勲章は橘の花をデザインしたものだ

The Order of Cultural Merit

The Order of Cultural Merit, passed into law in 1937, is given to those who have made significant contributions to the development of science and the arts. Beginning from 1949, awards are presented on November 3rd, Culture Day. The awards are presented at a formal ceremony surrounded by mandarin blossoms, the flower of culture. The recipients are recommended by a committee designated by the Ministry of Education, Culture, Sports, Science and Technology from candidates consisting of "distinguished contributors to culture," with the final decision being made by the cabinet.

The Order of Cultural Merit does not have the various levels of other awards, but it is considered the greatest honor in the science and artistic communities. In addition to the honor, the recipients receive an annual pension of 3.5 million yen from the government. In 1969, the three astronauts on Apollo 11 who walked on the moon became the first non-Japanese to receive the award.

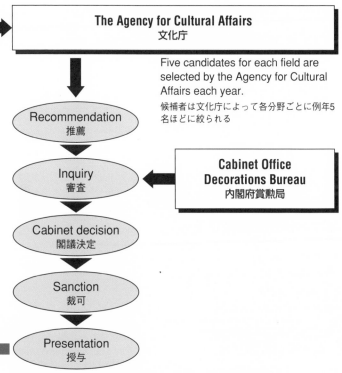

The Agency for Cultural Affairs
文化庁

Five candidates for each field are selected by the Agency for Cultural Affairs each year.
候補者は文化庁によって各分野ごとに例年5名ほどに絞られる

Recommendation
推薦

Inquiry
審査

Cabinet Office Decorations Bureau
内閣府賞勲局

Cabinet decision
閣議決定

Sanction
裁可

Presentation
授与

Awards are given by the Emperor at the Imperial Palace.
皇居で天皇から直接渡される

葬儀社のしくみ

　葬儀というと、当然暗くて沈滞したムードになる。しかし、誰もが暗く悲しんでいては葬儀は進行しない。葬儀社は悲しむ肉親に代わって葬儀を取り仕切るとともに、そこに厳粛さと一種の安心感を与えなくてはならない。まさに裏方の仕事だが、万一の場合に備えて24時間寝台自動車を待機させたり、各宗派の僧侶や葬儀場の手配など迅速さが求められる難しいビジネスでもある。

　1996年には、葬儀を演出する専門知識や技能を証明する「葬儀ディレクター」が政府認定資格となった。高齢化社会の日本で、2000年には1兆1000億円産業に拡大した。

In former years the industry was notorious for the numbers of one-man firms greedy to squeeze as much yen out of people as they could. However, with the large funeral undertaker firm, Kōeki listed in the stock market, the industry has managed to improve its image.

かつてはボッタクリ的な個人事業者も目立った葬儀社だが、最大手の公益社の上場によりイメージがアップした

Funerals require a number of people to carry out various practical duties.

葬儀には実行部隊が必要

Local Governments
地方自治体

These also give help to local residents, mostly with ward funerals and city funerals.

区民葬・市民葬が一般的

Mutual Assistance Associations
互助会

Mutual assistance associations, numbering 300 nationwide, held with all sorts of ceremonial occasions including weddings and funerals. Nōkyo, Agricultural Cooperatives, and Seikyō, Life Cooperatives, also help.

全国に約300以上ある冠婚葬祭互助会のほか、農協や生協も参入している

Businesses
事業者

There are roughly 4500 private funeral companies nationwide, but most are small- to mid-size type enterprises with close ties to the local community.

民間の葬儀社は全国に約4500社あるが、地域密着型の中小企業がほとんどだ

Funeral Undertakers

The word "funeral" inevitably produces a somber, rather depressed mood. But if everybody just gave themselves over to gloom and sadness, funerals would never get off the ground. The funeral undertakers see to all the details of the funeral ceremony while the relatives of the deceased get on with their grieving. They also make sure the proceedings have an air of solemnity and a kind of soothing atmosphere. The work that the undertaker has to do is thus the epitome of a behind-the-scenes job, but it is also quite demanding. For example, a car has to be kept ready to rush off to collect the body of the deceased at any hour of the day, communications have to be made promptly with clergy of various religious sects, and arrangements have to be made speedily at the place where funeral is to be held.

In 1996, the specific qualification of "Funeral Ceremony Director," proof that a person had the specialist knowledge and capability to officiate at funeral ceremonies was recognized by the government. In the year 2000, the funeral industry in Japan (an "aging society") has swelled to an industry worth 1.1 trillion yen.

Average funeral expenses 平均葬儀費用		
Total expenses: ¥2,060,000 総額206万円		
Fee paid to temple, ¥510,000	Meal and reception expenses: ¥430,000	Payment to funeral undertakers: ¥1,120,000
寺院への費用 51万円	飲食接待費用 43万円	葬儀社などへの支払い 112万円

A comparison of funeral expenses from region to region shows that Tokyo is the most expensive place to hold a funeral. The Chūgoku region in the main island of Japan, on the other hand, is apparently quite reasonable. According to statistics from the government, the number of deceased in 1996 was about 900,000. The number of people dying annually is predicted to increase by 2 or 3% every year, so by 2025, we can foresee that 1,790,000 will die annually.

葬儀費用を地域別に比較してみると、物価に比例して東京が一番高い。逆に中国地方はかなり安いそうだ。なお、政府によると96年の死亡者数は約90万人。今後2～3％ずつ増加していく見通しで、2025年には約179万人が死亡すると推定されている

葬儀社のしくみ……2

Changes in the style of funeral ceremonies
お葬式形態の変化

Since people's residences (apartments, condominiums etc) tend to be on the small side, funerals are rarely held at home.

マンション等では手狭なため、自宅での葬儀が少なくなってきた

Funerals at funeral halls
斎場での葬儀

Ward funeral halls, temple funeral halls, municipally managed funeral halls

区民斎場、寺院斎場、都道府県の公営斎場

More and more people are going in for self-arranged funerals.

手作り葬儀が増える傾向にある

Funerals in local facilities
地域社会での葬式

In various ward and city centers, In public halls

区民・市民センター、公民館

High-tech funerals
ハイテク葬

Funeral costs for a top-level executive of a company are likely to reach 15 million yen—at the very least. Some company funerals cost 100 million yen range. Recent years have seen the appearance of "high tech" funeral services, which use laser light for special effects, and which are broadcast via satellite on TV stations nationwide.

社葬にかかる費用は上場企業の経営者で最低1500万円。なかには1億円クラスの社葬もある。最近はレーザー光線を使ったハイテク葬を衛星放送で全国に生中継するケースも

Self-arranged funerals
自分葬

Ironically, the person who is the central protagonist of a funeral often has very little say in how it is to be held. Nowadays many people think that they should have more control in the arrangements of this once-after-a-lifetime event, and more and more funeral companies are offering arrangements allowing a person to draw up a contract with them before death specifying the details of the ceremony.

自分のことなのに思うにまかせないのが葬儀。まさに"一生に一度"だから自分で仕切るのは当然ということで、葬儀の生前契約システムも登場している

The funeral business: increasing systematization
システム化される葬式ビジネス

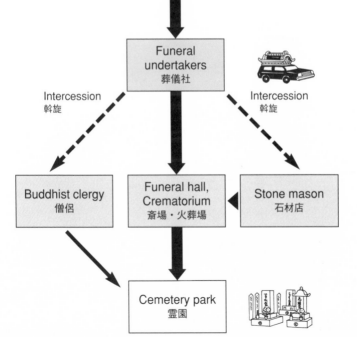

Hospital
病院

Certain bizarre practices occur in the funeral business in cities—for example, Buddhist priests wining and dining funeral undertakers, or paying them rebates in order to assure that they get business.

都市部では僧侶が葬儀社を接待したり、リベートを支払ったりする珍現象も

Permission from the Minister of Land, Infrastructure and Transport is required for funeral undertakers to conduct business involving a funeral hearse.

葬儀社が霊柩事業を行うには国土交通大臣の許可が必要である

Funeral undertakers
葬儀社

Intercession
斡旋

Intercession
斡旋

Buddhist clergy
僧侶

Funeral hall, Crematorium
斎場・火葬場

Stone mason
石材店

Cemetery park
霊園

法事のしくみ

　法事は死者の霊をとむらう儀式である。大別すると仏式、神式、キリスト教式の3種があるが、わが国では仏式が最もなじみが深い。そこで、仏式を例にとって法事のプロセスを見てみると、忌明けの法要である四十九日法要までは七日毎に、それ以後は毎月の命日に霊をなぐさめるというしきたりになっている。これは、故人の霊が安らかにあの世に旅立てるようにする遺族のつとめで、その大きな区切りが一年後の祥月命日にとり行われる一周忌法要である。以後の法要は次第に間隔が長くなるが、一周忌の次の三周忌はなくなってから二年目という起算（正月が経過することで一年と数える）のしかたをする。法事は五十回忌をもって完了するのが慣例である。

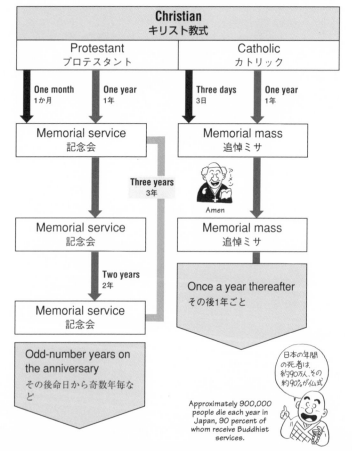

Christian
キリスト教式

| Protestant プロテスタント | Catholic カトリック |

One month 1か月　**One year** 1年　　**Three days** 3日　**One year** 1年

Memorial service
記念会

Memorial mass
追悼ミサ

Three years 3年

Amen

Memorial service
記念会

Memorial mass
追悼ミサ

Two years 2年

Once a year thereafter
その後1年ごと

Memorial service
記念会

Odd-number years on the anniversary
その後命日から奇数年毎など

日本の年間の死者は、約90万人、その約90%が仏式

Approximately 900,000 people die each year in Japan, 90 percent of whom receive Buddhist services.

Memorial Service

Memorial services are held to pay respect to the spirit of the deceased. The three main categories are Buddhist, Shinto, and Christian services, Buddhist services being the most common in Japan. In Buddhism, the mourning period lasts for 49 days, with ceremonies held by the family on every seventh day during that period, and then once a month on the obit. It is the responsibility of the family to carry out these rites to help the deceased proceed to the other world. A memorial service is held on the first anniversary after passing, called the shōtsuki-meinichi. After the first year, the length of time between rites gradually increases, and following the first year rites is the third year rites, which is in the second year after the death. (In the year when a person passes away, the passing of New Years is counted as one year.) It is not uncommon for the extended mourning period to end on the 50th anniversary of death.

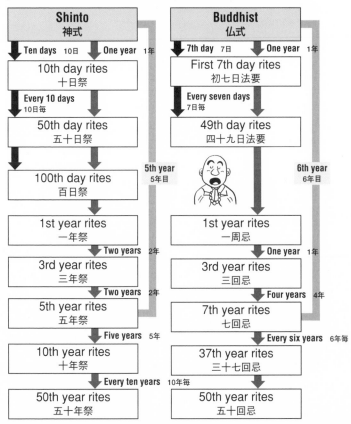

Shinto 神式	Buddhist 仏式
Ten days 10日 — **One year** 1年	**7th day** 7日 — **One year** 1年
10th day rites 十日祭	First 7th day rites 初七日法要
Every 10 days 10日毎	**Every seven days** 7日毎
50th day rites 五十日祭	49th day rites 四十九日法要
	5th year 5年目
100th day rites 百日祭	
	6th year 6年目
1st year rites 一年祭	1st year rites 一周忌
Two years 2年	**One year** 1年
3rd year rites 三年祭	3rd year rites 三回忌
Two years 2年	**Four years** 4年
5th year rites 五年祭	7th year rites 七回忌
Five years 5年	**Every six years** 6年毎
10th year rites 十年祭	37th year rites 三十七回忌
Every ten years 10年毎	
50th year rites 五十年祭	50th year rites 五十回忌

遺産相続のしくみ

　遺産相続は、被相続人の死亡（失踪宣言制度により死亡とみなされるものも含む）によって、開始される。遺産の相続分については遺言による指定相続分と、それがない場合の法定相続分とがある。さらに遺言がない場合は、相続人の協議・合意による分割も可能だ。遺産とはいえ、なかには借金などのマイナス財産が含まれているケースもある。その場合は、相続を放棄することもできる。

　また、遺産相続にともなう節税対策として、生前に多数の人と養子縁組をする"かき集め養子"が一時流行したが、現在はこういう手は使えない制度になっている。相続税の申告期間は原則として10か月間となっているので、この間に相続分の確定と納税が必要だ。

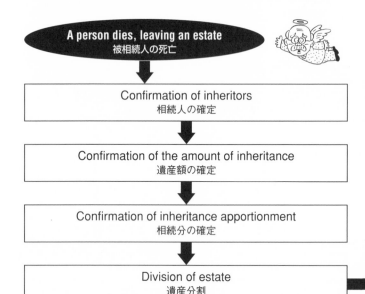

A person dies, leaving an estate
被相続人の死亡

Confirmation of inheritors
相続人の確定

Confirmation of the amount of inheritance
遺産額の確定

Confirmation of inheritance apportionment
相続分の確定

Division of estate
遺産分割

The basic rate of deduction for inheritance tax involves a fixed deduction of 50 million yen, and then 10 million yen for every inheritor.
For spouses of the deceased, however, tax exemption applies to the legally recognized inheritance, or up to 160 million yen.

● 相続税の基礎控除は、定額控除5000万円、相続人1人当たりの比例控除は1000万円

● 配偶者に対しては、法定相続分または1億6000万円までは非課税

Property Inheritance

Property inheritance commences on the death of the person from whom property is to be inherited (and this includes cases where a person is declared by law to have "absconded" or "disappeared"). Inheritance covers both those sections of a person's property laid down in a will, and parts for which no will has been drawn up, in which case the apportionment is decided in accordance with provisions in the law. In cases where there is no will at all, property division is carried out through division based on discussions and agreement of inheritors. Of course, it is often the case that debts are inherited by the individuals who inherit property and estate. In this case, the inheritors may choose to abandon their inheritance.

At one time, as a strategy to decrease the burden of tax that inevitably accompanies inheritance, it was common to enter into adoptive relationships with a number of people while one was still alive (this practice was known pejoratively as "corral adoption"). Nowadays, however, it is not possible to take recourse to this measure. The period allowed in which one has to submit a report for tax purposes is 10 months; during this time one should both file a final tax report and pay the requisite taxes.

It is possible to abandon one's inheritance to avoid inheriting a person's debts. In such cases, one submits a petition to the family court within three months of the commencement of inheritance.

借金を相続しなければならないときは、相続放棄ができる。その場合は、相続の開始を知った日から3か月以内に家庭裁判所へ申し立てる

Inheritance
IOU

Obligatory within 10 months from the day after the inheritee's decease.

死亡の日の翌日から原則として10か月以内に行うこと

Inheritance tax return and payment

相続税申告・納税

Tax Office
税務署

"In principle, inheritance tax should be paid in one lump sum, but remedial measures are available that enable payment in installments, as well as payment in kind."

納税は一時払いが原則ですが、分割払いや物納の救済措置もあります

第**3**章

街でなじみの ランド・マーク

しくみを知ると、いっそう親しみが湧くぞ！

Chapter 3

Common City Landmarks

A Little Knowledge
Goes a Long Way

宝くじ販売のしくみ

　宝くじは、全国都道府県および政令指定都市によって発売され、金融機関によって発売代行される。まず、発行元の自治体が年間の発売計画を議会にかけ、了承を得る。次に総務省に発売計画を申請し許可を得た時点で、受託金融機関を公募する。受託銀行は、地方自治体の販売計画にそって公告し、売捌人に販売を委託する。売捌人は街頭などの宝くじ販売所で、券を販売するというプロセスを経る。

　購入した宝くじの当選発表は新聞などで行われ、当選券は受託銀行で当選金と交換される。「宝くじ世論調査」によると、年間100億円もの賞金が、引取人もなく１年の時効期間を過ぎて販売元の地方自治体に納付され、公共事業に役立てられているそうだ。

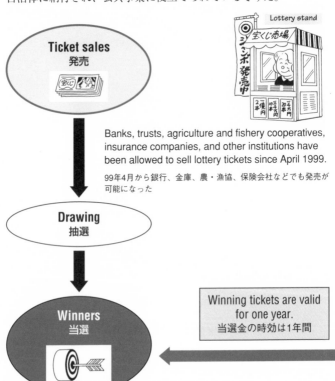

Ticket sales
発売

Lottery stand

宝くじ売場

Banks, trusts, agriculture and fishery cooperatives, insurance companies, and other institutions have been allowed to sell lottery tickets since April 1999.

99年4月から銀行、金庫、農・漁協、保険会社などでも発売が可能になった

Drawing
抽選

Winners
当選

Winning tickets are valid for one year.
当選金の時効は1年間

Tickets that qualify for winnings of 10,000 yen or less (50,000 yen or less at some stands) can be cashed in at the lottery stands.
売場で受け取れる当選金は1万円以下（一部の指定売場で5万円以下）である

Lotteries

Lottery tickets are sold in all prefectures and in specified cities through financial institutions. Each individual local government submits a sales plan to its council for approval. Upon receiving approval, it recruits financial institutions that then begin selling the lottery tickets in accordance with the sales plan. Those who wish to buy lottery tickets can find stands on the street and elsewhere.

Winning numbers are made public in the newspaper, and the winning lottery tickets are cashed in at specified banks. According to a white paper on lotteries, local governments annually profit some 10 billion yen from lottery tickets that are not cashed in.

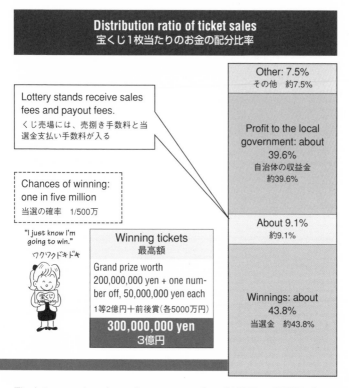

Distribution ratio of ticket sales
宝くじ1枚当たりのお金の配分比率

Lottery stands receive sales fees and payout fees.
くじ売場には、売捌き手数料と当選金支払い手数料が入る

Chances of winning: one in five million
当選の確率　1/500万

"I just know I'm going to win."
ワクワクドキドキ

Other: 7.5%
その他　約7.5%

Profit to the local government: about 39.6%
自治体の収益金
約39.6%

About 9.1%
約9.1%

Winnings: about 43.8%
当選金　約43.8%

Winning tickets
最高額

Grand prize worth 200,000,000 yen + one number off, 50,000,000 yen each
1等2億円＋前後賞（各5000万円）

300,000,000 yen
3億円

The lottery numbers for each group range from 100000 to 199999. Some of the winning numbers have runner-up prizes. So if in group 1 the winning number is 100000, the runner-up prizes will go to the holders of the tickets numbered 100001 and 199999.

宝くじの番号は100000番から199999番を1組としている。そして、01組100000番の前後賞は100001番と199999番というように、組の中から出ることになっている

共同募金のしくみ

　赤い羽根でおなじみの共同募金は、1947年に始まった全国的規模の運動である。この運動の実施機関は、都道府県単位に組織されている共同募金会で、それぞれ独立している。その取りまとめ機関として中央共同募金があり、厚生労働省が管掌している。募金活動に従事する人は募金奉仕者と呼ばれ、全国に約200万人いる。募金の実施期間は、毎年10月から12月までの3か月間で、募金方法は街頭募金、法人募金、戸別募金、学校・職域募金、興行募金、バッジ募金、歳末たすけあい募金などの種類に分かれる。こうして寄せられた募金総額は、年間およそ300億円にものぼり、児童福祉、生活援護、身障者福祉などに役立てられている。

The organization behind joint fund-raising
共同募金の実施機関

Central Joint Fund-raising Committee
中央共同募金会

Joint fund-raising committees of local governments
各都道府県の共同募金会

Distribution
配分

Setting of fund-raising targets
目標額の設定

Money raised
集金

Chapters 分会:	Towns, villages, school districts 町村・校区単位
Support committees 支会:	Counties, cities 郡市部単位

Joint Fund-raising

The so-called red-feather fund-raising campaign was started nationally in 1947. This campaign is organized for each local government unit under independent joint fund-raising committees. The process is overseen by the Central Joint Fund-raising Committee under the direction of the Ministry of Health, Labour and Welfare. Throughout the country, there are approximately two million fund-raising volunteers. The campaign is conducted three months a year, from October to December. Money is collected in various ways, including street campaigns, company contributions, house-to-house collection, school and workplace collections, fund-raising performances, badge campaigns, and year-end charity campaigns. Approximately 30 billion yen is collected every year and used to provide support to children, the disabled, and others.

How money is collected
募金の方法

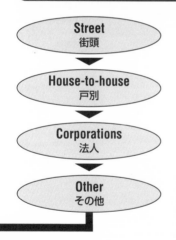

Street
街頭

House-to-house
戸別

Corporations
法人

Other
その他

Please contribute.

A little more than two percent of the money collected comes from street collections. This amount is declining each year. Individuals contributing more than 10,000 yen are given deductions on their income tax.

街頭での募金は全体の2%強で、年々その比率は低くなってきている。個人の大口寄付者(1万円以上)は、所得税が安くなる

Details concerning the money raised and how it is used are made public in newspapers.
募金および配分については、共同募金会が新聞等による公示をする

書店のしくみ

　書店で売れ残った本は、一定期間を経て返品できるというのが、わが国独特の委託販売制度である。返品が自由であるため、書店は勢いたくさんの本を仕入れてしまう。その結果、書籍の4割強が返品の憂き目にあっているのだ。なかには、店頭に並べられないまま、返品されてしまう本もある。

　書店に配本するのは取次会社で、配本数は書店の売上実績をもとに決定される。これをパターン配本という。本の発行部数によっては、小さな書店には配本されない場合も多々ある。

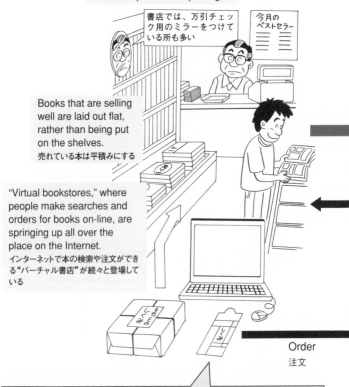

Many bookstores are fitted with mirrors to prevent shop-lifting.

書店では、万引チェック用のミラーをつけている所も多い

今月のベストセラー

Books that are selling well are laid out flat, rather than being put on the shelves.
売れている本は平積みにする

"Virtual bookstores," where people make searches and orders for books on-line, are springing up all over the place on the Internet.
インターネットで本の検索や注文ができる"バーチャル書店"が続々と登場している

Order
注文

The order goes to the distributor on an order slip, and the bookstore pays for the book (which then becomes non-returnable).
取次会社への注文は注文票によって行い、買い切りである

Bookstores

In Japan, books that are remaindered at bookstores can be returned to the publishers after a set period of time through the so-called "Sale or Return" system (sales on consignment basis), which is unique to this country. Since the return of items ordered is so easy, bookstores tend to buy far more stock than they can actually foresee selling. As a result, well over 40% of all publications meet the fate of being returned as unsold goods. Some books are returned without even reaching the stage of being laid out on the shelves.

Books are brought to the bookstores by distributing agents, who decide on the number of books to be distributed depending on the particular bookstore's sales records. This is known as pataan (pattern) book distribution. Often, certain books will not even be distributed to the smaller bookstores, which tend to sell fewer copies.

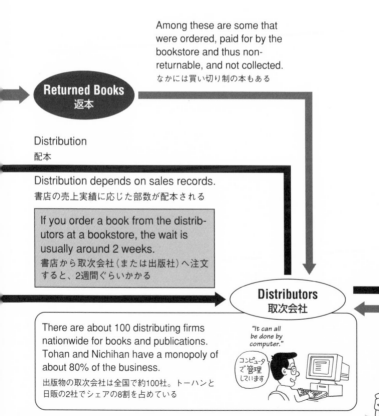

Among these are some that were ordered, paid for by the bookstore and thus non-returnable, and not collected.
なかには買い切り制の本もある

Returned Books
返本

Distribution
配本

Distribution depends on sales records.
書店の売上実績に応じた部数が配本される

If you order a book from the distributors at a bookstore, the wait is usually around 2 weeks.
書店から取次会社（または出版社）へ注文すると、2週間ぐらいかかる

Distributors
取次会社

There are about 100 distributing firms nationwide for books and publications. Tohan and Nichihan have a monopoly of about 80% of the business.

出版物の取次会社は全国で約100社。トーハンと日販の2社でシェアの8割を占めている

"It can all be done by computer."
コンピュータで管理しています

Accounts are settled taking into account returned books and sales proceedings (once the commission for distribution has been taken out). The usual consignment period between distributing companies and publishing companies is 3 months for magazines, 2 months for journals, and 6 months for new titles.

返品および売上代金決済（取次マージン差引）。取次会社と出版社間の委託期間は、月刊誌3か月、週刊誌2か月、新刊書籍は6か月が原則

Publishing House
出版社

Distribution to bookstores is usually carried out on the pattern distribution model, in which distributors decide on the basis of various kinds of data which bookstores should have copies sent to them. Occasionally a publisher will designate a particular bookstore where they want a book to be sold.

書店への配本は、取次会社が各種のデータにもとづいて行うパターン配本が一般的だが、出版社が書店を指定するケースもある

Recently many bookstores have been forced to close because of generally depressed book sales and the upsurge of superstores. In 1999 about 600 new stores came into being and 1300 closed down. This seems to be the trend for the foreseeable future.

近年、出版不況と大型書店の乱立で、閉店する書店が増加している。1999年は出店数約600店に対して、閉店数約1300店で、こうした傾向は今後も続くと見られている

The period for book consignment from the distribution agency to the bookstores for new titles is generally 4 months. In this returnable sales system, the bookstore takes the profit made on sales and then reimburses the distributors. Since invoices are sent to bookstores immediately after distribution, the bookstores tend to return books rather quickly in order to get credit for the invoices, creating a vicious cycle.

取次会社から書店に対する新刊本（書籍）の委託期間は、4か月を原則としている。これは売れた分だけ小売マージンを差し引き、取次会社へ支払いをする「返品条件付き売買」なのだが、書店には取次会社からすぐに請求書が送られてくる。そのため、書店は防衛のために早々と見切りをつけて返品するという悪循環が一部に見られる

There are about 26,000 bookstores nationwide. The major publishing houses and distribution agencies tend to concentrate their focus on the larger bookstores, using a ranking distribution, which means that new titles often do not get delivered to smaller bookstores.

全国の書店数は約2万6000店。大手出版社と取次会社は大型店を中心に重点配本する"ランク配本"を行っているため、小さな書店には新刊が回らないことも多い

古書店のしくみ

　学生時代には、古書店にお世話になった人も多いに違いない。特に、発売されて間もない新刊本が割安で買えるというメリットが、古書店にはある。これは特価本といって、専門の問屋があり、そこから卸し値で仕入れてくるため安く売ることができるのである。古書店は、一般の書店ほどにお客はいない。それでも経営が成り立っているのは、仕入と販売に独特のしくみがあるからだ。中でも仕入は、古書店の生命線といえる。ちなみに、「古書を高価で買入れます」という看板につられて本を持ちこんでみたら、二束三文の値踏みをされた、という苦い経験をもつ人も少なくないはず。「安く仕入れて安く売る」。これがどうやら古書店の商売の原則のようだ。

"We're on a very tight budget."

なかなか大変な商売です！

High Prices
For Old Books.

古本高価で買入れます。

There are around 24,000 second-hand bookstores nationwide. Over 40% of them are concentrated in Osaka and Tokyo.

古書店は全国に約2,400店あるが、その4割が東京と大阪に集中している

Purchase of stock 仕入

Second-hand booksellers' union markets 古書組合の市場
Bargain price book dealers 特価本の問屋
Exchanges between second-hand book dealers 同業者間での交換
Purchases of books from individual customers 個人からの買入れ

Second-hand Bookstores

Many people will doubtless have frequented second-hand bookstores in their student days. One great feature of second-hand bookstores is that they often offer brand new titles at knock-down prices. These books are called "bargain price books," and the reason they can be sold so cheaply is that they will have been purchased at trade prices from specialist dealers. Second-hand booksellers tend to have fewer customers than ordinary bookstores, and they manage to stay in business only because there are special arrangements regarding purchase of stock and sales. Purchase of stock in particular is a key to second-hand bookstores' survival. Incidentally, quite a few people may be fooled by the placards placed outside bookstores that say "High prices for old books." They take in their books hoping for a handsome sum, and emerge thinking they've been tricked! The truth is, the real motto of the second-hand book trade is cheap sales and cheap purchases.

In order to carry on a business as a second-hand book dealer, one has to obtain a License for the Sale of Second-hand Articles issued by the police.
古書店を開業するには、警察の古物商許可証が必要

Every second-hand bookstore has its own particular clientele to whom it directs its sales. These customers are the lifeline of its business.
古書店はそれぞれ得意先をもっていて、こちらが商売の本命

Sales
販売

Store sales
店売り

Displays at spot sales and exhibitions
即売会出品

Sales from mail orders through listings
目録による通信販売

Unsolicited sales to universities and libraries
大学や図書館などへの持込み

画廊のしくみ

　株や土地とともに投資の対象として、絵画が注目され、一時、市場規模は1兆円になろうかという勢いだった。絵画を買おうとするなら、まず画廊へ足を運ぶのが常識。だが、画廊のしくみを知らないと、話にならない。さりげなく掛けてある絵が、何千万円などということもあるのだ。一般の画廊の場合は、店頭販売以上に外商に力を入れている。いわゆる得意客を相手にした商売が主体になっているのだ。

　ちなみに画廊をのぞいてみると、閑散としている所も結構ある。それでも潰れないのは、外商で稼いでいるからだ。絵画の値段は、号単価という日本独特の慣習によって決められているが、画商の世界は不動産屋と相通じていそうだ。

この絵はいくら!?

Very often, the price of a picture will not be shown.

絵には価格が表示されていないことが多い

A painting's price is calculated according to a fixed price unit covering 1 go (a measurement about the size of a postcard): the price of the painting will be the price of 1 go multiplied by the number of go in its size. Artists are ranked according to the price fetched by a single go unit of their paintings.

絵の値段は、1号（葉書きの大きさ）単価×号数で計算する。1号当たりの単価は、画家ごとに評価が定めてある

Well-known artists who are members of Japan Arts Academy may often be able to sell their paintings for a more expensive sum than the value of land, with prices in the several tens of thousands of yen for something the size of a postcard.

日本芸術院会員クラスの洋画家の作品は、号当たり数十万円もし、地価より高いことも

It's not the quality, it's the go that counts!

作品の善し悪しに関係なく号いくらで計算するんじゃ

Art Galleries

Paintings have joined shares and land as a favorite object of investment, and in fact, at one time a few years ago, they were so popular that the scale of the market was reaching the trillions of yen. If one decides that one wants to own a painting, the first thing to do is to betake oneself to a gallery. But unless one is aware of the customs and protocol that pertain in such places, one may make a fool of oneself. Prices are often high, and a painting hanging seemingly casually up on the wall may well cost several millions of yen. The general art galleries expend quite a lot of effort on purchases and sales apart from the sales they make on the premises, and their main business is conducted with a regular clientele.

A peek inside a gallery may give one the impression that absolutely nothing is going on. The fact that galleries manage to make ends meet is because they make their real earnings in sales to outside customers. In Japan there is a unique system of pricing paintings, according to particular units, or go. In many ways, trade in paintings has much in common with the real estate business.

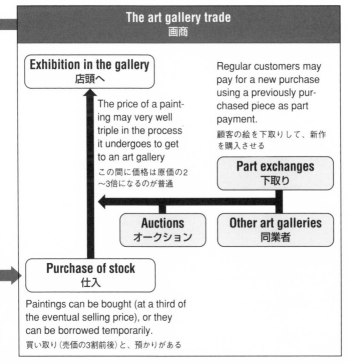

The art gallery trade
画商

Exhibition in the gallery
店頭へ

The price of a painting may very well triple in the process it undergoes to get to an art gallery
この間に価格は原価の2〜3倍になるのが普通

Regular customers may pay for a new purchase using a previously purchased piece as part payment.
顧客の絵を下取りして、新作を購入させる

Part exchanges
下取り

Auctions
オークション

Other art galleries
同業者

Purchase of stock
仕入

Paintings can be bought (at a third of the eventual selling price), or they can be borrowed temporarily.
買い取り（売価の3割前後）と、預かりがある

自動販売機のしくみ

　自動販売機は、今や街の広告塔といってよいほど目につく。清涼飲料、タバコ、酒類が自動販売機のメイン商品であるが、生花・保険商品・玩具・宝くじ・ストッキングなどを売る機械も登場している。変わったところでは、あたたかいおにぎりを売る自動販売機で、これは電子レンジを内蔵した食品電子レンジ加熱調理システムと言うそうだ。すでに市場に出回り始めているが、流通面では過当競争という状態で、採算がとれない機械が多いことも事実。変わり種の自動販売機ほど、採算がとれないとも言われる。

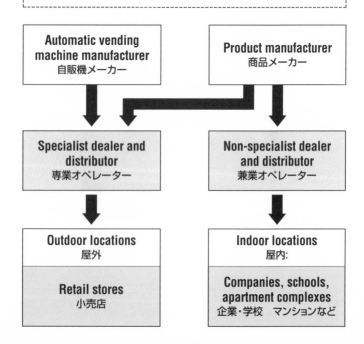

Automatic vending machine distribution
流通のしくみ

Companies called "operaters" determine the locations and supply the goods for the automatic vending machines.
自動販売機のロケーションと商品の供給は、オペレーターと呼ばれる会社が行う

Automatic vending machine manufacturer 自販機メーカー	**Product manufacturer** 商品メーカー
Specialist dealer and distributor 専業オペレーター	**Non-specialist dealer and distributor** 兼業オペレーター
Outdoor locations 屋外	**Indoor locations** 屋内:
Retail stores 小売店	**Companies, schools, apartment complexes** 企業・学校　マンションなど

Automatic Vending Machines

Automatic vending machines have now become such a common sight on the streets, they're like yesterday's billboards. The main items on sale in these machines are refrigerated beverages, cigarettes, and various kinds of alcohol, but some machines also offer items like fresh-cut flowers, insurance, toys, lottery tickets, and stockings. The strangest kind of vending machine offers freshly made o-nigiri rice-balls. Apparently, such machines, which are already on the market, are fitted with a special apparatus called a Microwave Heating and Cooking System. However, they have to compete with so many other types of vending machines that few of them actually make any profit. Indeed, one could probably say that the more eccentric the goods offered by a vending machine, the more difficulty it has in making money.

"It won't be long before we see snazzy vending machines like this."

自動販売機のしくみ……2

Vending machines are as a rule purchased or leased by people who install them on their premises (one machine costs roughly ¥500,000). Nowadays, however, competition amongst manufacturers has led to more machines being leased and installed free of charge.

機械は原則的に、設置者側の買い取り（1台約50万円）やリースだが、業者側の競争が激しいため無償貸与というケースが増えている

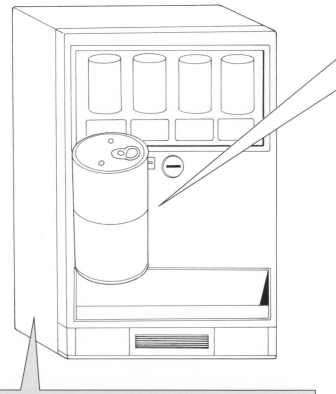

At one time, bulky vending machines that jutted out onto the pavement became something of a problem, so now manufacturers are putting their efforts into developing slimmer versions.

歩道へのはみ出し自販機が問題になっているおりから、製造業者は薄型タイプを開発中

The contents of a canned drink
缶飲料の中身

50% cost of ingredients, profit etc.

50% 原材料代・利益など

50% cost of the can, distribution

50% 容器代流通コスト

Canned coffee beverages are divided into 3 varieties–coffee, coffee beverages, and chilled coffee drinks–depending on the amount of actual coffee beans used. Usually, the smaller the can, the greater amount of real coffee it will contain.

缶コーヒーは豆の使用量でコーヒー、コーヒー飲料、コーヒー入り清涼飲料の3種に分類される。生豆の量と缶の大きさは反比例する傾向がある

The machine is so designed that cans are not damaged as they drop down.

缶が落下してもつぶれないように、ボックス内の構造は工夫がしてある

When the 5% Consumption Tax came into effect in April 1997, beverage manufacturers announced that they would assume all extra costs themselves to keep the price of a canned drink the same. The subsequent deterioration in their revenues, however, forced them to add ¥10 to the price of a regular canned drink.

飲料メーカー各社は97年4月の消費税率引上げの際、増税分を自社負担として価格を据え置いたが、収益の悪化で98年3月に1本10円の値上げを実施した

JAのしくみ

　JA（農業協同組合）は、総合農協と専門農協に大別される。総合農協は、信用・購買・共済・厚生・技術指導などの各事業を兼営するもので、ほぼ町村単位に組織されている。専門農協は、果樹や酪農など一定の作物に専門化された組織で、信用事業の兼営は認められていない。市町村レベルの単位農協の上には、都道府県レベルの連合会があり各事業ごとの連合会が組織されている。さらに全国レベルの各事業組織として、JA全農、JA経済連、全信連、厚生連、各種専門農協連などがあるほか、特殊法人農林中央金庫・社団法人家の光協会がある。そして、これらを統括するのが全国農協中央会で、日本有数のマンモス組織・JAを背景に強大な政治力を持っている。

Central Union of Agricultural Cooperatives 全国農業協同組合中央会 （JA全中）	**National Federation of Agricultural Cooperative Associations (JA Zennoh)** 全国農業協同組合連合会 （JA全農）
Prefectural Union of Agricultural Cooperatives 農業協同組合中央会 （JA中央会）	**Prefectural economic federations** 経済農業協同組合連合会 （JA経済連）
	City, town, and village co-operatives 単位農業協同組合

At the end of 1996, there were 2,242 cooperatives throughout the country.
単位農協は全国に2242（96年末現在）ある

JA

The National Federation of Agricultural Cooperative Associations consists of two parts, the general cooperatives and the professional cooperatives. The general cooperatives, organized for the most part by town and village, carry out such tasks as providing loans, purchasing services, insurance, social welfare, and technical assistance. The specialized cooperatives focus on a specific product such as fruit or dairy goods, and do not get involved in loans. Above the local city, town, and village cooperatives, there are prefectural federations, and federations are also established for each type of business. At the national level, there are various other organizations such as the National Federation of Agricultural Cooperative Associations, the Prefectural Economic Federation, the Zenshinren Bank, the Prefectural Public Welfare Union of Agricultural Cooperatives and various specialized federations, in addition to the Norinchukin Bank and Ienohikari Association. All these bodies are organized under the Central Union of Agriculture Cooperatives, forming one of Japan's largest organizations, and also one of the most politically influential organizations.

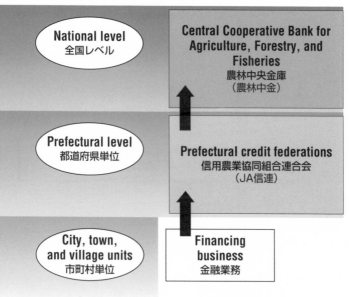

National level
全国レベル

Central Cooperative Bank for Agriculture, Forestry, and Fisheries
農林中央金庫
（農林中金）

Prefectural level
都道府県単位

Prefectural credit federations
信用農業協同組合連合会
（JA信連）

City, town, and village units
市町村単位

Financing business
金融業務

JA has about 50 trillon yen in total assets and 78 trillion yen in deposits.

農協金融は総資産約50兆円、預金78兆円を背景にしている

生協のしくみ

生活協同組合（生協）の売上高が急伸している。特に生協のプライベート・ブランドである"CO-OP"商品は、組合員以外の一般消費者にも好評だ。ところが、生協が経営するスーパーマーケットは、本来は組合員以外は利用できない定めになっている。

生協スーパーは、一般のスーパーが「大規模小売店舗法」によって規制を受けるのに対して、出店も自由で利益に対する税率も低い。これは、生協が組合員の出資にもとづいて運営されているためで、その利益還元は当然であるとの措置にほかならない。監督官庁も生協スーパーは厚生労働省、一般のスーパーは経済産業省という違いがある。生協商品が安いのも、実はこんなところに理由があるようだ。

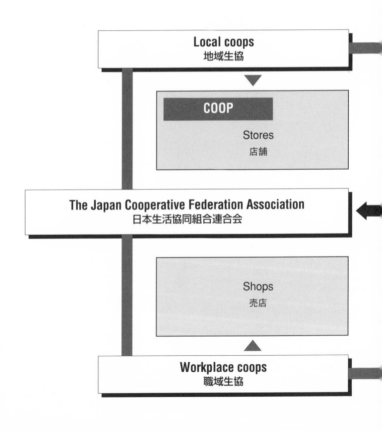

Local coops
地域生協

COOP

Stores
店舗

The Japan Cooperative Federation Association
日本生活協同組合連合会

Shops
売店

Workplace coops
職域生協

The Japanese Consumers' Cooperative Union

Sales by the Japanese Consumers' Cooperative Union (JCCU) are rising sharply. The COOP brand is especially popular with non-member consumers. Originally, non-members were not allowed to shop at the Coop supermarkets throughout the country.

While general supermarkets must adhere to the Large Store Law, the Coop is able to open stores without restrictions and the tax on profits is low. This is because the Coop is managed through investments from the members, and so it is considered only natural that the profits be returned to the investors. The Coop is regulated by the Ministry of Health, Labor and Welfare, while general supermarkets are under the Ministry of Economy, Trade and Industry.

Local coops are controlled mostly by housewives.
主婦を中心とした地域単位の生協

The Coop develops it's own products that reflect the desires of the members. Many of the products with the Coop brand are quite popular.

生協は、組合員の希望を反映した独自の商品開発を行っていて、その商品は CO-OP のプライベート・ブランドとして好評である

Products can also be ordered from the Coop through catalogs.

カタログで注文をとり、宅配する協同購入方式もある

Many colleges and companies also have coops.
大学や職場ごとにつくられている生協

公衆浴場のしくみ

　街角から姿を消しつつある商売がある。その最たるものが「公衆浴場」だ。自家風呂の普及とともに需要が急速に落ち、経営難から廃業する浴場も多い。東京都の場合は、最盛期には１日平均1000人が利用していたのが、現在はその４分の１に減ってしまったという。

　浴場数は東京都内の場合、最盛期には約2600軒を数えたが、今や1300軒ほどに減ってしまった。浴場名でいちばん多いのは「松の湯」。かつては街のランド・マークだった煙突が１本、２本と減ってゆくのは寂しい限りである。

Now that 9 out of 10 households in Japan have their own bathrooms, the number of public baths is decreasing yearly. As a community gathering place, however, the bathhouse is irreplaceable.
自家風呂の普及率9割の現在、公衆浴場は年々減少している。だが一方では、街のコミュニティ・スペースとして重宝されてもいる

Public baths
公衆浴場

はぎの湯
ゆ
男　女

Public Baths

Of all the various businesses gradually disappearing from the towns and cities in Japan, the public bathhouse is the one that many people will be sad to say goodbye to. Now that most houses are being built with their own bathrooms, the demand for public baths has decreased markedly, and many public baths have simply gone out of business, unable to make ends meet. At one time in Tokyo, when the bathhouse business was at its peak, a public bathhouse might have been able to expect about a thousand customers a day, but now the number has dropped to about a quarter of that amount.

Similarly, whereas at the peak of the business the public bathhouses in Tokyo numbered around 2,600, now the number has dropped to about 1,300. "Pine Baths" is one of the most popular names used by public bathhouses. A common landmark in towns and cities in the past, the tall chimney rising up from the furnace of the public bathhouse will one day no longer be seen.

The standard temperature for the hot water in public baths is 42 degrees; this was set after the war as a temperature that killed syphilis germs. The temperature most suitable for the human body is, however, around 39 degrees, so most people regard the standard temperature as too hot, and the actual temperature is usually decided by by-laws put out by local governing bodies. In Tokyo the by-laws for public baths have been revised for a number of reasons: to lower the temperature of the water, to do away with the limited opening hours of bathhouses, and even to have open-air baths recognized officially.

浴槽内の温度は42℃が標準だが、この標準温度は終戦直後に梅毒の熱湯消毒のために設定されたそうだ。人体への適温は39℃前後であり、熱過ぎるというのが一般論で、自治体ごとに条例で温度を定めている。東京都では条例を改正し、湯の温度や営業時間の制限を撤廃したほか、露天風呂も認めるなどの対策を講じている

"God, that's hot!"

アッチチ アッチチッ ちょっと熱すぎない!?

風呂の栓を故意に抜くと、器物破損罪が適用される場合もある

Purposely removing the plug from the bath is a punishable offense— the "Crime of Damage to Fixtures."

駅のしくみ

　駅の省力化が進んでいる。そこで、駅の機械のしくみを中心に紹介してみたい。まず筆頭に挙げられるのが、券売機である。お金を入れ、ボタンを押すと約2秒ほどで切符が出てくるが、この機械の裏側をのぞくチャンスはめったにないと思われるので、ここで公開しよう。面白いのは、切符がそのつど印刷、カットされて出てくることだ。関西の近鉄では音声認識機能を持った機械の実用化に着手している。

　自動改札機は関西方面では早くから採用されていたが、関東では比較的最近になって登場した機械である。わずか0.7秒で改札業務を処理するが、切符だけでなく定期券もチェックできることから、キセル防止にも役立っている。

A peek inside the ticket vending machine
券売機の裏をのぞくと

Monitor panel

This device keeps a close check on each section of the machine, and if there's any trouble, shows it with a light that goes on. The device for marking the date of ticket issuance is also here.

Function control

This part of the machine functions to indicate and explain any source of trouble. The off/on switch is also located here.

Cassette for coin dispensary

This has reserves of 10 and 100 yen coins, and also circulates the coins inserted.

Printing mechanism

Once the ticket has been printed out using a thermal treatment, it is carried by conveyer belt to the outlet.

Recording mechanism

This records both the total number of daily ticket sales, and the number of times any problems occurs with the machine.

Deposit box for coins received

Once sufficient coins have been collected for change, this keeps extra coins received from ticket purchases.

Stations

Reduction of unnecessary manpower at train stations is proceeding apace, helped by the introduction of several interesting pieces of equipment, which are worth explaining. First of all, of course, there is the ticket vending machine. You insert coins, press the requisite button, and in the space of just two seconds a ticket pops out. A look at the drawing below gives you an idea of what goes on inside the machines—something that people rarely get the chance to see. What is amazing is that a ticket gets printed out and cut every time a button is pressed. In the Kansai region, there are machines in use that respond not only to the touch of a button but also to voice commands.

Automatic wicket machines were adopted early in the Kansai region, but only relatively recently have they made an appearance in the Kanto region. The ticket goes through the machine in less than 7/10s of a second. These machines check tickets, and they also check season passes, so they are a good way of catching people attempting to steal rides.

Ticket paper roll

Each roll has the capacity to issue 8000 tickets.

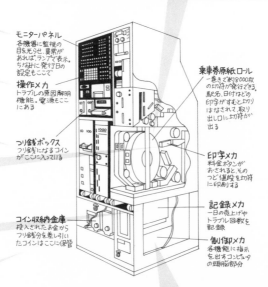

モニターパネル
各機器に監視の目を光らせ、異常があれば、ランプで表示。ちなみに発行日の設定もここで

操作メカ
トラブルの原因解明機能と、電源もここにある

つり銭ボックス
つり銭になるコインがここに入っている

コイン収納内金庫
投入されたお金からつり銭分を差し引いたコインはここに保管

乗車券原紙ロール
一巻きで約8,000枚の切符が発行できる。駅名、日付などの印字がすむと切りはなされて、取り出し口に切符が出る

印字メカ
料金ボタンがおされると、そのつど値段を切符に印刷する

記録メカ
一日の売上げやトラブル回数を記録

制御メカ
各機能に指示を出すコンピュータの頭脳部分

Control mechanism

This is the brains of the vending machine, sending out commands to each part.

駅のしくみ……2

How the automatic ticket wickets work
自動改札機のしくみ

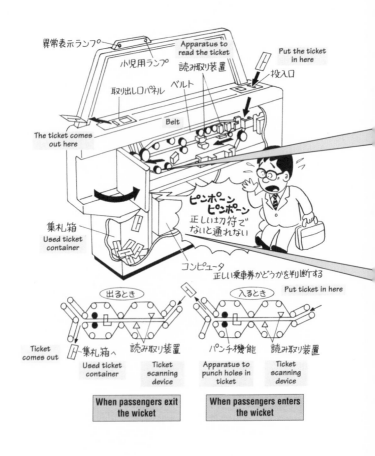

異常表示ランプ

Apparatus to read the ticket

Put the ticket in here

小児用ランプ

読み取り装置

投入口

取り出し口パネル　ベルト

Belt

The ticket comes out here

集札箱
Used ticket container

ピンポーン
ピンポーン
正しい切符でないと通れない

コンピュータ
正しい乗車券かどうかを判断する

出るとき

入るとき

Put ticket in here

Ticket comes out

集札箱へ　読み取り装置

パンチ機能　読み取り装置

Used ticket container

Ticket scanning device

Apparatus to punch holes in ticket

Ticket scanning device

When passengers exit the wicket

When passengers enters the wicket

How passengers are able to buy tickets for JR, subway and private railways all in one.
相互乗入れのしくみ

If a ride involves multiple connections between JR, private railways and the subway you can still buy a single ticket. Settlement between the different companies involves total payments being calculated by the railway company of the station where the ticket was issued, and then reimbursement being paid accordingly.

JR・私鉄・地下鉄などの相互乗入れ駅間の合算運賃の精算方法は、発券した駅が属する鉄道会社から他の鉄道会社へまとめて支払われる

Door

When a wrong ticket is put into the machine, or if anyone tries to go through the wicket without a ticket, this door automatically shuts, and an alarm goes off.

Computer

This checks to see whether the tickets passing through are as they should be.

If you want to take a pet on a JR train, you must put it in a carrier that is less than 70 cms in length and 90 cms in height, and also purchase an extra ticket for "personal effects."

ペットを電車に乗せる場合は、タテ・ヨコ70センチ、高さ90センチ以内の入れ物に入れて、手回り品切符を購入するきまりになっている（JRの場合）

カラオケボックスのしくみ

　今や全国津々浦々に普及しているカラオケボックス。第1号が登場したのは1988年で、わずか10年で第3次といわれるブームをつくった。ちなみに第1次ブームはカラオケスナック、第2次ブームはホームカラオケが引き金になった。

　カラオケボックスは全国に1万店舗、部屋数15万室にのぼるとされ、これは人口800人当たり1室の計算になる。そして、この第3次ブームを推進して来たのが「通信カラオケ」である。従来のレーザーディスク・カラオケに比べて新譜のリリースが早く、曲数も圧倒的に多いのがユーザーにうけて、カラオケボックスの大半が導入している。この業界もマルチメディア時代を迎えているのだ。

On-line Karaoke
通信カラオケシステム

There are two types of on-line karaoke systems: one is the "on-demand" system, where one downloads a tune from the host computer to be used at that very moment; the other is the "save and store" system, where the information that is downloaded can be stored on a suitably formatted hard disk.

リクエストのたびにホストコンピュータから情報を引き出す「オンデマンド型」と、あらかじめ端末のハードディスクに情報を蓄えておく「蓄積型」の2タイプがある

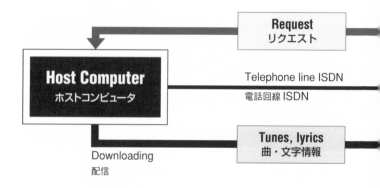

Request
リクエスト

Host Computer
ホストコンピュータ

Telephone line ISDN
電話回線 ISDN

Tunes, lyrics
曲・文字情報

Downloading
配信

Karaoke Boxes

The "karaoke box," a set of soundproofed rooms to which customers go to sing karaoke songs. Even now these places continue to proliferate, and can be found in every nook and corner of the land. The very first karaoke box made its appearance in 1988, and since then, in just ten years, there have been at least three "booms" in the business—the first occasioned by the appearance of "karaoke snack bars" where people go to drink and sing, the second by the invention of "home karaoke" sets used to practice and sing at home.

There are about 10,000 "karaoke box" establishments in Japan. If one counts the individual soundproofed rooms, the number comes to something like 150,000, meaning a ratio of 1 "box" for every 800 people in the nation. A further stimulus to the most recent boom in karaoke-box singing has been "on-line karaoke." Up till now karaoke boxes had to rely on laser disks to reproduce the tunes, but now users can download the very latest hits and releases in no time at all, and the number of songs available is immeasurably greater. The majority of karaoke box bars have started to make use of this system. The changes brought by the age of multi-media have made themselves felt even in the karaoke industry.

Formatted disk
端末

The images shown on the screen to accompany the song are played from laser discs and CD-ROMs. The task now is to make it possible to download clear pictures as well as tunes and lyrics from communication systems.

背景の映像はレーザーディスクやCD-ROMプレーヤーで再生するが、鮮明な動画を配信可能にするのが課題だ

第**4**章

どうなってるの？
この仕事 長年の謎が解けるかも!?

Chapter 4
Who Does What
Questions about Jobs You've
Always Wanted to Ask

コンパニオンのしくみ

ショービジネスの花形であるコンパニオンは、若い女性に人気の高い仕事である。そのため近頃は、風俗営業の世界でもこの名称をつかって募集しているケースが多く、紛らわしいことこの上ない。しかし本来のコンパニオンは、誰もがすぐになれる職業ではない。オーディションに合格し、少しずつキャリア・アップをしていかなければならない厳しい競争世界なのだ。

下積み時代を経たコンパニオンの晴れ舞台は、イベントの演出にもかかわるナレーションコンパニオンである。

Dispatch 派遣

人材派遣会社

Registration 登録

宴会や街頭キャンペーンのコンパニオンは、モデルクラブから派遣されることが多い

新発売
キャンペーンガール

Mild Five Stars: now on sale

受付嬢

ここまではコンパニオン見習いで、日当が1万円前後。正式なコンパニオンになると、日当は倍増する

コンパニオン

イベントのマニュアルにそった言動が要求される

MOTOR S

ナレーションコンパニオン

ナレーション原稿づくり、演出も担当し、コンパニオンの頂点だ

"Companions"

The job of a "companion," or the decorative show-girl who attracts customers to items on show in trade galas and events, is quite popular amongst young women. Indeed its popularity has led strip joints and prostitute parlors to start using the term "companion" in their recruitment advertisements—a situation that real companion girls do not take at all kindly to. But in its proper meaning, the term "companion" refers to a job that requires no mean ability and determination. The world of companion girls is a competitive one, in which even after the original audition, a woman progresses slowly up the ladder toward success.

After all her preparatory training, the companion girl makes her final and most glamorous debut as a "narration companion," involved in the displays of galas and trade events.

Recruitment company

Companions who attend banquets or who conduct advertising campaigns (as "campaign girls") on the streets will usually have been dispatched from a club for models.

Campaign girl

Receptionist

Up to this point the companion girl will be in her apprenticeship, and only earning around ¥10,000 a day. When she finishes her apprenticeship, her daily wage is doubled.

Companion

The companion girl is required to speak the patter and make certain gestures that accord with rules written down in a company manual.

Narration companion

The daily fee paid to narration companions, who are responsible both for composing the script of their patter and for its presentation, are top of the companions.

石焼芋屋のしくみ

　冬の街角の風物詩といえば、石焼芋屋をその筆頭に挙げる人も多いだろう。この石焼芋屋は東北などからの出稼ぎ人である場合が多く、親方のもとで営業している。親方は、売り子に屋台を貸し、営業コースを割り当て、原料のサツマイモを卸す権利を持つ。この方式は、フーテンの寅さんのようなテキヤと同じである。元手のない寅さんが地方で商売ができたのは、テキヤの親方から商品と売場を借りたから。売れた分の手数料稼ぎである。

　もっとも焼芋屋の場合は、テキヤの売人とは違って、サツマイモを仕入れるための元手が必要になる。しかし、それ以外は自分の取り分。営業努力次第で、儲けることも可能な商売なのだ。

Stone-baked potatoes
Net price per kilo

Materials
材料

「イーシャーキ、イーモ」のかけ声は15秒間で、というのが流儀とか

値段は1kg当たりの相場が決められているが、最終的には売り子の裁量に任されている

おまけをしてくれる焼芋屋さんも多いわよ

燃料になるマキは、廃材を集めてくる

サツマイモは親方から仕入れ、1日平均で40kgほど持って出るのが普通だ

朝9時頃にカマに火を入れ、石を焼き始める。カマは重さが30kgほどで、リヤカーの総重量は約180kgになるというから、石焼芋の売り子の仕事はかなり重労働である

"Most vendors will give you an extra potato for free."

The vendor gets his supply of sweet potatoes from his boss. He usually takes out a load of about 40 kilos daily.

The Stone-Baked Sweet Potato Vendor

Surely many people would name the man who travels the streets with his cart selling stone-baked potatoes as one of the most typical sights on a cold winter's day.

These stone-baked potato sellers, many of whom originate from the Tohoku region in the northeast of Japan's main island of Honshū, come to Tokyo to make a living, and they carry out their business under the auspices of a boss. The boss provides the wheeled booth, allots the vendor his particular route, and he also holds rights over the sweet potatoes the vendor bakes and sells. The potato seller thus conducts his business in much the same way as Tora-san, that famous character in the movies, who also travels from place to place as a type of street vendor. The only reason the penniless Tora-san can set up his trade in the countryside is because he has a boss who lends him the goods and a stall. His earnings are taken out of the amount he manages to sell.

Of course, stone-baked sweet potato sellers have to have at least enough capital to buy supplies of sweet potatoes. But apart from that, their earnings are their own. It's the kind of trade in which how much you earn depends on how much effort you are willing to put into the work.

The vendor often has a taped ditty "Stone-baked, stone-baked potatoes" playing at fifteen-second intervals from the stall.

The firewood in the furnace is gathered from scrap wood.

The price is usually fixed at a per-kilo rate, but in the end the charge is left to the seller's discretion.

At around 9 A.M. the vendor lights the furnace in his cart and starts to heat the stones. The furnace itself weighs around 30 kilos so the total weight of the cart he pulls as he plys his trade is around 180 kilos. The work of the stone-baked potato seller involves hard labor!

落とし物処分のしくみ

　落とし物を拾った場合、もよりの警察へ届け出るのが国民の義務。届け出なかった場合は、犯罪者になることを覚悟しなければならない。しかし、落とし物が発見されるのは、周囲に誰もいないときが多いのである。そこで、落とし物は、拾った人の善意によって届けられるのを原則としている。

　法的には、拾ってから（施設内では、24時間以内にその施設の占有者へ届けたうえで）7日以内に警察へ届けないと「遺失物横領罪」にあたるとされているが、この猶予期間は、刑の執行猶予の先どりとでもいうべきニュアンスもあって、微笑ましい。だが、この罪に問われる人は極めて少ないのではと、誰もが推測してしまうのではあるまいか。

Pocketing the lost property makes you a violator of the Law of Misappropriation of Lost Property.

届け出ずに自分のものにした場合遺失物横領罪に問われる

On premises 施設内	**Users of the premises** 施設占有者
Within 24 hours　24時間以内	Within 7 days (on JR premises, the article is kept in Lost Property for 5 days; in the subway, for 3 days). 7日以内（JRは5日間、地下鉄は3日間保管）

Public thoroughfare etc. 一般路上
Within 7 days　7日以内

"To report, or not report—that is the question."

届けるべきか届けざるべきかそれが問題だ！

交番　Police Station

小悩んでいいのは7日間だけですよ！

You have 7 days to mull the question over!

Police Station 警察署
Articles are kept for a period of 6 months. （保管は6か月間）

Treatment of Lost Property

It is the moral duty of any citizen on coming across an article of lost property to report it to the nearest police station; failure to do so is actually a crime. However, it often happens that one comes across lost property, dropped or mislaid, when no one else is around. In this case, the law assumes that the good conscience of the person who discovers the lost property will direct him to report it.

Legally speaking, one is obligated to report a lost article to the police within 7 days of its discovery (on public premises, the discovery has to be reported within 24 hours, to the owners or users of the premises)—otherwise one is regarded as having committed the Crime of Misappropriation of Lost Articles. This period of grace given before one has to do what is lawful seems very much like the reprieve that should come after the crime, and one has to smile as one considers the reasoning behind it. And of course, as anyone can imagine, very few people are actually punished for this crime.

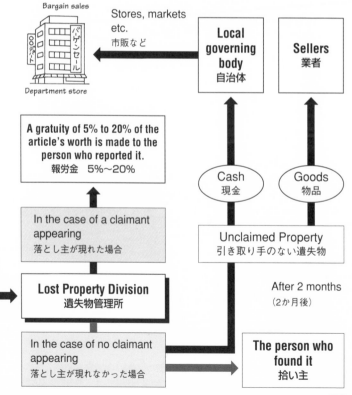

Bargain sales

Department store

Stores, markets etc.
市販など

Local governing body
自治体

Sellers
業者

A gratuity of 5% to 20% of the article's worth is made to the person who reported it.
報労金　5%〜20%

Cash
現金

Goods
物品

In the case of a claimant appearing
落とし主が現れた場合

Unclaimed Property
引き取り手のない遺失物

Lost Property Division
遺失物管理所

After 2 months
（2か月後）

In the case of no claimant appearing
落とし主が現れなかった場合

The person who found it
拾い主

邦人保護のしくみ

　湾岸戦争で、イラクが人質を楯にとり、国際世論の避難を浴びたことは、まだ記憶に新しい。ところで、海外での日本人の安全・保護対策は、大使館と総領事館が担当している。トラブルや緊急事態に即応して邦人の安全を守り、保護・援助するための事前準備や諸対策が主要な任務である。海外の在留邦人は約80万人で、出国者は年間約1700万人にものぼる。なかには、政情不安な国に滞在しなければならない企業戦士もいる。

　そうした国の在外公館の責務は極めて重い。一方では、海外で事件や事故に遭遇する日本人旅行者の数がこのところ激増している。外国は、日本ほど安全ではないことを、旅行者は覚悟しておかねばならない。

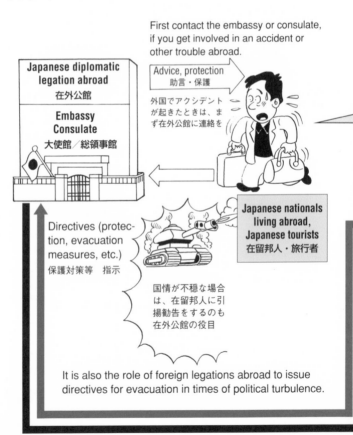

First contact the embassy or consulate, if you get involved in an accident or other trouble abroad.

Japanese diplomatic legation abroad
在外公館

Embassy Consulate
大使館／総領事館

Advice, protection
助言・保護

外国でアクシデントが起きたときは、まず在外公館に連絡を

Directives (protection, evacuation measures, etc.)
保護対策等　指示

Japanese nationals living abroad, Japanese tourists
在留邦人・旅行者

国情が不穏な場合は、在留邦人に引揚勧告をするのも在外公館の役目

It is also the role of foreign legations abroad to issue directives for evacuation in times of political turbulence.

Protection of Japanese Nationals

The memory of the hostages taken and used as human shields by Iraq in the Gulf War is still fresh in people's minds, and of course it was the cause of much worldwide criticism. When Japanese nationals go abroad, measures regarding their protection and safety are the responsibility of the Japanese embassy and the Japanese consulate in the country concerned. The main duty of the embassy and consulate is to see to the safety of Japanese nationals as soon as any trouble or a tense situation arises, as well as to take measures for their protection and assistance. The number of Japanese who live abroad is about 800,000, and the number who travel abroad every year is as high as 17 million. Among them are business men "company samurai," who have to live in countries where the political situation is highly unstable.

The responsibility of the diplomatic establishments abroad in such countries is thus extremely important. Meanwhile, the number of Japanese tourists who encounter incidents and accidents when traveling abroad is soaring. Japanese tourists should go abroad only with the awareness that other countries are not necessarily as safe as Japan.

What is taken for granted in Japan does not necessarily apply in other countries. The number of Japanese tourists who travel with the same kind of nonchalance as they do at home country—and who meet with trouble as a result—is increasing.

外国では日本の常識は通用しない。日本にいるような気分でアクシデントに巻き込まれる日本人旅行者が増えている

| Ministry of Foreign Affairs 外務省 |
| Protection of Japanese Nationals Division 邦人保護課 |
| Crisis Center 邦人特別対策室 |

The Ministry of Foreign Affairs keeps a check on the political situations in areas and cities of countries deemed unstable and/or dangerous, and issues information on their findings with a ranking system of 1 to 5. The directive to postpone travel for tourist purposes is Danger Rank 2.

外務省は治安が悪く危険な国や地域、都市を5段階に分け、情報提供を行っている。観光旅行延期勧告は危険度2クラスだ

In charge of protecting Japanese nationals from incidents of international terrorism.

国際テロ組織などから邦人を守る部署

Report
報告

119

高速道路料金のしくみ

　高速道路の料金値上げのたびにささやかれるのが、国と道路公団の約束違反。たとえば、東名高速道路は当初の約束では無料で開放されるべきなのに、逆に便乗値上げをしているという批判である。日本道路公団が建設・管理をする高速道路の料金は、40年後の償還を前提に算出されている。つまり、借金が帳消しになるまでの間、利用者がその分を負担してくださいということだったはずなのだ。これが実行できない理由は、赤字路線があるからだという。これでは永遠に約束が実行されそうにない。

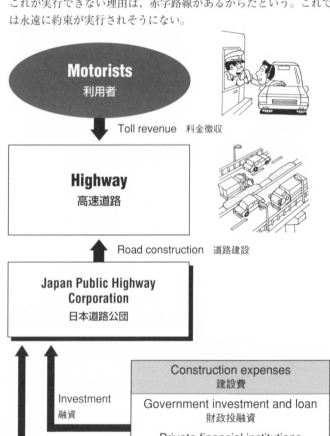

Motorists
利用者

Toll revenue　料金徴収

Highway
高速道路

Road construction　道路建設

Japan Public Highway Corporation
日本道路公団

Investment
融資

Construction expenses 建設費
Government investment and loan 財政投融資
Private financial institutions 民間金融機関
Special national account 国の特別会計

Interest rate subsidy
利子補給

Highway Tolls

When highway tolls are raised, the murmuring it causes is in opposition to a contract between the government and the Japan Public Highway Corporation. According to this contract, the tolls for highways built and operated by the corporation were calculated based on repaying loans in 40 years that the corporation took out to build the highways. In other words, motorists were to bear the burden of repaying the construction loans only until they were paid back. This is why people criticize the fact that tolls on the Tomei Expressway go up even though by now it is supposed to be free of charge. The reason tolls can't be eliminated is reportedly that some highways operate in the red. So it looks as though tolls are going to be around for a while.

> The tolls are calculated based on the repayment over 40 years of loans for construction.
> 高速道路の料金は、建設に要した借金を40年間で返済するという前提で算出されている

> When the loan is completely paid off, the roads will fall under national control, and can then be used free of charge, but...
> 借金完済時には、道路は国の管理になり、無料で利用できる約束だったが…

> According to the "Toll Pool" system introduced in 1972, a fixed amount of toll revenues is diverted to unprofitable and new roads. Therefore, making the highways free of charge to motorists is a hopeless dream.
> 1972年に導入された「料金プール制」によって料金収入の一定限度を不採算路線や新規路線に回す措置がとられたため、無料化の実現は絶望的である

Profitable highways include the Tomei, Chuo and Tohoku Expressways. Of these, the Tomei Expressway is extremely profitable. For every 13 yen it costs to maintain the road, it makes 100 yen. On the other hand, unprofitable highways include the Tokai Hokuriku, Sanyou, and Douou. The Tokai Hokuriku costs as much as three times its operating revenue.

採算路線は、東名・中央・東北などで、東名高速道路は100円を稼ぐために13円のコストで済む超黒字路線。一方、不採算路線は東海北陸・山陽・道央などで、東海北陸自動車道は3倍以上のコストがかかっている

新聞拡張業のしくみ

　日本のマスコミは質よりも量、数がものをいう世界である。新聞各社は"発行部数こそが世論"とひたすら部数拡大の路線を歩む。この最前線が、新聞販売店である。ここでは毎日、食うか食われるかの熾烈な読者獲得合戦が展開されている。販売店主にとって自店の担当地区の配達部数を減らすことは、経営難にも結び付く。系列販売店主なら、本社からクビを宣告されることもある。かくして、減る以上に増やすことが至上命題になる。ここに、新聞拡張団の存在意義が生じてくるわけだ。

　店主が必要とする部数を確実に達成するのが拡張団の目的であるため、手段を選ばぬ勧誘をしてひんしゅくを買うケースもある。

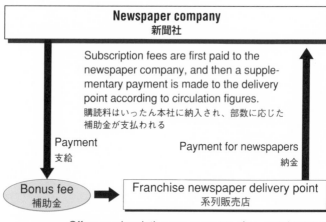

Newspaper company
新聞社

Subscription fees are first paid to the newspaper company, and then a supplementary payment is made to the delivery point according to circulation figures.
購読料はいったん本社に納入され、部数に応じた補助金が支払われる

Payment
支給

Payment for newspapers
納金

Bonus fee
補助金

Franchise newspaper delivery point
系列販売店

Offers a subscription agreement to sign　販売申込契約の提出

The supplementary payment is supposed to cover any and all extra charges in the canvassing of newspaper subscriptions. The money that delivery points invest in such canvassing is said to be 30 to 50% of the supplementary payment. This is a business where expanding sales by just one newspaper may cost several tens of thousand of yen.

補助金には増紙対策費も含まれる。販売店が拡張のために投入する費用は補助金の3〜5割といわれる。1部増やすために数万円かける業界なのである

From 1991, a law regarding house-to-house sales, also covering sales of newspapers, came into effect, which permitted an 8-day "cooling off" period after a contract is signed, allowing the customer unilaterally to cancel.

1991年から新聞にも「訪問販売法」が適用され、契約後8日以内なら一方的解約（クーリング・オフ）ができる

Newspaper Subscription Canvassing

In Japan, it is quantity rather than quality that rules the mass media: this is a country where numbers win the day. All the newspaper companies thus try desperately to outdo each other to increase circulation numbers, the idea being that whoever sells the most holds the most sway over public opinion. At the very forefront of this process stands the local newspaper delivery point, where every day a fierce battle to capture readers, a very battle for survival, is waged. For the owners of these delivery points, any decrease in the subscriptions to the newspapers in the district puts the survival of the business into question. For the operator of a franchise, it may mean a notice of dismissal from headquarters. It is thus a categorical imperative to keep the number of newspaper subscriptions greater than the number of cancellations, and for this job, the groups who go from door to door canvassing for subscriptions play a vital role.

Newspaper sales agents must reach a particular quota, a certain number of subscriptions, set for them by the owner of the delivery point, so they are occasionally criticized for being too pushy in their attempts to get subscribers.

The group of newspaper sales agents that covers a delivery point's particular area ranges from one person to several dozens. There are subscription canvassers who are not bound by any one company and who work for any or all newspapers.

拡張団は1名～数十名規模で、販売店の担当区域内に投入される。頼まれればどの新聞でもやる見識のない拡張団もある

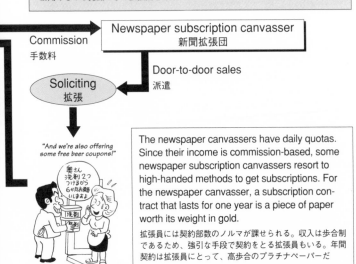

Commission
手数料

Newspaper subscription canvasser
新聞拡張団

Door-to-door sales
派遣

Soliciting
拡張

"And we're also offering some free beer coupons!"

奥さん
洗剤2つ
つけるから
6ヶ月お願い
いたします

洗剤

Laundry detergent

The newspaper canvassers have daily quotas. Since their income is commission-based, some newspaper subscription canvassers resort to high-handed methods to get subscriptions. For the newspaper canvasser, a subscription contract that lasts for one year is a piece of paper worth its weight in gold.

拡張員には契約部数のノルマが課せられる。収入は歩合制であるため、強引な手段で契約をとる拡張員もいる。年間契約は拡張員にとって、高歩合のプラチナペーパーだ

123

野犬処分のしくみ

　ペット愛好者が増えている。だが、その一方で、飽きると捨ててしまう人も多い。まるで遊び飽きたオモチャを捨てる幼児のように…。この現代人の幼児性のためにペットたちの受難史が始まった。たとえば、野犬である。法律では「鑑札や予防注射済票をつけないまま放し飼いになっている犬は"抑留"しなければならない」のである。そのために、捕獲され引き取り人のない野犬は下のような安楽死へのコースをたどることになる。"かわいそうに"と思いながらも、関係者は涙をのんで処分をしているそうだ。

Once taken into protection
捕獲

ガルルルルワンワン

Any dog considered to harbor a risk of rabies has to be caged and observed for a two-week latency period for the disease.
狂犬病のおそれがある犬はオリに入れて、潜伏期間の2週間、観察する

**The Public Health Center:
Animal Supervision Office**
保健所／動物管理事務所

Once a dog is taken into custody, it has to be kept for a required 6 days, during which it will be shifted from cage to cage. There is no cage for dogs that remain for more than this time.
捕獲後は原則として6日間抑留し、毎日オリが変わる。7日目のオリはない

Day One 1日目	
Day Two 2日目	
Day Three 3日目	
Day Four 4日目	
Day Five 5日目	
Day Six 6日目	
Day Seven 7日目	

The Treatment of Stray Dogs

The number of pet owners is increasing, which means, of course, that the number of people who tire of and simply abandon their animals is also on the rise. It's just as if pets were a kind of toy that one could throw away on a whim. Such is the childish nature of people in modern society, and the cause of much tragic suffering of pets. Take stray dogs, for example. By law, any dog that is on the loose, without its owner, and in a collarless and unvaccinated state, must be interned. Those animals which are interned and not claimed by their owners or taken in by others, have to follow the course ending with euthanasia outlined to the below. The people whose job it is to do away with such dogs say they do so fighting back tears of pity.

Claiming one's dog or becoming a new owner
引き取りと譲渡制度

Often, the owners of dogs (particularly dogs with pedigrees) taken into custody will contact the center themselves, and come and collect their pets. Also, puppies of up to 2 or 3 months brought in by owners are kept for 2 months so that they can be given to anybody who decides they want to become the new owner.

野犬として捕獲されても、血統書つきの犬の
場合は飼い主が連絡してきて引き取ってゆく
ケースが多いそうだ。また、飼い主から持ち
込まれた生後2、3か月の犬に限り2か月以内
なら希望者に譲渡してくれる

The animals are put to death
by gas and then cremated.
ガス室で安楽死させたあと焼却炉へ

Transferal to the Animal Protection Center　移動

125

マンガ制作のしくみ

　読者には娯楽でも、制作現場は修羅場。売れっ子のなかには出版社の編集者泣かせのマンガ家も多い。原稿が間に合わず掲載不可になることを「落ちる」というが、編集者はこの恐怖を常に味わっている。

　そこで原稿ができ上がるまで、マンガ家の仕事場に泊まり込んでひたすら監視に努めることになる。編集長からは矢のような催促がくることも覚悟しなければならない。まさに板ばさみの苦しみを味わう破目になるわけで、そうなると笑いごとでは済まされないのだ。

XX Publishers

○○出版社

"Boy's Comic"

「少年COMIC」新連載企画会議

Plans for a new series
Theme
Author
Artist

Editor-in-chief: "We'd like you to do our new comic strip."

先生、新連載よろしくお願いします

編集長

"It's an honor to meet you."

よろしくお願いします

"This is Kurata, the editor you'll be working with."

担当編集者の大西です

ストーリー＆アイディア

"Uh, let me see, 'Once upon a time...'"

原作・作画とも

Story and pictures

原作付き

An existing story

Pictures only

The Production of Manga

We all know that comic books are a delight to read, but production can often be sheer hell. Many of the best-selling comic book artists are the bane of an editor's life. The biggest and a rather common terror an editor can undergo is the possibility that the artist will not in time for press.

Sometimes the editor will camp out with the artist to make sure the manga gets done on time. In the meantime the editor also has to suffer barbed comments—insinuations of his own incompetence—from the chief editor. Between a rock and a hard place, it's hard to laugh, no matter how funny a manga may be.

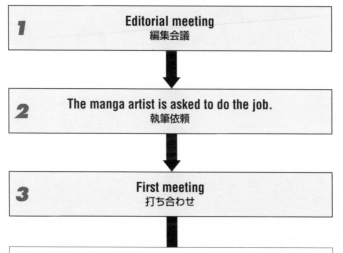

1 Editorial meeting
編集会議

2 The manga artist is asked to do the job.
執筆依頼

3 First meeting
打ち合わせ

The artist may be asked to think up an original story, or he may merely have to design pictures.
ストーリーを考えるところから始めるケースと、原作があって作画だけの
ケースがある

With the manga, the editor rushes them to be photo-typeset.

Photo-typesetting

The artist divides the story roughly into scenes (called "rough continuities"), and then creates the captions.

印刷会社

ネームが上がったら、事前に写植をうっておくんだ

シナリオにあわせて、コマ割り(ラフコンテ)をし、フキダシのネーム(せりふ)を上げていく

4

"Oh yes, sir, it'll be ready in a jiffy!"

はい、編集長　もうすぐに上がると思います

"Could you possibly do ours first? Pleeze?"

先生どうか うちの社のを先にお願い

えんぴつで下描きをする

5

Done by the manga artist in pencil.

Best-selling artists may work on several series at once.

売れっ子マンガ家になると、数本の連載を同時進行で進めていく

One of the editor's duties is to hang around waiting for the manga to get done.

でき上がりを待つのも編集者の大切な仕事

アシスタントが、背景を描いたり、コマワクを描いたり、トーンを貼ったり、細い作業をする

Assistants

下描きをなぞりながら、ペンでインク(スミ)をいれていく

6

The draft pictures are traced over in ink pen.

INK

9

8

7

○○印刷

Printers

フキダシに写植を貼って完成だ!!

最後に細部を手直しをして、できあがり

○○書店

写取次店

PAPER CEMENT

Bookstores　Distributors

Once the captions are stuck onto the photo-typeset pictures, the comic strip is ready.

The final task is to add the finer details by hand.

4   **Layout**
コマ割り

5   **Draft pictures**
下描き

6   **Inking in**
スミ入れ

7   **Final details**
仕上げ

8   **Captions added**
ネーム貼り

9   **Printing, binding, distribution**
印刷・製本・配本

アニメ制作のしくみ

　テレビのマンガ番組としておなじみのアニメーションの制作には、実に膨大な時間と手間がかかっている。たとえば、キャラクターの1秒間の動作を表現するには原則的に24枚の動画が必要となる。30分番組（正味23分ほど）では、約3万3000枚の動画が描かれ、それと同数のセル画がトレース・彩色されることになる。これとは別進行で背景画も描かれるわけだから、撮影する以前に必要な画だけでも気の遠くなるほどの量である。見るのはアッという間だが、制作のしくみを考えると、これほど贅沢な話はない。

Planning
企画

A plan that includes production costs, screen time, and story takes shape.

制作費、上映時間、どんな作品をつくるかなどのプランを構成する

Script
シナリオ

A script is written according to the plan.

企画にそって脚本を書く

Design
設計

The large and small props are designed.

大道具や小道具をデザインする

Cutting
カット割り

The director cuts the script with the final editing in mind.

監督が編集のことを考えながら脚本をカットごとにわける

Creation of continuity pictures
絵コンテ作成

According to the cuts, the film with people movement, elements, and dialogues are made.

カット割りにしたがって、人物の動き、構成、セリフなどをつけてフィルムのもとをつくる

The Production of "Anime"

The TV animated shows we know and love actually involve an immense amount of time and effort to make. A mere one second's worth of a character's movements or gestures requires 24 drawings. For a program of roughly thirty minutes 33,000 drawings are required, and the same amount of celluloid pictures traced and colored in. At the same time, in a separate process, the background pictures have to be created. So even before the filming takes place, a mind-boggling amount of work has to be done. The action on your screen flows by, but this is actually an extravagant art form.

"I want viewers to be in tear."

この部分は盛り上げて……ここは……

脚本家

Designer
デザイナ

Director
監督

scratch, scratch

セリフ, 効果音 ナレーション など

秒やコマ

Dialogue, musical effects, narration, etc.

Continuity pictures
絵コンテ

Seconds and frames

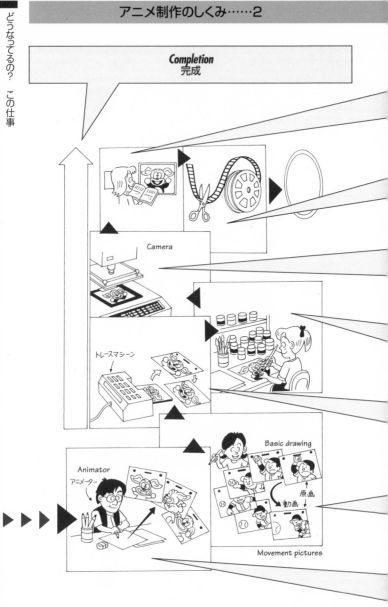

Completion
完成

Camera

トレースマシーン

Animator
アニメーター

Basic drawing

原画

動画

Movement pictures

After-Recording
アフレコ

Voice actors record their voices to match the words and actions taking place on the screen.

声優がスクリーンの絵に合わせながらレコーディングする

Editing
編集

Editing is carried out in much the same way as for movies.

映画と同様にフィルムを編集する

Filming
撮影

Each celluloid picture is placed one after another on a background picture, and then filmed.

背景の上にセルを重ね、1枚ずつ撮影する

Coloring
彩色

The celluloid tracing are then painted in on the reverse side.

トレースしたセルに裏から色をつけます

Tracing
トレース

All the pictures are then transfered to the celluloid.

原動画をセルロイドに写す

Creation of moving drawings
動画作成

The pictures that go between the movement pictures are then created.

動作の中間部を描いていく

Creation of basic drawings
原画作成

Animators draw pictures showing the key points of the characters, following the designs shown in the continuity pictures.

絵コンテにしたがって動作の基本部分を描きます

視聴率のしくみ

　各テレビ局が血道をあげているのが、視聴率競争だ。民放局の場合は、1か月平均1%アップすれば、数千万円の売上増加に結びつくといわれているので、真剣にならざるを得ない。1ケタの視聴率が続くと、スポンサーから苦情がくる。

　わが国では、ビデオリサーチとニールセン・ジャパンという2つの調査会社が関東、関西、名古屋などの地区で行う世帯視聴率調査をもとに視聴率が算出されている。だが、この調査サンプル数が地区で200〜600世帯という少数であり、"猫がテレビを見ていた場合も視聴率に含まれる"という皮肉も語られるほどだった。しかし、調査世帯に関する資料は"門外不出"だ。

Household viewership rates
世帯視聴率

Each member of the monitor households chooses the programs they want to see. When viewing a program, each member watching pushes a personal button, and a sensor identifies how many people are watching the program. This is called the people meter (PM) system.

モニターとなった家族1人ごとに番号を決め、視聴するときは各人のパーソナルボタンを押してもらい、センサーで人数を確認する。ピープル・メーター（PM）というシステムである

Individual viewership rate
個人視聴率

A device is attached to the reception equipment in each monitor household to automatically record what programs are watched. The monitor households are changed every three years (in the case of Video Research). This data determines the fate of programs.

モニターの家庭のテレビ受像機に機械を取りつけ、どの番組をいつ視聴したかを自動的に記録する。3年ごとに調査世帯が入れ替わる（ビデオリサーチの場合）が、このデータは放送番組の運命を左右する

TV Audience Ratings

Television stations are obsessed with winning the battle for audiences. An average 1 percent increase per month in viewership will lead to an increase in sales of tens of millions of yen, so you can't blame them for fretting so much over a few points. Whenever audience ratings drop into the one-digit range, the stations can expect to hear from their sponsors.

Video Research and Nelsen Japan are the two television audience rating services that provide figures for Kanto, Kansai, Nagoya, and other parts of the country. The number of sample households in each area is between 200 and 600. This means that even households where the TV is on and only the cat is watching have a large influence on the outcome. However, any information gathered from the individual households is considered top secret.

How TV audience ratings are calculated
視聴率の出しかた

• Example using five households　5世帯の例

(Total)　Station A = 2／Station B = 1／Station C = 1
（合計）　A局＝2、B局＝1、C局＝1

Households　世帯	No.1	No.2	No.3	No.4	No.5
No. of televisions　テレビ台数	2	3	1	1	2
Station A　A局		2	1		
Station B　B局					1
Station C　C局					1
Television ON/OFF テレビON/OFF	OFF	ON Station A A局 1	ON Station A A局 1	OFF	ON Station B Station C B局 1 C局 1

• Station audience ratings　各局の視聴率

Station A: 2 households/5 households = 40%
Stations B and C: 1 household/5 households = 20%

（A局）2世帯／5世帯＝40%
（B局・C局）1世帯／5世帯＝20%

• Program average viewership　番組平均視聴率

Total of combined viewership for each minute of broadcast time/number of broadcast minutes.

放送時間内での1分ごとの視聴率の合計／放送分数

天気予報のしくみ

　テレビ番組の天気予報が面白くなってきた。以前は気象庁の発表をそのまま放映していたが、局独自の見解を出してもいいことになったからだ。といっても基礎データは気象庁提供という制約はある。それを気象予報士の資格者が分析して予報するわけだが、局によって当たり外れがあり、番組的にも興味深いところだ。

　ところで、予報の発信源である気象庁は、国土交通省の外局である。両者の関連性は不思議な気もするが、天気予報は船や飛行機などの運行に密接に関係しているからだそうだ。

Weather observation
on the ground
地上気象観測

Weather satellite
("Himawari") observation
気象衛星観測（ひまわり）

Regional weather observation
stations (known as "Amedasu,"
1,335 locations nationwide)
地域気象観測所（アメダス）1335か所

天気予報の種類	Types of weather forecast
短期予報（毎日5回）	Short-range forecasts (five times a day)
週間予報（毎日1回）	One-week forecasts (once a day)
1か月予報（月3回）	One-month forecasts (three times a month)
3か月予報（月1回）	Three-month forecasts (once a month)
暖候期予報（年1回・3月）	Warm season forecasts (once a year in March)
寒候期予報（年1回・10月）	Cold season forecasts (once a year in October)

Weather Forecasts

Weather reports on TV have become much more fun to watch nowadays: whereas before TV stations used to broadcast the reports exactly as they were received from the Meteorological Agency, now each station adds its own interpretive opinions. That said, the basic data still come from the Meteorological Agency—that same restriction still applies. Qualified weather forecasters analyze that data and make their own predictions, which means that some of them may make forecasts that are slightly off sometimes, so it's fun to watch and see how well they do.

The Meteorological Agency, which is the source for all statements about the weather, is actually an external organ of the Ministry of Land, Infrastructure and Transport. At first sight, it may seem a little hard to see what relation they have to each other, but apparently it's because weather conditions have an intimate bearing on the operations of means of transport like ships and airplanes.

Meteorological Agency
気象庁

A diagram is made.
天気図をつくる

The computer puts out a weather forecast diagram.
コンピュータで予想天気図をつくる

Meteorological data is put together.
気象の資料を集める

A weather forecast is made.
天気を予報する

TV Station
放送局

A meeting is held to discuss how the weather forecast should be broadcast, based on details from the Meteorological Agency.

気象庁のデータをもとに生放送の打合わせ

Weather Forecaster
気象予報士

TV Studio
スタジオ

Giving the weather forecast used to be the easy way for young female TV announcers, so-called "new faces," to make their debut. Nowadays, though, weather forecasters have to be properly qualified.

天気予報はかつて新人アナウンサーの"顔見せ"番組だったが、現在は気象予報士の資格がないとできなくなった

From 1995, it became possible for anybody involved in weather forecasting to give general weather forecasts. For a person to give his or her own particular forecast as well, it became necessary for the forecaster to obtain a national qualification in weather forecasting. This exam is extremely difficult to pass, both on a technical and a scientific level.

95年から予報業者による一般向けの天気予報が自由化された。あわせて独自の天気予報を行うには、国家試験をパスして気象予報士の資格を得ることが必要になった。ただし、この試験は実技、学科とも超難問である

有線放送のしくみ

　スナックなどの飲食店が店内で流している音楽は、たいがい有線放送番組である。この放送所は全国に約800か所あり、そこから各契約者へ番組が流れるしくみになっている。番組といっても放送所に録音スタジオがあるわけでなく、キー・ステーションから同軸ケーブルを通じて送られてくる番組を中継する役目である。

　放送所はユーザーからの電話リクエストに応じてレコード音楽を流すサービスや、モーニングコールなどのサービスをしたりもする。有線放送は、誰でもが加入することができ、設備もマルチチューナーをアンプにつなぐだけという手軽さから、最近では一般家庭での加入が増えてきているそうだ。

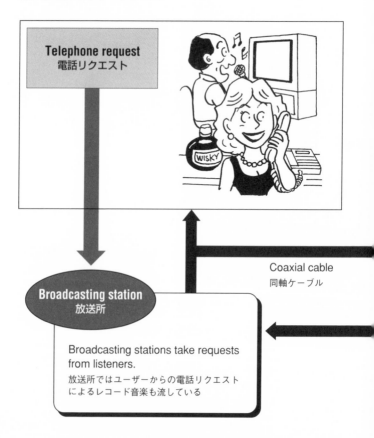

Telephone request
電話リクエスト

Coaxial cable
同軸ケーブル

Broadcasting station
放送所

Broadcasting stations take requests from listeners.
放送所ではユーザーからの電話リクエストによるレコード音楽も流している

Cable Broadcasts

Much of the music that you hear in bars and restaurants in Japan is by way of cable broadcast. There are about 800 stations around Japan from which such broadcasts are sent to listeners. These stations do not have actual recording studios, but instead act as intermediary stations that receive the programs via coaxial cable from key stations. These stations also take requests by telephone and even provide morning calls. Individuals can also sign up for the service, and since all you need to do is connect a multi-tuner to an amplifier, the number of households enrolled in the service has been on the increase.

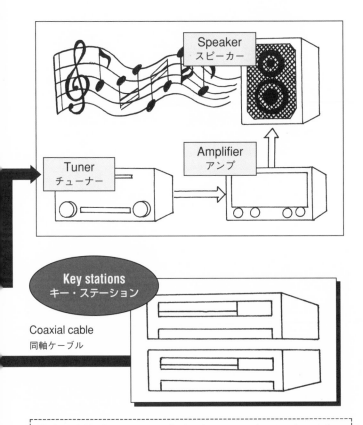

Speaker
スピーカー

Amplifier
アンプ

Tuner
チューナー

Key stations
キー・ステーション

Coaxial cable
同軸ケーブル

Music is dubbed onto tapes at the headquarters and sent to key stations throughout the country. The music is then sent to the broadcasting stations.
番組は本社がテープにダビングして全国のキー・ステーションに送る。それを放送所へ流す

141

第**5**章
知っててよかった 業界のウラオモテ

これであなたもギョーカイ通!?

Behind the Scenes at the Industrial Level *Now You Know It All*

コンビニのしくみ

　コンビニエンスストア（コンビニ）は、都市部では異なるチェーン店が軒を並べているという光景さえ珍しくない。コンビニはそれほど儲かる商売なのだろうか？

　コンビニの経営は、本部直営店とフランチャイズ店の2種類に大別される。ほとんどの店は後者で、酒屋などの小売店から転じたオーナー店長が多い。消費者の多様なニーズに応じるという点で、コンビニ経営は時流にかなった商売といえそうだが、最近は過当競争で従来ほどにウマ味のないビジネスになり下がってしまった。

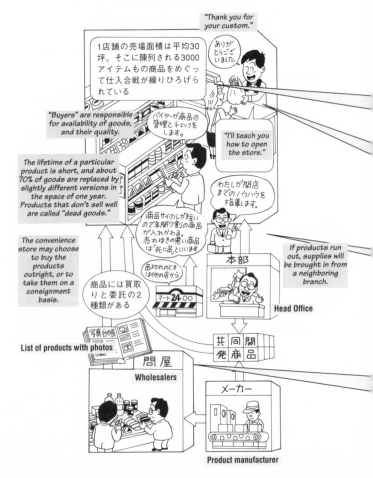

"Thank you for your custom."

1店舗の売場面積は平均30坪。そこに陳列される3000アイテムもの商品をめぐって仕入合戦が繰りひろげられている

ありがとうございました

"Buyers" are responsible for availability of goods, and their quality.

バイヤーが商品の管理とチェックをします。

"I'll teach you how to open the store."

The lifetime of a particular product is short, and about 70% of goods are replaced by slightly different versions in the space of one year. Products that don't sell well are called "dead goods."

わたしが開店までのノウハウを指導します。

商品サイクルが短いので年間7割の商品が入れかわる。売れゆきの悪い商品は"死に品"といいます

The convenience store may choose to buy the products outright, or to take them on a consignment basis.

品切れのときは他の店から

商品には買取りと委託の2種類がある

本部

Head Office

If products run out, supplies will be brought in from a neighboring branch.

写真台帳

List of products with photos

共同開発商品

問屋
Wholesalers

メーカー

Product manufacturer

Convenience Stores

It is now not at all uncommon in many Japanese towns and cities to see several convenience stores belonging to different chains lining the sides of the street. Why the proliferation—is it because running a convenience store makes so much money?

There are two ways to run a convenience store business: the first is where the store is run directly from a main office; the second is where the store is run independently as a franchise. Nearly all convenience stores fall into the second category. Many owners are people who take up the job after having had experience of running their own small store, for example a liquor store. Convenience stores have to meet the needs of a great variety of consumers, and so in that sense one might say it's a business that matches the times. But recently the fierce competition has rather detracted from the attraction.

The average selling space in one convenience store is often no more than a mere 90 sq. meters. In this space, as many as 3000 items are displayed on the shelves—items for which a fierce battle will have been waged between various buyers.

The requirements for becoming a store owner are that he or she is married; that he or she be between 20 and 50 years in age; that he or she has personal funds of at least 2.5 to 3 million yen.
オーナー店長の条件は家族2名（夫婦）以上、20〜50歳、自己資金最低250〜300万円などが原則だ

Dispatches a delegate to help set up a store
開発員派遣

Products carefully selected by someone from the head office of the convenience store chain are entered onto a list, which will then become the basic products available in all the other branches of that particular chain.
本部の担当者が厳選した商品は台帳に掲載され、これに基づき各店は品揃えする

パチンコ店のしくみ

　パチンコ業界の年間総売上は30兆円といわれる。自動車業界は20兆円だから、それをしのぐ巨大産業だ。だが、これは表向きの数字で、いわゆる過少申告だという声も多い。

　パチンコ業界は、80年代に登場したフィーバー機やデジ・パチ機によって急速に売上を伸ばした。ギャンブル性が高くなったぶん、お客がつぎ込む金額がアップしたからだ。今や、1回2万～3万円を使うのが普通だという。となると、出玉を換金する傾向が強まるのは当然。だが、「風営法」はパチンコ店が客に提供した商品を買い取ってはならないと定めている。そこで例の独特の換金システムがとられているわけだ。

The merchandise used for prizes is bought from specialist suppliers, but many pachinko parlors also use a system whereby one ball can be used as 4 yen to buy more pachinko balls.

景品は専門の納入業者から仕入れるが、玉1発4円の貸玉料と等価交換するところも多い

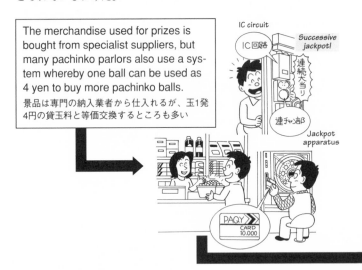

IC circuit

IC回路

Successive jackpot!

連続大当り

連チャン部

Jackpot apparatus

PAQY CARD 10.000

The pre-paid card system
プリペイドカード

The pre-paid card system was brought in to put the business on a clear and above-board footing, and both Tokyo and Osaka have one firm each that conducts the business. These companies are also workplaces where high-ranking police officials are re-appointed to work after retirement. Many pachinko parlors have had to accept this system under the administrative guidance of the police.

経営の明朗化を図るために導入されたプリペイドカードシステムを運営するカード会社は、東京と大阪に1社ずつ。警察幹部の天下り先にもなっている。警察の行政指導で、やむなく店の一部に導入しているところも多い

Pachinko Parlors

The total annual earnings of the pachinko (Japanese pinball) industry are said to be 30 trillion yen, exceeding even the total earnings of the automobile industry (20 trillion yen). But actually, these are merely the official figures, and many consider that a large part of the actual income in this industry remains undeclared.

It was in the 1980s, with the appearance of the new so-called "Fever machines" and "Digital pachinko machines," that the pachinko industry started to increase its earnings at a terrific rate. These machines had an increased element of high-risk high-returns, with the possibility of huge winnings—with the result that pachinko devotees poured large amounts of money into the game. Now, apparently, people commonly spend 20 or 30 thousand yen in a single round. And of course this means that more people want to make exchanges of pachinko balls for cash. But the Law Concerning the Sex and Gambling Business forbids the exchange of prize goods for money, and this accounts for the bizarre system of exchange.

> 90% of the pachinko prizes are "special-purchase prizes" for the specific purpose of exchange for cash, but legally speaking one cannot make such exchanges in the pachinko parlor.
> 景品の9割は換金のための特殊景品に換えられているが、法律上パチンコ店では換金できない

Special purchase prizes
特殊景品

Exchange for cash
換金

The rate of exchange is 2.5 yen per one pachinko ball. In Tokyo, many pachinko parlors also offer gold ingots as special prize gifts, and the exchange depots are located outside the store, under the ownership of other parties. In some cases, these exchange depots become a source of funds for yakuza hoodlums.

換金のレートは玉1個につき2円50銭が相場。東京では純金の地金を特殊景品にする店も多く、換金所は店外の第三者に委託。この換金所が暴力団の資金源になっているケースもある

小売業界のしくみ

　小売業界が様変わりしつつある。変化のキー・ワードは、「価格破壊」だ。この先鞭をつけたのがディスカウントストア (DS) なのはいうまでもないが、今や大手スーパー、デパートなども自ら価格破壊をうたう時代になった。

　もっとも、消費者にとってはより安いことが絶対条件になるわけだから、ディスカウントは本来、消費者に指示されるのが当然なのだ。この当然のことができなかったのは、商品流通の複雑なしくみがあったためである。メーカーから小売店に商品が届くまでには、問屋などの流通経路がある。中間の流通コストを削減すること、これが小売店のディスカウント販売の第一歩なのである。

Discount stores
ディスカウントストアの業態

Discount stores
ディスカウントストア

Discount stores undersell their competition by buying direct, buying in bulk, and paying in cash.
直取引、大量仕入れ、現金決済がディスカウントストアの価格破壊の秘密だ

Retail Trade

The retail business is now undergoing great changes. The keyword is "price destruction." Needless to say, discount stores (DS) have taken the initiative, but major supermarkets and department stores are also starting to sell products at lower than suggested consumer prices.

Since consumers put a high value on value-for-money, a new discount store is always welcomed. The reason that this change did not occur earlier is because of an intricate distribution system. For a product to reach a retailer from a manufacturer, it usually goes through a distribution channel that includes a wholesaler. The first step toward discount sales is to reduce the intermediate distribution cost.

Category killer
カテゴリー・キラー

These shops sell a variety of products only in specific categories in order to keep prices low.

取扱商品の分野を限定し、品揃えを多くして低価格販売をする

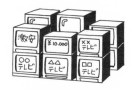

Power center
パワーセンター

Shopping malls that consist of five or more category killers and that have over 30,000 square meters of retail space.

カテゴリー・キラー5店舗以上を核とし、売場面積3万m²以上のオープンモール型のショッピングセンター

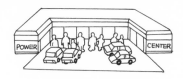

New types of discount stores
ニュータイプの小売業態

Hyper market
ハイパーマーケット

This type of store, usually found in the suburbs, covers an area of over 9,000 square meters, sells about 60,000 items, and offers discounts of between 10 and 30 percent.

郊外に立地し、店舗面積9000m²以上。約6万品目を揃え、10〜30％の割引販売をする

Clearance stores
オフプライス・ストア

Shops that purchase clearance goods from manufacturers, department stores, and specialty stores, and that sell items at discounts of 30 to 40 percent.

メーカー、デパート、専門店の在庫処分品や見切り品を仕入れて販売。定価の3〜4割引で店頭に出す

Outlet stores
アウトレット・ストア

Manufacturers set up this type of store to sell clearance items. In some cases, outlet stores do clearance of PB products.

メーカーが在庫処分を目的につくった店舗。PB商品の在庫処分用になっているケースも

Unrestricted consumer pricing is resulting in the emergence of new types of retail stores.

価格破壊の激しい波は、新しい形態の小売店舗を続々と生み出している

Dollar discount chain stores
ダラ・ディスカウント・チェーン

Chain stores that sell excess stock or defective articles at low uniform prices.

メーカーの過剰在庫品や傷物商品を、一定の価格に統一して低価格で販売する店舗チェーン

Home centers
ホームセンター

Self-service discount stores offering handicraft items, gardening goods, sporting goods, etc.

手工芸、園芸、スポーツ用品などの生活関連用品を幅広く揃え、セルフサービスとディスカウント販売が特徴

Wholesale clubs
ホールセール・クラブ

Warehouse-type stores that are able to sell items at low prices by cutting expenses and bulk buying. Open to members only.

倉庫型の店舗で、会員制によって運営する。大量仕入れ、コスト削減による低価格販売が特徴

Convenience stores are a rapidly growing form of retailing due to their ubiqity, product variety, and long business hours. As of 2000, there were 50,000 convenience stores throughout Japan.

最近の小売業でめざましい伸長を示しているのがコンビニエンスストア。地域密着型、品揃えの豊富さ、長時間営業の利便性がうけて、全国に約5万店（2000年）を数える

観光バスツアーのしくみ

　安い海外パック旅行のブームで、すっかり割を食ってしまったのが国内旅行。なかでも不況のあおりを受けて団体旅行がぐんと減った国内バスツアーは、その巻き返しに懸命だ。いずこの観光バス会社も、企画と料金の両面でのサービス競争を開始し出した。バスツアーといえば温泉が付きものだが、敷居が高かった高級温泉旅館も軒並み値下げに応じるようになって、高かろう悪かろうのバスツアーはちょっぴり影をひそめた感がある。とはいっても、旅先でハメをはずしてもらっては困るのだが……。

On any guided bus tour with several buses, the authority of the driver and guide in the first bus is paramount. Even when this driver makes a wrong turn and goes off the proper route, the buses behind must follow without question.

バスツアーで数台連ねて走るバスの1号車の運転手とバスガイドの権限は絶大。コースを間違えた場合も、後続車は文句を言わずについて行かなければならない

"Shouldn't we make a turn here?"

こっちが正しいルートじゃないんですか!?

"Just shut up and follow me!"

だまって1号車についてくればいいの

"Welcome! Get your hot meals and souvenirs here!"

いらっしゃいいらっしゃいお食事・お産産いかがですか

お食事　おみやげ　ドライブイン CARJACK

Meals/Souvenirs/Drive-in

The arrangement is that roughly 10 percent of the total sales of goods from drive-in restaurants and souvenir shops en route go to bus companies.

昼食をとるドライブインや土産物店からは、売上の10%前後のマージンがバス会社に入るしくみだ

Guided Bus Tours

The boom in cheap package tours abroad has taken a large bite out of the percentage of people who make trips within Japan. And now that the slump in the economy has so drastically reduced group travel, domestic bus tours are having to do everything in their power not to let it affect business. Wherever you look, tourist bus companies vie with each other to offer the best deal—whether in the particular features of each route or in the rates. Though a visit to a hot-spring resort is par for the course on any bus tour, now even inns that previously charged sky-high prices have reduced their prices to an average rate, and the bus tours that were once expensive rip-offs seem to have become fewer and far between. But remember, just because you save on the tour does not mean that you can let go and indulge in a spending spree at your destination!

Sticking to the rules about departures and arrivals
発着主義

Tourist buses have to pick up their passengers and let them off only within certain zones located in the vicinity of their business premises. Any business conducted outside these zones is illegal.

観光バスがお客を乗せて発着するのは、営業所のある区域内でなければならない。区域外の営業は違法行為になる

観光バスツアーのしくみ……2

"Let me pour, sir. You're the company president?"

"No, the president's the guy in his underpants over there."

Guided Bus Tours······2

When guided tour bus companies started showing videos of films during tours, a dispute arose between them and the Japan Copyright Association who demanded a copyright fee. Charges work out to roughly 4000 yen a day per video.

車中で放映する映画ビデオをめぐって、観光バス会社と日本著作権協会との間でトラブルが起きている。著作権使用料を支払えというのだ。ちなみに、使用料は1本ごとで1日約4000円ほどになる

The geisha's "Hana-Dai"
芸者さんの花代

Inviting geisha to carouse with you at parties will inevitably burn a large hole in your pocket. Rates for geisha, which are called "Hana-Dai," are calculated in units of thirty minutes, with a minimum time of 2 hours (four units)—and the going rate for one unit is around 3000 yen. Be aware that geisha usually come in couples, a young woman accompanied by an older woman, so even if you expressly request "One YOUNG woman, and ONLY one," her older chaperone will still come along.

芸者を呼ぶと当然、お金がかかる。この費用は"花代"と呼ばれ、30分単位(1本という)で計算され、通常は2時間(4本)が原則で、相場は1本3000円前後。なお、芸者は年増とヤングがコンビを組んでいることが多いので、"若いのを1人だけ"とはいかないことが多い

Geisha belong to a house called an okiya. At okiya in hot spring resorts, there is a manager called a kenban who dispatches geisha and collects the fee. This system is a vestige of Edo period.

芸者は"置屋(おきや)"という家に所属している。温泉街には置屋の元締めである"検番(けんばん)"があり、ここで派遣の取次ぎや代金の精算を行っている。このシステムは、江戸時代からの名残りである

タクシー業界のしくみ

　タクシー業界では利用者の保護・利便性の観点から、全国を77のブロックに分け「同一地域同一料金制」（1県が2つの区域に分割されており、区域内は同一料金）をとっているが、1993年5月に運輸政策審議会がその見直しを骨子とする答申をまとめ、タクシー運賃の規制緩和と増減車の弾力化が打ち出された。

　ところで、タクシー乗務員には、運転歴が3年以上ありタクシーを運転するために必要な第2種免許証を持っていれば誰でもなれる。地理の能力も必須で、東京と大阪では地理の試験がある。また、個人タクシーについては法人での一定期間の勤務経験（職業運転経験が10年以上）が必要だ。

> The taxi industry has been protected for many years by the Ministry of Land, Infrastructure and Transport. However, in the "Heisei" recession, individual companies have made fare cuts, heavily affecting the industry.
>
> 国土交通省によって保護されてきたタクシー業界だが、平成不況で各企業が交通費削減を打ち出し、その影響をモロに受けている

How taxi fares are revised　運賃改定のプロセス

Application from a business
事業者許可申請

District Transportation Bureau (reception)
陸運支局（受付）

 Submission　進達

Approval
認可

Transport Bureau (public notification, hearings, screening)
運輸局（公示・聴聞・審査）

 Request for decision　稟伺

Ministry of Land, Infrastructure and Transport (interior screening)
国土交通省（内部審査）

 Deliberation and pre-notification　協議・事前連絡

Cabinet Office (screening)
内閣府（審査）

 Submission　付議

Discussion by related cabinet members
関係閣僚会議

The Taxi Industry

For many years, taxi fares in Japan were set by dividing the country into 77 blocks, within which the fares were set uniformly for each individual block to protect taxi customers and make taxis more convenient. However, in May 1993, the transportation policy council reviewed this strategy and proposed a revision for deregulating taxi fares and making it easier to increase or decrease the number of taxis.

Anyone who has had a drivers license for more than three years and obtained the second-level drivers license can become a taxi driver. Knowledge of the streets is also necessary, and so would-be taxi drivers in Tokyo and Osaka have to pass tests. Those wanting to become private taxi drivers must have a certain amount of work experience as a driver (10 years of driving-related work experience).

Regulations have been lifted in stages.
規制は徐々に緩和されてきた

Regulations on new entry　参入規制

Getting a taxi business license was a troublesome process, but deregulation has gradually made it easier.

各地方運輸局から営業免許を受けるには厳しいチェックが必要だったが、徐々に新規参入が容易に

Uniform fares in zones　同一地域同一運賃

Fares were regulated under administrative guidelines. However, the introduction of zones has diversified fares and competition is now heating up.

行政指導による事実上の運賃規制。だがゾーン制導入で運賃は多様化し、競争は熾烈になる模様

Out-of-zone regulations　発着規制

When drivers leave their zone of business, they cannot, in principle, pick up clients. That's why some taxis may not stop to pick you up.

自分の営業区域から出た場合は原則として客を乗せられない。乗車拒否が意外に多いのはこの規制のため

Regulations on additional taxis　増車規制

Regulations on the number of taxis were introduced to help maintain profits. A 1997 revision has made it possible to increase fleets by 10 percent.

供給過剰による事業者の採算悪化を防ぐのが目的。97年度からは1割までの増車が認められた

In Tokyo, taxi companies are ranked based on the number of complaints from clients to the Modernization Center, which oversees taxi driver training.

東京では、業界の研修・指導を行っている「近代化センター」に苦情が寄せられ、これをもとに各社のランクが決められる

タクシー業界のしくみ……2

Where taxi fares go (in Tokyo)
タクシー料金の原価の内訳（東京の場合）

Other expenses: 12.6%
Profit: 2.3%
利潤2.3%
その他 12.6%
燃料 4.5%
Fuel: 4.5%
人件費 80.6%
Labor: 80.6%

ほとんどが人件費なんですよ

How much do taxi drivers make? 乗務員の年収は？	
	Annual income (1993) 年収（93年）
Kyoto 京都	4.11 411万円
Osaka 大阪	4.43 443万円
Tokyo 東京	5.16 516万円
	(Unit: million yen)

Zone fare system
ゾーン運賃制度

Since April 1997, requests to discount fares to 10% below the maximum limits are approved automatically.

97年4月から政府が決めた上限値から10%以内の割引は自動的に認可されるしくみに

There are approximately 213,000 company taxis on the roads (7,200 companies), and about 47,000 private taxis for a total of 260,000. In 1974, the number of rides given peaked at 4 billion, and now the number is around 3.2 billion per year, accounting for about 10 percent of public transport.

法人が約21万3000台（約7200社）、個人タクシーが約4万7000台の計約26万台のタクシーが走る。輸送量は74年の40億人をピークに減少し、現在は年間32億人程度。日本の陸上輸送の約10%だ

The Taxi Industry……2

Where taxis pick up clients 多様なタクシーの営業形態	
Driving around 流し	Drivers patrol the streets around office and government building areas. 一定の時間を決めて、オフィス街や官庁街を走る
Train stations 駅待ち	Drivers pick up clients at specified train stations (usually two or three). 特定の駅（2〜3か所）を中心にお客を拾う
Night life areas 辻待ち	From evening until late at night, drivers look for clients in busy night life areas. 夕方から深夜にかけて盛り場の辻で客待ちをする
Wireless dispatch 無線配車	People who stay out drinking and miss the last train often call for a taxi. 終電に乗り遅れた飲み屋の客などが数多く利用する
Waiting for calls 車庫待ち	In smaller cities, taxi drivers often wait at the company garage for calls to come in. 中小都市では会社への電話を待つ、この形態が多い

Tokyo
東京の場合

Fares for consumption tax-exempt businesses (including private taxis): 650 yen for 2 km.
消費税の免税業者（個人を含む）は2 km まで650円

Hi-no-maru Taxi (from April 1997): Starting fare of 340 yen
日の丸自動車が97年4月から初乗り340円

Standard taxi: 660 yen for 2 km.
標準的なタクシーは2 km まで660円

MK Taxi of Kyoto (from November 1997): 600 yen for 2 km.
京都のMKタクシーが97年11月から2 km まで600円

ブライダル業界のしくみ

　ブライダル業界とは一般に結婚情報サービス業や結婚相談所といった結婚相手の紹介業から、結婚式場紹介業、結婚プロデュース業、結婚式場、ホテル、さらに結婚式や披露宴用の貸し衣裳業界、結婚写真業者、エステティックサロンなども含まれてくる。百貨店や旅行会社もブライダル業の周辺業界として重要だ。そして、これらの業界が密接に絡み合って提携しながらマーケットを拡大しているのが特徴。なんといっても結婚は人生の最大のセレモニーで、平成不況のいまも結婚に投資する費用は平均700万円（三和銀行調べ）という。5兆円産業になったブライダル業界は、結婚という「金のなる木」の演出家なのだ。

"It's my wedding—I don't care how much it costs!" "It ought to be expensive—it's a once in a lifetime event!" This is the kind of customer the wedding industry loves.
「結婚式なら多少カネがかかっても」「一生に一度だから」という顧客の深層心理をうまくついて、各種産業が群がる

Marriage Introduction Services
結婚情報サービス業

Tie-ups with various related businesses
異業種との提携

Tasks and Strategies
課題と戦略

ブライダル
情報サービス

Variations in recruitment systems
入会システムの工夫

Better management of personal information
個人情報の管理の徹底

Expansion of corporate requirements
法人需要の拡大

Perfection of counseling services
カウンセラーの充実

Reduction of exaggerated advertising
誇大広告の自主規制

Thorough observation of the "cooling-off" period between prospective couples
クーリングオフの徹底

Reduction of problems surrounding membership contracts
契約トラブルをなくす

The Bridal Industry

The bridal industry includes services that introduce prospective marriage partners to each other, so-called marriage consultation services, and marriage information services, and services surrounding wedding ceremony halls, the services that offer help in holding weddings, the wedding halls themselves, hotels, the shops and services that rent out clothing for wedding ceremonies and receptions, the photographers who specialize in wedding photographs, and bridal beauty salons. Also important as peripheral industries are department stores and the travel industry. Further, it should be noted that all these industries continue to expand their markets, and one of their notable features is that they offer their services in combination with each other. A marriage is the greatest ceremonial event in a person's life—even now, when we are supposed to be in a recession, the average amount of money poured into a marriage is apparently 7,000,000 yen (Sanwa Bank survey). An industry that in its totality is now worth 5 trillion yen, weddings are the trees upon which money grows.

The role of the bridal consultants
ブライダル・コンサルタントの役割

Wedding ceremony information center
結婚式場紹介所

結婚式場説明

(1) To help the couple decide where to hold the ceremony by explaining with the aid of pamphlets the various choices available
(2) To give an idea of the costs, bearing in mind the number of guests and the type of cuisine at the banquet
(3) To help decide the date of the wedding

①各種のパンフレットを見せながら式場を決める
②出席者数や料理を決めて予算をはじき出す
③日取りを決める

Wedding ceremony hall
結婚式場

(1) To give an estimate of the budget, and to print up the wedding invitations
(2) To calculate the number of people who will accept the invitations, and to come up with a seating plan
(3) To carry out final confirmations

①予算の見積りを出すとともに招待状を作成する
②出席者数を確認し、席次表を作成する
③最終確認を行う

ブライダル業界のしくみ……2

Peripheral services and trades

Jewelry and accessory stores
宝石・アクセサリー業

An engagement ring should apparently cost 3 times one's monthly salary. This kind of market never bottoms out.

指輪の相場は給与の3倍とか。永遠の安定市場だ

Department stores
百貨店

Bridal corners always have a high earnings ratios. They handle gifts for guests, clothing rental, and daily household items.

ブライダルコーナーは収益率が高い。引出物や衣装・生活用品も取り扱う

Wedding production services
結婚式プロデュース業

These businesses specialize in making all the arrangements for wedding banquets and other parties after the wedding.

披露宴や2次会を盛り上げる専門集団

Catering services
ケータリングサービス

All kinds of cuisine are possible, from Japanese to European and Chinese.

和・洋・中華・無国籍とあらゆる料理を用意する

Credit card companies
クレジットカード会社

These form alignments with other businesses in the trade, such as wedding production services. Some offer special deals for newlyweds.

結婚式場紹介所などと提携。新婚特典サービスも

Real estate trade
不動産業

Newly weds tend to go for middle-sized condominiums. They offer support to newlyweds.

2DKクラスが人気。新婚生活をサポート

Engagement
婚約

Choosing where to hold the wedding ceremony
式場選び

Wedding Ceremony
結婚式

Wedding Reception
披露宴

Life for the Newlyweds
新婚生活

The Bridal Industry·······2

結婚を演出する周辺企業

Wedding information services
結婚情報サービス業

These dating services arrange meetings between men and women. Exorbitant membership fees can be a problem.

男女の出会いを演出。会費が高いとの批判も

Wedding ceremony information centers
結婚式場紹介所

These provide pamphlets and information on the various places to hold weddings, and they also deal with parties after the wedding as well as weddings held abroad.

提携する各式場の資料をそろえており、2次会や海外挙式も取り扱う

Wedding ceremony halls
結婚式場

These fall into the main categories of private ceremonial halls, hotels, and public halls.

民間の式場、ホテル、公営の会館に大別できる

Wedding outfit rental services
貸衣裳・レンタル業

These have everything from kimono to wedding dresses and suits.

着物、ウエディングドレス、スーツ等をそろえる

Staffing services
人材派遣

These send out the various professional people who help bring off a wedding banquet—emcees, musicians, photographers and video-cameramen.

司会・ビデオ撮影・音効など披露宴のプロを派遣

Travel companies
旅行会社

Honeymoon travel never seems to go out of fashion, no matter how expensive it may be.

新婚旅行は多少高くても売れるおいしい市場だ

生保業界のしくみ

生命保険は、明治時代初期に福沢諭吉がヨーロッパの制度を紹介したことに始まる。そして第2次世界大戦後、生保は「安心」と「保障」を売り物に急速に拡大していく。生保の考え方の基本は相互扶助の精神。このため生命保険会社は、株式会社より相互会社の形態を取るケースが多いのが特徴。

本来、生保という商品は死亡や病気など万一に「備える」ためのものなのだが、一時払い養老保険や変額保険のような利息追求型の保険の登場で、その性質が変化してきている。

また、96年10月より生損保の兼業・相互乗り入れが認められたことにより双方が子会社方式でお互いの業務に参入している。

As the Japanese economic bubble ended, life insurance companies, a symbol of Japanese affluence, arrived at an abrupt turning point.

「ザ・セイホ」と呼ばれ、豊かなジャパンマネーの象徴だった生命保険会社も、バブル崩壊で大きな曲がり角に

Life insurance companies
生命保険会社

Office workers
内勤者

They deal with maintenance and management of insurance contracts, development of new policies, and asset investment. Salaries are much higher than those in other business fields.

契約の維持・管理のほか商品開発や資産運用を担当。給与水準は他業種よりぐんと高い

 Management 管理

Sales staff
外務員

Over 400,000 people are working throughout Japan selling policies through their connections with relatives and with people in their local communities.

全国に40万人以上いるとされ、地縁・血縁を頼りに果敢なセールス活動を展開

Working conditions 【待遇】

They receive a regular salary and a commission on sales and bear their own expenses under a work contract.

基本給と歩合給の組合せ。営業経費は自己負担。契約社員に近い立場

The Life Insurance Industry

The life insurance business in Japan was started in the early Meiji era when Yukichi Fukuzawa introduced the European system. Companies in this field rapidly expanded after WWII by emphasizing security and emergency support as selling points.

The fundamental concept of life insurance is the spirit of reciprocal aid. Accordingly, mutual companies are more common than stock corporations. Though the original purpose of life insurance is to prepare for an emergency such as illness or death, this feature was now changing because of newly developed policies with higher dividends, such as endowment or variable plans.

Since October 1996, non-life and life insurance companies have been allowed to merge with each other. Both types of company have started to expand into other fields, having subsidiary companies dealing with other business.

"Hey, you're not supposed to die!" — Insurer

	Customers 顧客
Insurance payout 保険金等の支払い	
Premium payment 保険料支払い	**Corporate body** 法人 Selling policies to prepare for retirement allowance or to invest assets 退職金準備として保険販売。その他、資産運用も
Business activities 営業活動	**Business area** 職域 Selling insurance to employees by visiting companies 企業等を訪問して従業員に保険加入をすすめる
Business activities 営業活動	
Business activities 営業活動	**Local area** 地域 Door-to-door sales to medium and small firms and to households within an assigned territory 一定テリトリー内の中小企業・住宅を訪問セールスする

生保業界のしくみ……2

Life insurance business faces heated competition
競争が激化する業界の構図

Stock corporations
株式会社

Sony Life Insurance Co. Ltd., Nihon Dantai Life Insurance Co. Ltd., etc.
ソニー生命、日本団体生命など

Mutual companies
相互会社

Most of insurance companies such as the Nippon Life Insurance Company and the Dai-ichi Mutual Life Insurance Company.
日本生命、第一生命など大半の保険会社がこの形態

Cooperatives
共済

JA Kyosai (National Mutual Insurance Federation of Agricultural Cooperatives), Zenrosai (National Federation of Workers and Consumers Insurance), etc.
JA（農協）共済、全労災など

Foreign-affiliated insurers
外資系生保

Medical insurance policies are well developed. Unlike domestic companies, the sales representatives are mostly male.
医療保険が充実。国内保険と違って男性が営業の中心

Post offices
郵便局

Postal life insurance has more advantages because it is not sold for the purpose of making money.
簡易保険は営利を追求しない分、有利な点が多い

The principle of a mutual company is to have all policyholders as its members and to have them participate in management through meetings of representatives. However, in reality this concept is becoming nothing more than an obstacle to making information open to the public.

保険契約者をすべて社員とし社員総代会を通じて経営に参加できるのが相互会社の建前。だが、形骸化が著しく、かえって情報開示の妨げになっているとの声も

The Life Insurance Industry······2

Comparison
内容を比較してみると

	Advantages 長所	Weaknesses 欠点
Domestic companies 国内生保会社	Possible to receive meticulous service and support from the sales representative. 外務員のこまめなサービスとメンテナンス	Premium is relatively expensive. Dividends have recently been lowered. 保険料が割高で、最近は配当も低迷している
Foreign-affiliated companies 外資系生保会社	Low premium. Possible to buy a small coverage policy. 保険料が安く、小口の保障額でも加入できる	No dividend. No personal annuity policy available. 配当がなく、個人年金保険を扱っていない
Post offices 郵便局	Numerous windows make it easier to pay and receive money. 窓口が多く加入および保険金受取りが簡単	The amount of coverage is limited. 保険金額に限度がある
Cooperatives 共済	Low premium. Wide variety of policies. 掛金が安いうえに各種保障もしている	Membership in the cooperative required. Inconvenient procedures. 組合員になる必要があり、加入手続きが不便

The per capita insurance coverage in Japan is about 15 million yen. Compared to the United States and Canada, tied in second place, with coverage equivalent to 5 million yen, this data shows that the Japanese tend to purchase very expensive policies. Four life insurance companies went bankruptcy in 2000, and life insurance is graduatlly losing reliability.

"I'll take his head!" 頭はウチのものだ！ *"The legs are mine!"* 足はウチのものよ

わが国の1人当りの保険金額を見ると、何と約1500万円。第2位の米国やカナダが約500万円なので、いかに日本人が世界の中で突出して高い保険をかけているかがわかる。2000年は、生命保険会社4社が破綻し、生命保険に関する信頼性が弱まりつつある

テレビ放映権のしくみ

　テレビのスポーツ中継にはテレビ局から放映権料が支払われる。今やアマチュアスポーツの祭典・オリンピックは、この放映権料抜きでは開催できないとまで言われているのだ。放映権料の出所は、もちろんNHKなら受信料、民法ならCM収入である。

　話は変わって、プロ野球中継が尻切れトンボになるのはテレビ局が欠陥商品を売っているようなものだとの論議がかねてからある。プロ野球機構ではゲーム進行のスピード化を指導しているが、放映時間内に試合を終わらせようという狙いか？

Live broadcasts of baseball games are a prime source of income for TV stations. There are differences in the broadcasting fee according to the popularity of the baseball team.

プロ野球中継はテレビ局にとっても大きな収入源。放映権料は球団の人気によって差がある

TV Station
テレビ局

The fee paid by the TV station goes to the home team of the baseball game.

テレビ局から支払われる放映権料は、試合の主催球団（ホームチーム）の収入になる

Broadcasting fees 放映権料	
Giants games 巨人戦	40 to 50 million yen per game. Giants games are a cash cow for other Central League teams. 1試合について4000〜5000万円。巨人戦はセ・リーグ他球団のドル箱カードだ
Other games その他のカード	10 to 20 million yen per game. Fee for the Pacific League are relatively low. 1試合について1000〜2000万円。パ・リーグは比較的安い

TV Broadcasting Rights

When sports events are broadcast live by satellite, a broadcasting rights fee is paid by the TV network. Nowadays especially at the biggest amateur sports events the Olympic games, things have even reached the point where it is said that such events can't actually be broadcast without the funds raised by such fees. Such broadcasting fees are paid for by the TV owner's fee in the case of NHK, and by commercials in the case of commercial television networks.

It often happens that live TV broadcasts of baseball games have to stop before the game has come to an end, something that has caused viewers to accuse stations of the equivalent of advertising defective goods. The Professional Baseball Organization is advocating a speeding up of games, but should games really be made to fit into the broadcasting times?

Revenue from commercials
CM収入

Contracted with TV sponsors every season. Advertising revenue is 30 milion to 100 milion yen (for the Japan series), providing a large income source for private TV stations.

シーズンごとのスポンサー契約をしている。全国ネットでは1試合について3000万〜1億円（日本シリーズ）の広告収入が見込めるので、民放局の大きな収入源だ

Reasons that a baseball broadcast might get cut off before the game's end
プロ野球中継が尻切れとなる理由

When a game goes beyond the set time, it is common for Japanese TV station simply to stop broadcasting it. There are two reasons for this: one is that editing and broadcasting of the program is done by computer, and it is thus very difficult to make any changes. The second is that adjustment from sponsors is said to be very difficult.

放映時間をオーバーして試合が続いた場合、最後まで中継しないのが日本の放送局の流儀だ。これは番組編成や放送がコンピュータ処理されているため変更するのが大変なことと、スポンサーの調整が難しいという、2つの理由からだ

Professional soccer is now posing a threat to the primacy of baseball games. The broadcasting fees in this case go first into the funds of J-League, and they are then divided evenly among all the teams.

プロ野球中継を脅かしているのがプロサッカー中継。こちらは放映権料がいったんJリーグに入金され、全チームに均等に配分されるしくみだ

Chapter 6
What Will Change
with Deregulation
Who'll Be Happy and Who Not

車検制度のしくみ

わが国の車検制度は、ムリとムダが多過ぎるとさんざん指摘されてきた。たしかに安全という面から、車を定期的に点検・整備すべき義務は持主に課せられるべきである。だが、それにも程度がある。車検の前に、国土交通省が認証・指定する工場で点検・整備する義務まで課すのは行き過ぎというものだ。しかも、この義務に乗じて整備工場は直す必要もない部位まで整備し、多額の点検・整備費をユーザーに請求してくるケースも多かった。

1995年7月からの制度改正は、こうした車検制度の改善を図る規制緩和なのだが、「いっそのことなら車検制度そのものを廃止すべき」との強硬論も多い。

The car safety inspection system was simplified in July 1995. Car owners may go to national automobile safety inspection centers by themselves for "user safety inspections."

1995年7月から車検制度が簡素化されるとともに、ユーザーが自分で国の車検場に行く「ユーザー車検」が可能になった

The period of validity for a safety inspection was extended to 2 years for family cars owned more than 11 years.

購入11年を超える自家用車は、車検の有効期間が2年に延長された

Reforms
改正点

The six-month inspection requirement was abolished.

6か月点検の義務付けが廃止された

Automobile Safety Inspection

The Japanese automobile safety inspection system has been widely criticized for its incredible waste and lack of common sense. Of course, from the standpoint of safety, owners should be obliged to regularly inspect and service their cars, but there is already a system in place to handle this. Motorists are required to have their cars inspected and serviced at authorized service stations prior to the actual safety inspection, and this is considered by many to be overkill. Moreover, these service stations sometimes perform unnecessary maintenance, and owners are often asked to pay expensive inspection and maintenance fees.

Reforms aimed at deregulating the safety inspection system were instituted in July 1995, but many people take the hard-line view that "The safety inspection system should be abolished altogether."

Pre-inspection/post-maintenance has become accepted.
前車検・後整備が認められるようになった

Maintenance followed by a checkup (pre-maintenance, post-safety inspection) was obligatory for 24-month inspections. However, these are separated, so items that do not pass the safety inspection may be serviced.

従来24か月点検はまず整備を行い、次に検査を行う（前整備・後車検）ことが義務付けられていたが、この2つは切り離されて車検の後で不合格になった部位を整備すればよいことになった

The number of items previously on the 12-and 24-month inspection checklist was reduced by half. The set-up of the 24-month inspection has also been changed.
従来の12か月、24か月点検の点検項目が半減。24か月点検のしくみも変わった

A user inspection is now accepted for the 24-month inspection, and direct inspection is possible at the National Automobile Safety Inspection Centers (91 locations nation-wide). Also, light cars can be inspected at the Light Car Inspection Association (74 locations nation-wide).

24か月点検ではユーザー車検が認められるようになって、国の車検場（全国に91か所）で直接受検できる。ただし、軽自動車は軽自動車検査協会（全国74か所）で受検することになる

車検制度のしくみ……2

Inspection process
車検のプロセス

Used cars must be inspected every two years. 中古車の場合は、2年ごとに車検を受ける	New cars must be inspected from the third year after purchase. 新車の場合は、購入後3年目に車検を受ける

Ongoing inspections
継続検査

Owner
ユーザー

Inspection station

The number of businesses offering inspection services at rock-bottom prices is increasing rapidly. However, safety is one thing you don't want to treat lightly.

ユーザー車検を格安で代行する業者が急増している。だが、安かろう危なかろうでは困る

No inspection or maintenance
点検・整備をしない

Owners may re-inspect and repair their own cars and then take them to a government inspection station or have the cars inspected and repaired by a certified garage.

ユーザーが点検・整備をやり直して国の車検場に持ち込むか、指定整備工場で整備・検査を受ける

Repair and completion inspection

When inspection is not passed
不合格になった場合

整備・完成検査

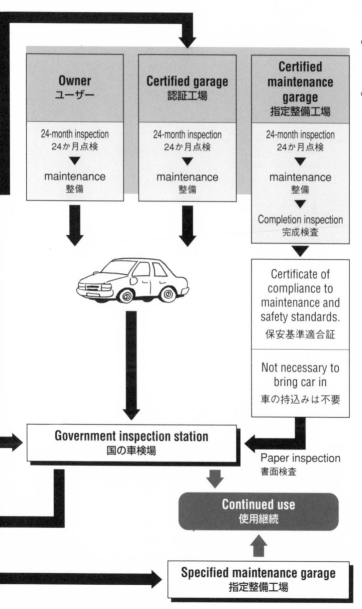

Owner
ユーザー

24-month inspection
24か月点検
▼
maintenance
整備

Certified garage
認証工場

24-month inspection
24か月点検
▼
maintenance
整備

Certified maintenance garage
指定整備工場

24-month inspection
24か月点検
▼
maintenance
整備
▼
Completion inspection
完成検査
▼

Certificate of compliance to maintenance and safety standards.
保安基準適合証

Not necessary to bring car in
車の持込みは不要

Government inspection station
国の車検場

Paper inspection
書面検査

Continued use
使用継続

Specified maintenance garage
指定整備工場

ガソリンスタンドのしくみ

ガソリンスタンドには、過当競争を防ぐために「指定地区制度」が設けられ、新規参入が制限されていた。この規制、実は税収を確保するためのもの。なにしろガソリン料金の約半分は税金。競争が激化し、お尻に火がついたガソリンスタンドが増えれば、税収が落ち込んでしまうからだ。だが、「特石法」の廃止に合わせ、規制緩和の動きが出てきた。1996年4月からは商社などにもガソリン輸入が解禁され、2001年中には「石油業法」が廃止され、完全自由化になる予定だ。

In April 1998, the ban on self-service stations under the Fire Service Law was lifted.

1998年4月から消防法の関連で規制されていたセルフ方式のガソリンスタンドが解禁された

Gasoline distribution
ガソリンの流通

Oil-producing countries
産油国

Oil companies	Importers
石油会社	輸入業者

Primary wholesalers (special agents)
一次卸（特約店）

Secondary wholesalers (special agents)
二次卸（特約店）

Retailers
小売店

General consumers
一般消費者

Gas Stations

To prevent excessive competition, a "designated area system" was implemented to limit the entry of additional gas stations. This system was implemented in order to secure tax revenue. In fact, about half of the price paid for gas goes to the government. Heavy competition and more gas stations will likely decrease tax revenue. However, with the phasing out of the Provisional Measures Law on the Importation of Special Kinds of Refined Petroleum Products, there is a trend toward deregulation. Changes were made in April 1996 to allow trading companies and others to import gasoline. The Petroleum Industry Law will be abolished in 2001 and the gasoline distribution will be totally deregularized.

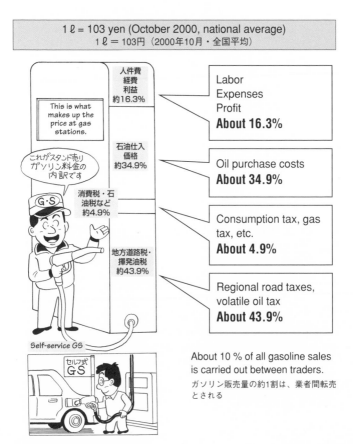

1 ℓ = 103 yen (October 2000, national average)
1 ℓ ＝ 103円 （2000年10月・全国平均）

人件費
経費
利益
約16.3%

This is what makes up the price at gas stations.

これがスタンド売り ガソリン料金の 内訳です

石油仕入 価格 約34.9%

消費税・石 油税など 約4.9%

地方道路税・ 揮発油税 約43.9%

Labor
Expenses
Profit
About 16.3%

Oil purchase costs
About 34.9%

Consumption tax, gas tax, etc.
About 4.9%

Regional road taxes, volatile oil tax
About 43.9%

Self-service GS

About 10 % of all gasoline sales is carried out between traders.
ガソリン販売量の約1割は、業者間転売 とされる

ガソリンスタンドのしくみ……2

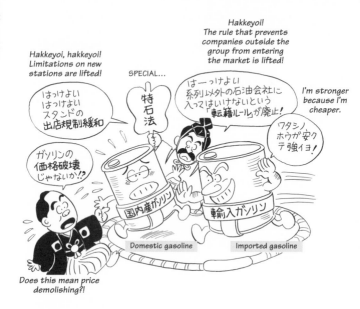

*Hakkeyoi, hakkeyoi!
Limitations on new
stations are lifted!*

*Hakkeyoi!
The rule that prevents
companies outside the
group from entering
the market is lifted!*

SPECIAL...

*I'm stronger
because I'm
cheaper.*

Domestic gasoline   Imported gasoline

*Does this mean price
demolishing?!*

Deregulization of gasoline sales started from March 1996.
Gasoline was initially seen as all being of the same quality, but
gasoline companies are now developing new products to differ-
entiate themselves.

96年3月からは販売の自由化がスタート。従来は品質に差がなかったのが、
新商品の開発で石油会社間の差別化も進む

Oil companies are trying to curtail the gasoline price war because
their business is depressed by the increase of the cost of oil. They
ceased giving rebates to gas stations from April 2000.

石油元売り会社は、原油価格が上昇していることで経営が圧迫され、ガソリン乱
売合戦の解消を図っている。2000年4月からはガソリンスタンドに対するリベー
トの廃止を打ち出した

**Excessive service at gasoline stations is needed
to maintain prices.**

There are so many workers!
Why don't you have self-service and lower the price?!

Japanese like all the extra service.

Put an end to excessive service!

銀行サービスのしくみ

　規制緩和の眼目の一つであった銀行の預金金利が完全に自由化されたのは、1994年10月だった。だが、期待に反して都市銀行の普通預金の金利は、ほぼ横並び状態。抜け駆けは許さないという業界の体質は、いっこうに変わらない。

　その代わりというわけでもあるまいが、同時に景品等のサービスに関する自主規制が緩和された。金利は上げられないので、こんなところでご勘弁をと言いたげな銀行業界。所詮は、この程度のサービス精神なのだろうか。

Lifting of self-imposed regulations by banks in 1994 was aimed at improving service.

1994年から銀行業界の自主規制の緩和によって、顧客向けサービス向上が図られた

Considerable attention was focused on Jonan Credit Association (Tokyo) when they announced their Super Fixed Deposit plan with one lottery ticket for every 100,000-yen deposit. In June 1996, the limit on money that banks could give was increased to 100,000 yen, while the value of gifts was lifted to 10 percent of the deposit amount. But of course, what most clients receive is much less than this.

城南信用金庫（東京）が発売した「懸賞金付きスーパー定期預金」は、預け入れ10万円（1口）単位で1本の抽選券付き、1等は10万円の賞金ということで人気を呼んだ。96年6月から銀行での懸賞金の上限が10万円、景品は預金額の10%以内と景品規制が緩和されたが、この通りのサービスを受けている人はごく少ないのでは？

Bank Services

As part of the move lifting regulations, the interest rates on bank savings accounts was completely deregulated in October 1994. But the interest on savings accounts at the major city banks has unexpectedly remained the same. The concept of keeping in line with the industry has not changed at all.

When interest rates were deregulated, so were the giving of gifts and other such services by banks. So while they can☐t give higher interest rates, banks ask their customers to be happy with small gifts. Perhaps asking for higher interest rates is asking too much.

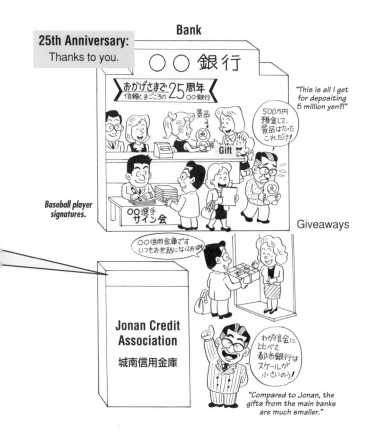

25th Anniversary: Thanks to you.

Bank

"This is all I get for depositing 5 million yen?!"

Baseball player signatures.

Giveaways

Jonan Credit Association

城南信用金庫

"Compared to Jonan, the gifts from the main banks are much smaller."

銀行サービスのしくみ……2

Why are so many no-teller banks being built?
近頃、銀行の無人店舗がどんどんできているわけは？

Regulations on the number of branches from the Ministry of Finance
財務省による出店規制

Banks are limited to opening one new branch or business office every two years.

銀行が支店や営業所を出店する場合、2年間に1店舗を原則とするとの規制がある

When there are more than four different financial unions, such as trust associations and credit unions, within 600 meters of each other, new bank branches are not allowed.

信金・信組など違う種類の金融機関が直径600m以内に4つ以上ある場合、新規出店することはできない（都区内や政令指定都市ではさらに厳しい規制がある）

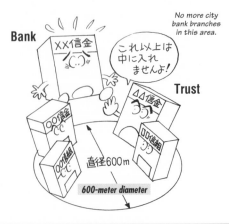

There are about 62,000 CDs and ATMs
belonging to city and regional banks.

都銀・地銀のCD・ATMは合計で約6万2000台（96年）

CDs are automatic cash dispensing machines, and ATMs
are automatic cash deposit
and dispensing machines.

CDは現金自動支払機、
ATMは現金自動預け払い機

**No-teller banks have many
advantages for banks.**

無人店舗は銀行にとっては、
メリットが多い

**As a means of
deregulating the opening
of branches, banks are
allowed to open no-teller
branches.**

出店規制の緩和策として、
無人店舗の出店が認められた

For example...
たとえば…

(1) Banks can save on labor costs.
(2) There is no need to provide extra services.
(3) Banks profit from the service fees.

①人件費がかからない
②サービスの必要がない
③黙っていても手数料が入ってくる

食品表示のしくみ

　加工食品などには、製造年月日を表示することが義務付けられていた。だが、製造年月日表示の慣習がない諸外国から「見えない障壁だ」と非難されたことがきっかけとなって、1995年4月から期限表示に変わった。

　ところで、出来立てのものと時間が経ったものを一緒に並べると、消費者は新しいほうを選ぶ。その結果、古いものは売れ残り、まだ十分に食べられるのに捨てるハメになる。小売業者の間では、「この日までなら食べられます、という期限表示に変えれば、もっと安く売ることができる」と期限表示を支持する声が強いが、一部の消費者からは製造年月日の併記の要望も強い。

Take the example of packaged milk
パック牛乳の場合…

Milk Producing Company
メーカー

Manufacture
製造

Inspection
検査

Date stamping
日付打ち

It is no longer necessary to indicate the date of inspection for colon bacilli, which takes a whole day. To answer to the needs of the consumer who values freshness above all else, the date of manufacture is sufficient.

消費者の鮮度重視ニーズにこたえるため、出荷前に1日かかる大腸菌検査の日を製造年月日にして出荷するケースはなくなる

It has now left up to the manufacturer whether to show the date of manufacture, but obligatory to show the "best consumed before" time on the package.

従来の「製造年月日」の表示が任意表示になり、いつまで飲食できるかの「消費期限」「賞味期限」表示が義務付けられた

Food Labeling

It was always the case in Japan that the date of manufacture was shown on packages of processed foods. But there was criticism from various foreign countries that did not make this a practice that it was one of the invisible barriers preventing importation of their food-stuffs, with the result that from April 1995, the expiration date rather than the date of manufacture came to be shown.

When faced with an array of fresh goods and goods that were made some time before, the consumer will always go for the freshly made item. As a result, the older items will remain on the shelves, unsold, and have to be thrown away, even though in fact they are still quite edible. Shop and supermarket owners support the idea that all that is needed is the expiration date, which would show the last date before which a product can be consumed safely, so that it could still be sold at a cheaper rate. But no small number of consumers still demand that the date of manufacture as well as the date of expiration should still be shown on the package.

Retailers
小売店

"This is still okay!"
まだ安心ね

Delivery
出荷

The risk of goods being left unsold on the shelves (as when the date of manufacture is shown) goes down.
製造年月日表示のように、日付が少しでも古いと売れなくなるというリスクがなくなる

The milk industry started to consolidate its policy to one of expiration date from October 1995, but consumer groups and cooperatives objected, saying that this would take away the consumers' means of judging the freshness of the product. Many places still continue to show the date of manufacture on their products for PB milk, so for a while it looks like inconsistency will rule.

牛乳業界は95年10月に期限表示に一本化する方針を出したが、鮮度を判断する手掛かりがなくなると消費者団体や生協が反発。PB牛乳には製造年月日表示を続けているところも多く、混乱は当分続きそうだ

"Best Consumed Before" labeling

Best Consumed Before 賞味期限	**Quality Guaranteed Until** 品質保持期限（1）
Label is marked. It is not advisable to consume such goods after this date. ○年○月○日と表示。この日付以後は、飲食を避けたほうがよい	Label is marked. The manufacturer guarantees the product's quality until this date. ○年○月○日と表示。この日までは、メーカーが品質を保証する

Processed foodstuffs that do not keep well, such as the rice and sundry items in lunchboxes and half-cooked noodles. 弁当、ゆでめん類など、日持ちが悪い加工食品	Processed food that lasts for several weeks, such as ham and fish-paste products. ハム類や練り製品など、数週間日持ちする加工食品

賞味期限の表示のしかた

Quality Guaranteed Until 品質保持期限（2）	**Products for which such labels are unnecessary** 表示は不要
Label is marked. The manufacturer guarantees the product's quality for the month previous to the indicated day. ○年○月○日と表示。この月以内なら、メーカーが品質を保証する	 Table Salt Sugar
Processed food that lasts for many months, such as pouch-packed and frozen food. レトルト食品、冷凍ものなど、何か月も日持ちする加工食品	These foodstuffs will keep for years. 砂糖、塩など、何年も保存しておいて使える加工食品

賞味期間とは充分おいしく食べられる期間という意味です

"Best consumed before" indicates the period during which the product can be consumed with little deterioration in taste."

187

飼犬登録のしくみ

　ペットブームも今やすっかり定着した感がある。家庭や企業に犬や猫を貸し出す「ペットレンタル」なるニュービジネスも誕生したほどだ。なんでも、オフィスにペットがいると、従業員の人間関係が和やかになるとか。

　それはさておき、飼い主をわずらわせている犬の登録制度が変わった。いくらかわいい愛犬のためとはいえ、毎年毎年、登録手続きを行うのは面倒なもの。だが、1995年4月から、犬を飼うときに1度登録するだけで済むようになった。

　ただし、狂犬病予防注射の義務はなくならない。人間の安全を守るための規制は緩和されないのである。

After April 1, 1995, it became possible to license one's dog on a one-time basis. But annual rabies vaccinations are still necessary.

1995年4月1日以後の飼犬登録は、1回だけすればその後はしなくてもよいが、狂犬病の予防注射は毎年必要だ

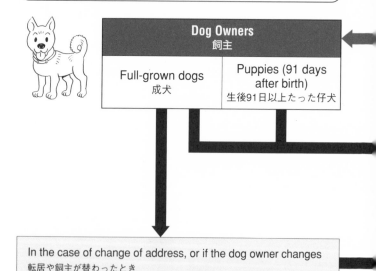

Dog Owners
飼主

Full-grown dogs
成犬

Puppies (91 days after birth)
生後91日以上たった仔犬

In the case of change of address, or if the dog owner changes
転居や飼主が替わったとき

After April 1995, dog licensing, previously carried out annually, was shifted to a once-only system. This is a boon to the dog owner, who used to have to pay a fee every time the license was renewed.

95年4月から、従来は毎年1回行われていた犬の登録が、犬の生涯に1回すればよいことになった。毎回の登録手数料だけでもバカにならないので、飼主には朗報となった

Dog Licensing

Owning a dog or a cat as a pet has become quite the fashionable thing nowadays—so fashionable, indeed, that a new type of business, "Rent-A-Pet," has come on the scene, where families and businesses can rent pets for a while, rather than owning them. We all know how the presence of an animal is great for bringing about a more relaxed, trusting atmosphere between employees in an office.

And thank goodness the licensing system, the bane of all dog owners' lives for so many years, has changed. It was such a nuisance to have to go, each and every year, to fill out the forms for licensing—no matter how beloved one's little Fido or Patch might be. Finally, from April 1995, it became possible to get the whole procedure over in one visit.

However, the obligation to revaccinate one's dog against rabies every year remains the same. It might be a nuisance, but human safety is paramount, and no law would put that at risk.

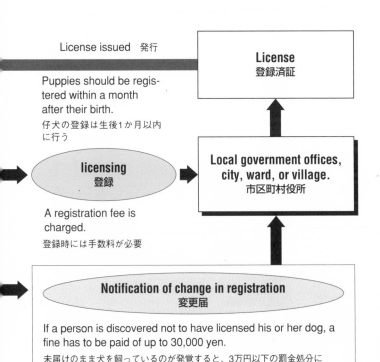

License issued　発行

License
登録済証

Puppies should be registered within a month after their birth.
仔犬の登録は生後1か月以内に行う

licensing
登録

A registration fee is charged.
登録時には手数料が必要

Local government offices, city, ward, or village.
市区町村役所

Notification of change in registration
変更届

If a person is discovered not to have licensed his or her dog, a fine has to be paid of up to 30,000 yen.
未届けのまま犬を飼っているのが発覚すると、3万円以下の罰金処分に

189

飼犬登録のしくみ……2

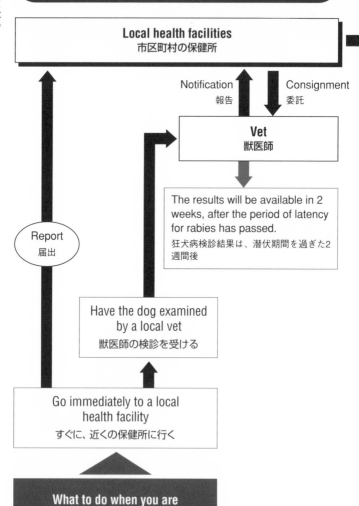

All you need to know about Rabies vaccination
狂犬病予防接種のしくみ

Local health facilities
市区町村の保健所

Notification
報告

Consignment
委託

Vet
獣医師

The results will be available in 2 weeks, after the period of latency for rabies has passed.
狂犬病検診結果は、潜伏期間を過ぎた2週間後

Report
届出

Have the dog examined by a local vet
獣医師の検診を受ける

Go immediately to a local health facility
すぐに、近くの保健所に行く

What to do when you are bitten by a dog.
犬に咬まれたときは、こうする

Notification
通知

→

Owner
飼主

↓

It is supposed to be the case that dog owners would take their dogs to the vet's for a rabies vaccination at their own convenience. Nowadays, special Rabies vaccination days are arranged and the dog owners have to accommodate the vet's convenience.

本来、犬の予防接種は飼主が直接獣医師の所へ飼犬を連れていくのが建前なのだが、何かとわずらわしくなるため、集合接種を行っている

Vaccination en masse
集合接種

The vaccination fee is around 2,500 yen, of which about four-fifths goes to the veterinarian.

予防接種料は約2500円前後で、そのおよそ5分の4が獣医師に支払われる

Vaccine
ワクチン

The reason rabies vaccinations have to be carried out annually is simply that the vaccination's effectiveness only lasts one year.

毎年1回、狂犬病の予防注射をしなければならないのは、予防ワクチンの薬効期間が1年、という単純な理由からである

個人輸入のしくみ

　円高の追い風に乗って、個人輸入がブームになっている。80年代後半の第1次ブームを経て、超円高時代に入った最近の第2次ブームの勢いは、とどまるところを知らないかのようだ。政府は1994年4月から、個人輸入の促進のための規制緩和を行ったが、小手先の緩和ではなく、関税を引き下げてほしいという要望も多い。

　とは言っても、高い関税と高い送料（通常は商品価格の3～5割）を払っても、なお日本国内で買うよりずっと安い商品が多い。問題は、内外価格差の解消ということだ。

Catalogue
カタログ

Catalogue shop
カタログショップ

Manufactured Imports Promotion Organization (MIPRO)
（財）製品輸入促進協会（ミプロ）など

Import trade representatives 輸入代行業者	**Credit firm** 信販会社

Foreign mail order companies 海外通販業者	**Foreign shops** 海外小売店

One chooses the goods one wants from a catalogue. There are ways of ordering items directly from abroad, but it's safer for first-time purchasers to buy from catalogues. It's worth bearing in mind that the system of sizes is different from that used in Japan.
商品はカタログから選ぶ。海外から直接取り寄せる方法もあるが、初心者はカタログショップで入手するのが安心。サイズが日本と違うので要注意だ

Private Purchasing of Foreign Goods

The rise in the value of the yen has made the private importing of foreign articles into something of a boom. The first boom came in the latter half of the 1980s, and recently, with the value of the yen reaching rocket-high levels, a second boom has occurred, causing individual importation of foreign goods to reach an unstoppable rate. From April 1994, the government eased regulations so as to encourage individual importation of goods. But many consumers would prefer a lowering of the customs duties on importation rather than a mere simplification of the procedure.

Even with the high import tax (usually 30 to 50% of the value of the goods), it often still works out cheaper to import goods from abroad than to buy them domestically. And it will remain this way as long as the price of living in Japan remains so much higher than in other countries.

Customs formalities for imported goods costing more than 10,000 yen have been simplified, so the importing of goods by individual consumers has become much easier.

1万円以上の関税商品の通関手続きが簡単になり、個人輸入が従来よりもぐんとしやすくなった

Customs duties
関税

All imported goods are subject to taxation with the exception of certain specified items. The administration of this taxation is carried out by a public entity.

海外の商品を輸入する場合、一部の非課税品を除いて税金がかかる。この事務手続きを代行してくれる公的機関がある

Personal Import Information center
個人輸入通関相談センター

As part of the relaxation of import restrictions, this organization was established in April 1994 to facilitate personal import procedures. It often advises on customs procedures and acts as an inexpensive agent.

規制緩和の一環として、個人輸入の手続きを軽減するため、94年4月に開設された機関。通関手続きのアドバイスや安い手数料で代行をしてくれる

個人輸入のしくみ……2

From orders to receipt of goods—the process
注文から商品受取までのプロセス

Order
注文

Fill out the order form stapled into the catalogue with the items one wishes to purchase. Apart from purchases made with international credit cards, payment has to be made before the goods are delivered.

カタログに綴じ込まれている注文書を使って、申込みをする。国際カード以外の支払いについては、代金は前払いが原則

Costs
費用

(1) Cost of the article 商品代

The price, in the currency of the country where the article was sent from, must be shown.

現地通貨で表示された金額

(2) Shipping fee 送料

This usually includes an insurance charge.

保険料込みのケースが多い

(3) Handling charges 手数料

When going through an import agent, except when one is using an international credit card, packaging charges are also often made.

輸入代行業者を利用する場合、国際クレジット利用の場合のほか、商品発送の梱包代などを取られるケースもある

(4) Customs duties 関税

These vary according to the item.

商品によって違う

Shipping 発送

Sea mail 船便

Rates are low, but it can take from 2 to 3 months for the goods to arrive.

運賃は安いが、到着までに2か月から3か月かかる

Airmail 航空便

It takes from 2 weeks to 1 month for the goods to arrive.

到着まで2週間から1か月ほどかかる

International parcel delivery 国際宅配便

It takes from 1 to 2 weeks for the goods to arrive.

到着まで1週間から2週間ほどかかる

Receipt 受取

Items that can be delivered to the home
自宅に配達される商品

Non-taxed items and items taxed less than 10,000 yen

非課税または税額1万円以下の商品

Items consigned to import agents

輸入代行業者に委託した商品

Items that can not be delivered to the home
自宅に配達されない商品

Items taxed more than 10,000 yen, and not consigned to import agents have to be collected from the post office.

税額1万円を超える商品で、代行業者に委託しない場合は、郵便局等に受け取りに行かねばならない

再販売価格維持制度のしくみ

　価格の自由競争が原則となっているビジネス社会で、例外的にメーカーが小売店に対して商品の販売価格を指示できるのが、再販売価格維持制度である。わかりやすく言えば、小売店が勝手に定価の値引き販売をしてはならない商品があるということなのだ。

　この制度は本来、値引き販売競争によって、かえって消費者が不利益をこうむる恐れのある商品について「独占禁止法」の例外的措置として設けられたものである。だが、規制緩和の波はこの制度の抜本的改革を指向している。消費者にとっては朗報であるが、メーカー側がいったん獲得した恩典を簡単に手離すとは思えないのだが…。

Designated goods
指定商品

Literary works
著作物

Literary works that are commodities, such as newspapers and magazines

新聞、雑誌などの著作権が発生する商品

Literary works and the No-Discount Resale System
著作物と再販制度

Literary works can be bought at the same price throughout the country based on such flag-waving reasons as, "To spread and promote culture and protect freedom of speech." The Japan Fair Trade Commission came up with the idea of reviewing the system, which caused a reaction from economic organizations. However, music CDs are being introduced on a limited basis as resale products.

「文化の普及・振興や多様な言論を守る」という錦の御旗のもとに、著作物は全国どこでも同じ値段で買えるようになっている。公正取引委員会は制度の再検討を打ち出しており業界団体は反発しているが、音楽用CDではすでに期限付き再販商品も登場している

The Resale Price Maintenance System

In a business society, prices are determined by open competition. The exception to this is Resale Price Maintenance, in which manufacturers specify selling prices to retailers. Simply put, it means that for some products, retail stores cannot set prices themselves.

The reason for this is to set up a mechanism outside the Antitrust Law for goods over which price wars would harm consumers. However, a wave of deregulation is pushing this system toward radical reforms. This is good news for consumers, but manufacturers aren't expected to let go easily of special favors once they have them.

> Resale price maintenance on cosmetics and over-the-counter drugs was abolished in April 1997, but it still applies to literary works.
>
> 1997年4月から化粧品・一般用医薬品の再販制度が解禁されたが、著作物にはまだこの制度が適用されている

Goods that could not be sold at a discounted price until March 1997 97年3月まで値引き販売ができなかったもの	
Over-the-counter drugs 一般用医薬品 	Fourteen items including all cold and gastrointestinal medicines 総合感冒剤、総合胃腸剤など14品目が指定されていた
Cosmetics 化粧品 	Fourteen items including creams with a retail value less than 1,030 yen including tax, hair dressing, hair dye, and makeup. 消費税込みの小売価格が1030円以下のクリーム、整髪料、染毛料、化粧水など14品目が指定されていた

Mechanism for selling cosmetics
化粧品販売のしくみ

One might think that retail stores are able to decide prices themselves for products that are not designated by the Japan Fair Trade Commission based on the resale price maintenance system. However, manufacturers are always on the lookout for dumping.

再販売価格維持制度に基づく公正取引委員会の指定商品以外の商品は、小売店が自由に価格を決めてよいはずなのだが、メーカー側はダンピング販売に目を光らせている

Cosmetics manufacturers
化粧品メーカー

△□ Cosmetics

キレイ？！ ワタシ！

The beauty consultants at the counters of all cosmetics manufacturers at department stores are sent from sales companies under the manufacturers. It is said that about one-fourth of the cost for high-brand products goes to the beauty consultants. Some supermarkets are training their own beauty consultants in order to cut prices.

デパートにずらりと並んだ各メーカーの売場の美容部員はメーカー系列の販売会社の派遣店員だ。高級化粧品の原価の約4割が美容部員の人件費といわれる。自前の美容部員を養成して安売りを展開する大手スーパーも現れた

Due to deregulation of imports, discounting wars have started for products other than creams and lotions, thus stirring up competition.

化粧品の並行輸入の緩和で、乳液やローション以外の高級化粧品の値引き合戦も始まる。デパートは戦々恐々だ

The Resale Price Maintenance System……2

This is a unique system thought up by manufacturers to prevent discounts on cosmetics. However, there is a current call for reform.

化粧品の値引き防止のためにメーカー側が考え出した独特の方法だが、この見直しが叫ばれている

Dispatch of a beautician staff member
美容部員の派遣

Counseling agreement
カウンセリング契約

Sales subsidiary
販売会社

Self-service agreement
セルフ契約

Retail store
小売店

The discount price in manufacturers' retail outlets is about 70 percent of the catalogue price. For retail stores, this means that there must be high turnover at a low profit margin to initiate sales. Large supermarkets started discount sales of self-service products in the summer of 1995.

化粧品メーカーの小売店に対する卸値は、定価の70%前後といわれる。小売店にとっては、薄利多売でなければ商売が成り立たないしくみになっているのだ。セルフ契約商品については95年夏以降、大手スーパーが値引き販売を開始した

住宅容積率のしくみ

　３階建て、地下室付きの住宅が目につくようになった。いずれも住宅容積率の規制緩和の所産である。地価が下がったとはいえ、大都市部で土地を入手するとなると狭さを覚悟しなければならない。猫の額ほどの土地に建てられる家となると、従来の容積率ではせいぜい3LDKが一般的というところだった。狭い土地を有効活用するには、上下の空間利用しかないということで、上（３階）下（地下）に居住スペースを求めるのは、当然の成り行き。だが、一面では行政側の苦肉の策でもあるのだ。

In order to increase the amount of living space in cities and use land more efficiently, efforts are being made to increase floor-area ratios.

大都市部の居住空間を拡大するために、容積率の基準緩和による土地の有効利用が図られている

In the 1993 revision of the City Planning Law, 12 categories of land use were designated with floor-area ratio limitations ranging from 50 percent to 1,000 percent.

93年の「都市計画法」改正で土地の用途地域区分は12区分になり、各区分ごとに容積率は50〜1000％に分類されている

High-rise housing
高層住宅

Taller buildings on the same sized plot of land are now possible.

今までと同じ広さの土地でも、もっと高いビルが建てられるんです

In June 1995, the limit on floor-area ratio was raised from 300 percent to 600 percent in Tokyo and Osaka.

1995年6月から東京・大阪の高層住宅の容積率が300％から倍の600％に緩和された

Floor-area Ratio Regulations

In recent years, we have started to see more and more three-story homes with basements. This is the result of deregulation concerning floor-area ratio regulations which limit the height and depth of buildings. Although land prices in Japan have dropped, those wanting to build a home in one of the major cities can't complain about cramped quarters. It was generally believed that the biggest home you could build on a small plot of land was a 3-bedroom home with living room, dining room, and kitchen. And since landowners can only build higher or lower, there was naturally pressure to change the regulations. The deregulation was seen as a political last resort.

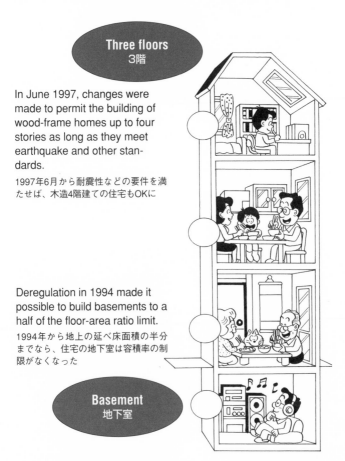

Three floors
3階

In June 1997, changes were made to permit the building of wood-frame homes up to four stories as long as they meet earthquake and other standards.

1997年6月から耐震性などの要件を満たせば、木造4階建ての住宅もOKに

Deregulation in 1994 made it possible to build basements to a half of the floor-area ratio limit.

1994年から地上の延べ床面積の半分までなら、住宅の地下室は容積率の制限がなくなった

Basement
地下室

第7章
ちょっと気になる
社会現象 知らないとソンするよ!

Chapter 7
Some Interesting
Social
Phenomena
The Whys and Wherefores

PL法のしくみ

　「PL法（製造物責任法）」は、1995年7月1日から施行された法律である。製品の欠陥によって生命や身体または財産に損害を受けた場合、それを証明すれば被害者はメーカーや販売業者に対して損害賠償請求ができる。

　従来は、被害者が製品の欠陥と製造者の過失との両方を証明しなければならなかったのに対して、PL法では事故の原因は製品の欠陥にあるということだけを立証すればよいことになった。その意味では、この法律は消費者重視の新法といえるだろう。

　なお、PL法は輸血用血液製剤についても適用される。この場合は、日本赤十字社が賠償義務者となる。

When, for example, your TV explodes and bursts into flames…
こんな時

BOOM!

PLセンター

When the PL Law went into effect, the government also set up "PL Centers" to give advice to consumers, and to provide mediation and arbitration between consumers and corporations.

政府はPL法施行に伴い、消費者の相談および企業との斡旋・調停のための「PLセンター」を設置した

Advice
相談

Before contacting the manufacturer, it's a good idea to get advice from local consumer associations.

メーカーに連絡する際に、消費生活センターなどに相談をしておくことが望ましい

Negotiation
交渉

With proof in hand of damages suffered (breakage, doctor's medical certificate, etc.), negotiate directly with the manufacturer.

被害の状況（破損・医師の診断書）をもとに、メーカー側と直接交渉をする

The Product Liability Law

The PL (Product Liability) Law went into effect on July 1, 1995. If deficiency in a certain product has caused injury or loss of life, or damage to property, this law allows the plaintiff, providing he or she has proof, to demand compensation for damages from the manufacturer or the distributor.

In the past, the plaintiff had to prove two things to get compensation: deficiency in the product and negligence on the part of the manufacturer. But now all that is necessary is to prove that the accident was caused by an inadequacy in the product. In this sense, the PL Law is very pro-consumer.

The PL Law also applies to artificial blood products used in blood transfusions. In this case, the Japan Red Cross becomes the party responsible to pay any compensation.

Product deficiency refers to an aspect of the product that makes it normally unsafe, but the manufacturers can be absolved of responsibility if it is proved that the deficiency was not predictable by the prevailing level of science and technology at the time of purchase.

製品の欠陥とは、通常あるはずの安全性を欠いている場合をさすが、製品引渡し時の科学・技術水準で欠陥が予見できなかったことが証明されれば、メーカー側の免責が認められる

Suing for compensation 賠償請求	Compensation can be sought up to three years after the victim is notified. 請求期間は、被害者が賠償義務者を知った時から3年間
	The period during which manufacturers are held responsible is 10 years. メーカーの責任期間は10年間

PL Insurance　PL保険

In response to the PL law, a new kind of insurance has appeared called New Product Liability Insurance, which is directed toward small and middle-level enterprises. Manufacturers can enter into group contracts with such bodies as the Japan Chamber of Commerce and Industry, which enables them to cover the costs of half of their individual contracts with insurance fees. As much as 300 million yen can be paid in insurance benefits.

中小企業向けの新型保険（PL保険）が登場した。この保険はメーカーが日本商工会議所などと団体契約をするのが特徴で、従来の個別契約の半分の保険料で済む。最高で3億円の保険料が支払われる。

悪徳商法のしくみ

いつの世にもはびこるのが悪徳商法。結局のところ、うまい話には乗らないことが肝腎なのだが、年々、その手口は巧妙になってきている。

最近の傾向としては、求人やアルバイト募集にかこつけて出資金や代理店契約料を集める "求人まがい商法" が横行している。レンタルビデオ宅配、学習塾経営、清掃メンテナンス、ブランド品販売などに、この手の商法が多い。給料どころか、出資金も戻ってこないので要注意。

Telephone soliciting
電話勧誘

"Really? I better hurry and sign!"

えーっ!ほんと!?すぐに契約しなくっちゃ!!

"If you take this course of lectures, you're exempt from having to take the national exam. The thing is, the deadline's today, so you better hurry and join up!"

この講座を受けると、国家試験は免除です ただし、今日が締め切りなので、あと1人で定員になります 急いだほうがいいですよ

"Mom, what'll I do? I have to pay 600,000 yen!"

どーしようお母さん 60万円もするのよ……!!

おめでとうございます 激安の海外旅行が当たりましたよ ○月○日までに当社におこしください…

"Congratulations! You just won a trip abroad at a knock-down price! Come to XY company on such-and-such a day!"

ウッソーほんとー!?

"I can't believe it! Really?"

英会話教材 ￥600,000

English conversation materials

Commercial Malpractice

Swindling and commercial trickery have been rampant since time immemorial. Ultimately, of course, the only way to protect oneself is not to be taken in by any talk that sounds especially tempting, but it's amazing how every year the tricks to lure people into getting duped get more and more skilful.

One very common type of commercial malpractice in recent years has involved a company that pretends to advertise for potential employees, and then collects money from them under the guise of gathering capital and fees for renting business premises. Another type of scam has involved people being persuaded to pay in advance for videos that never arrive, for classes that are never held or end halfway through, for cleaning and maintenance that is never done, or for expensive brand-name goods that don't exist. You may not only get paid, but also lose your investment.

Elderly people are easy victims
高齢者が狙われている

The easiest targets for commercial swindlers seem to be elderly people over 60. Elderly people are "highly favored customers" because they are often at home in the daytime when these crooks come calling, and another is that the elderly are seen as easy customers. Most common fraudulent products are bedding, telephones and fire extinguishers.

Elderly people can also often be enticed inside a shop by the prospect of a free gift, and then hypnotized into making purchases. It seems that by the age of sixty, one would know that there's nothing so expensive as what appears to be free.

悪徳商法のターゲットにされがちなのが60歳以上の高齢者。昼に家にいることが多いのと、情に流されやすいのが災いして、悪質な訪問販売の"上得意客"。被害が多いのは布団、電話機、消火器だ。

街頭で「ただで物をあげる」という誘い文句につられて、催眠商法の被害者になってしまうのも高齢者。"ただ"ほど高く付くとは、永年の経験でわかっているはずなのに……

悪徳商法のしくみ……2

"Catch Sales"
キャッチセールス

Catch sales makes clever use of group psychology and is sometimes called business by hypnotism.

集団心理をうまく応用したキャッチセールスは、催眠商法ともいわれる

A person entices a prospective customer in on a pretext, and then persuades them into making all sorts of purchases.

"We just happen to have some luxury feather bedding. Anybody who wants it, just raise your hand and say 'Yes!' in a nice loud voice."

"Yes please!"

"Madam, if you'll just come inside this building and fill in a questionnaire, you'll receive a lovely present."

"And on the second floor, we have some even greater deals!"

Commerce using extra-sensory powers
霊感商法

"You should pray for the repose of your ancestors' souls. If you just rub this vase once a day, they'll rest in peace."

Onomancy

"I can see from the number of strokes and combination of characters in your name that you're going to meet with disaster soon."

Commerce under the pretext of a party
ホームパーティー商法

"This set of fry-pans is the very thing to help you combat illnesses like cancer and diabetes! And it's so cheap!"

Topic: How to stay healthy for the rest of your life

相続税物納のしくみ

遺産相続に伴う相続税の申告と納税は、被相続人の死亡の日の翌日から原則として10か月以内に行わなければならない。生前に何らかの相続税対策を講じていたならまだしも、降ってわいたような相続税の支払いに苦慮する遺族も多い。現金がなく一括払いができない場合は最高20年間の延納（分割払い）が認められるが、それも不能なら物納ということになる。この物納は地価下落が始まった1992年頃から急激に増え、年間1万件を超える勢いである。バブルの後遺症はこんなところにも現れているのだ。

> Inheritance tax should as a rule be paid in cash, and all in one go, but one recourse for people without cash is to pay inheritance tax in kind.
>
> 相続税の納付は現金一括払いが原則だが、支払えない人のための救済措置として物納という方法がとられる

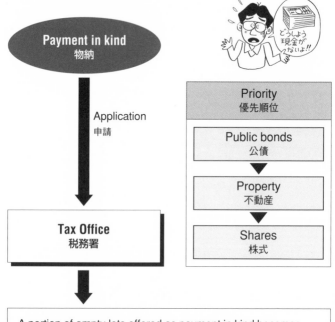

Payment in kind
物納

Application
申請

Tax Office
税務署

Priority
優先順位

Public bonds
公債

Property
不動産

Shares
株式

どうしよう
現金が
ないよ!!

A portion of empty lots offered as payment in kind becomes national land, and this can then be put up for sale.
物納された更地の一部は国有宅地として希望者に売却する

Inheritance Tax Payment in Kind

The declaration and payment of inheritance tax must be made within 10 months of death. And no matter what efforts are made before death, many bereaved families find themselves with an unexpectedly burdensome amount of tax when the event actually happens. If the family's wealth is tied up and no ready funds are available, the amount can be paid in installments over a maximum period of 20 years, but if this too is impossible, payment is made in kind. This method of paying inheritance tax has in fact increased markedly since the decrease in land prices, which began around 1992, and now there are over 10,000 such cases annually. The after-effects of the "Bubble Economy" have made themselves felt even here.

With payment of kind in land, the price is evaluated according to the land assessments price at the time of inheritance. It is a requirement upon submission for tax purposes that the land be cleared of buildings and made into an empty lot.

土地の物納では相続時の路線価で評価される。納める際は更地にするのが原則だ

In 1994, when the number of applications for extensions of payment of inheritance tax reached around 7,200, it became possible to switch from extended payment over many years to payment in kind as an exception.

94年度には相続税の延納申請約7200件について、延納から物納への切換えを認める特例物納が実施された

Fix price payment
定価売払

Every so often, advertisements for purchase of these lots are put up in regional financial bureaus. The sale of these lots is decided by means of an open lottery, with a contractual agreement that a building should be constructed on the land within 5 years of purchase.

地方財務局ごとに定期的に募集を行っている。公開の抽選によって売却が決定するが、売買契約後5年以内に建物を建てることが義務付けられる

自己破産のしくみ

　債務が多過ぎて返済しきれなくなった消費者が、自ら破産を申し立てること。80年代半ばにも、サラ金の苛酷な取り立てから逃れるための自己破産が急増した時期があるが、90年代に再び増え始めた自己破産は、複数枚のクレジットカードで身分不相応に高額な買物や遊興をくり返したケースが多い。1998年には、破産申し立て件数が10万件を突破。

　注意しなければならないのは、破産宣告されても「免責」が許可されないと、借金は帳消しにはならないということ。破産者は公務員（議員）、ガードマン、証券・保険の外務員にはなれないほか、株式会社や有限会社の役員にもなれない。

People who go bankrupt out of fraudulent trade practice, swindling, or simple extravagance are not permitted to become exempt from payment of their debts.

虚偽や詐欺行為、浪費による自己破産は、借金が帳消しになる「免責」の対象外だ

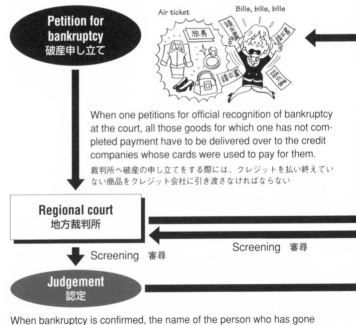

Petition for bankruptcy
破産申し立て

Air ticket

Bills, bills, bills

When one petitions for official recognition of bankruptcy at the court, all those goods for which one has not completed payment have to be delivered over to the credit companies whose cards were used to pay for them.

裁判所へ破産の申し立てをする際には、クレジットを払い終えていない商品をクレジット会社に引き渡さなければならない

Regional court
地方裁判所

Screening　審尋

Screening　審尋

Judgement
認定

When bankruptcy is confirmed, the name of the person who has gone bankrupt is published in an official gazette.

破産宣告がされると破産者の氏名が「官報」に掲載される

Declaration of "Self Bankruptcy"

People who find themselves in deep dept can declare themselves bankrupt. Around the middle of the 1980s, the number of people doing so to escape the ruthless so-called sara-kin, or loanshark companies from whom they borrowed money at exorbitant rates, soared, and it has soared again in the 1990s. In many cases the problem begins when a person has several credit cards, and uses them to make expensive purchases or to go on repeated trips that they can't afford. In 1998, the number of people who had to declare themselves bankrupt reached an all-time high of 100,000.

Be aware that even if you declare bankruptcy, you still have to pay off your debts, unless you are officially declared exempt. People who have gone bankrupt are barred thereafter from jobs as civil servants (government officials), security guards, securities and insurance sales agents, and also from becoming officers in companies.

Demand for payment
支払請求

Creditors
債権者

If permission is withheld 許可されないと	Debts remain, and the person is considered officially bankrupt for 10 years. 借金はそのまま残り、10年間は破産者となる
If permission is given 許可されると	Even though one is officially declared bankrupt, debts are written off. 破産者ではあるが、借金は帳消しになる

Application for exemption from debt
免責申し立て

It may take about 6 months for a screening.
審尋までは約6か月ほどかかる

In order to be exempt from paying off debts, it is necessary to file an official application.
借金返済の義務を免れるためには、「免責」の手続きが必要になる

過労死認定のしくみ

「働き過ぎの日本人」を象徴する言葉として《karoshi＝過労死》は欧米でもよく知られている。一般には、働き盛りのビジネスマンが、長時間の残業や休日なしの苛酷な勤務の末に突然死することを指す。

死亡の原因としては心筋梗塞や脳溢血が圧倒的に多いが、仕事の重圧が原因と考えられる自殺が過労死とみなされる場合もまれにある。

従来、過労死が労働災害として認定され、労災保険を受けられる割合は、きわめて低かった。だが、近年、過労死認定の基準が緩和される方向にあり、1995年2月から一部の見直しによる新基準が運用されるようになった。

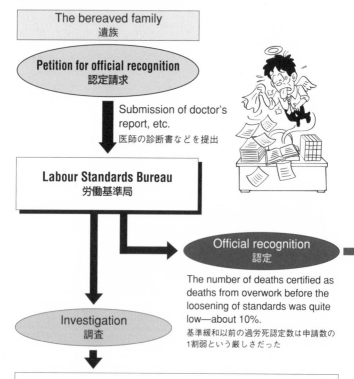

The bereaved family
遺族

Petition for official recognition
認定請求

Submission of doctor's report, etc.
医師の診断書などを提出

Labour Standards Bureau
労働基準局

Official recognition
認定

The number of deaths certified as deaths from overwork before the loosening of standards was quite low—about 10%.
基準緩和以前の過労死認定数は申請数の1割弱という厳しさだった

Investigation
調査

The death has to be recognized as a labor accident arising directly out of a person's work duties, which is sometimes very difficult to prove. However, it has become much easier to get recognition for cases where the person collapses and dies in the company.
死亡が業務による労働災害であると認められなければならないが、この因果関係を明らかにするのは困難だ。ただ、会社で倒れたケースは認められやすくなった

Death from Overwork

"Karō-shi," the Japanese term for "death from overwork," has become known even in the West as a phrase epitomizing the image of the Japanese company man who literally works himself to death. Generally, it refers to cases where a person at the prime of his working life is made to work for exceedingly long hours at his company, enduring a hard schedule without any vacation for a very long time—and then dies suddenly.

The actual causes of these deaths is overwhelmingly in most cases cardiac arrest or stroke. However, there are occasions when suicide due to unbearable work pressures is also officially recognized as the equivalent of karō-shi.

In years past, death from overwork was seen only in terms of "accidental death on the job," and the proportion of the bereaved who were able to claim insurance as a result was exceedingly low. However, the standard provisions regarding the qualifications of the term "death from overwork" have gradually been loosened, and in February 1992 there were revisions in part of the law that made new standards applicable.

After February 1995 when it was decided that stress could also be counted as a factor in evaluation, the standards for qualification as death from overwork were loosened somewhat.

ストレスも認定要因に加えられるなど、1995年2月から過労死認定の基準が一部緩和された

In previous years, the standard for certification of a death as karō-shi was set as "cases where within one week of death, the person had far more burdensome duties to carry out than colleagues in the same workplace." After the revisions, however, the qualifications for death from overwork were changed to admit that "the conditions resulting from well before one week of the person's illness, individual circumstances, as well as accumulated exhaustion and psychological stress" could also be taken into consideration.

従来は "倒れる前1週間以内に、職場の同僚などにくらべ過重な業務があった場合" が認定基準だったが、見直し後は、"発症1週間以前の状況や個別事情を考慮する、蓄積疲労や精神的ストレスを判断材料に加える" などと改善された

Besides being able to claim damages from the workplace of the person who has died from overwork, the bereaved family may be paid labor disaster compensation, and medical expenses.

遺族は本人が働いていた事業所などに対して賠償請求ができるほか、治療費や労災遺族補償年金などが給付される

定期借地権付き住宅のしくみ

　「一戸建てマイホームがこれまでの半額近くで手に入る」——そんな売り文句で注目を集めているのが定期借地権付き住宅。期限を決めて借りた土地に家を建てるというもので、1992年施行の「借地借家法」によって生まれた制度。ユーザーは地主と定期借地権契約を結び、契約時に保証金を預けて家を建て、月々の地代を支払う。ただし、一定期間（50年型が多い）が過ぎたら、土地を更地にして地主に返す義務が生じる。

　土地を購入する必要がないので、住宅購入当初の負担額は、土地購入型にくらべて格段に安くなるのも当然。ただし、この制度は92年7月31日以前の借地契約には適用されない。

定期借地権付き住宅のメリット

Land lessor
地主

Lessee
借地人

(1) A stable income can be obtained from the land and operation profit from the deposit. (2) Land tax is exempt, fixed asset tax burden is reduced, and inheritance tax can be paid in kind.	(1) Because the land does not need to be purchased, the cost of home ownership is decreased. (2) Fixed asset tax applies only to the home; the deposit will be returned upon completion of the contract.
①安定した地代収入と契約時の保証金の運用益が期待できる ②地価税が非課税、固定資産税が軽減され、相続税の物納も可	①土地を購入する必要がないので、そのぶん安い資金で済む ②固定資産税は建物のみ、保証金は契約満了時に返還される

Economic merits
経済的なメリット

House Built on Leased Land

"Get a new house at only half the regular cost." Such is the slogan used to attract would-be home buyers to a house built on leased land. The Leased Land and Rental House Law was passed in 1992, making it possible to build a house on land leased for a fixed period of time. The future homeowner signs a fixed-term lease contract with the landowner and makes a deposit to serve as a guarantee, and then makes monthly payments. When the fixed period ends (usually after 50 years), the land must be emptied and returned to the owner.

Because the land does not need to be purchased, the cost of building a home is much cheaper than usual. This system does not apply to land leased before July 31, 1992.

Merits of house built on fixed-term land leases

Land lessor 地主	Lessee 借地人
(1) When the fixed term is over, the land will be returned as an empty lot. (2) If specified in the contract, the building on the land may also be obtained.	(1) Chances of owning a home with a garden near to one's place of work increase. (2) If special terms are included in the contract, the lessee may add on and remodel and even sublet.
①契約期間が満了した時点で土地は更地として確実に戻ってくる ②契約時に特約を定めておけば、満了時の建物譲渡も可能	①通勤圏内でも庭付きの一戸建て住宅に入居できる可能性が大 ②契約時に特約を定めておけば増改築や転貸も可能

Land-use merits
土地活用上のメリット

定期借地権付き住宅のしくみ……2

What are land-lease rights?
借地権とは？

A lessee obtains lease rights when he or she rents land for the purpose of building a home. It includes rights of lease and land-surface rights. When a lessee has land-lease rights, the landowner does not have the right to refuse to renew the contract or evict the lessee.

住居を建てることを前提に土地を借りるところに生じる借地人の権利。土地の貸借権および地上権が含まれる。借地権が発生すると、地主の一方的な都合による契約更新の拒絶・立退き要求はできない

The underlying ground belongs to the landowner.

Under a fixed-term lease contract between a landowner and lessee, when the fixed term is over, the land-lease rights become null.

定期借地権契約とは、地主と借地人とが一定期間が過ぎれば借地権が消滅することを合意した契約である

House Built on Leased Land……2

Contract
契約

General fixed-term lease contracts, usually lasting at least 50 years, must be notarized.

契約期間は50年以上の一般定期借地権契約は、公正証書などの書面で行う

Land-lease rights
借地権発生

If trouble should ever occur between the landowner and the lessee, the district court is asked to arbitrate.

万が一、地主と借地人の間でトラブルが起きた場合は、地方裁判所に「調停」を申し立てる

End of term
期間満了

End of land-lease rights
借地権消滅

There are three ways rights can be terminated: (1) The building can be destroyed and the land returned. (2) The building can be transferred to the landowner. (3) The lessee can purchase the underlying ground.

その方法としては①建物を壊して更地にする　②建物を地主に譲渡する③地主所有の底地を購入する、の3つがある

廃棄物処理のしくみ

　ごみは、家庭やオフィスから出される一般廃棄物と工場などから排出される産業廃棄物の2つに大きく分類される。産業廃棄物については、行政サイドの規制が強化されつつある反面、一般廃棄物は行政が"せめて出すごみを分別して"とお願いをしているのが現状である。地方自治体はいずこもごみの最終処分場に困っていて、越境してごみ捨てに来たという自治体同士のトラブルまで起きている。資源の再利用という観点からも、ごみのリサイクルは急務の課題だが、やはり出す側の問題では……。

> With the revision in March 1995 of the Law Regarding the Disposal and Collection of Waste and Garbage, manufacturers were made to bear more responsibility for the disposal of their products.
>
> 1995年3月に改正された「廃棄物の処理及び清掃に関する法律」では、メーカーの処理責任が大きくなった

業者に持ちこまなければならない廃棄物

Home electrical goods
家電製品

Automobiles
自動車

According to the Law of Recycling Home Electrical Goods of April 2001, a fee must be paid for picking up such items as TVs, refrigerators, washing machines and air conditioners.

2001年4月施行の「家電リサイクル法」では、テレビ・冷蔵庫・洗濯機・エアコンの引き取り（運賃）が有料になる

Since cars count as industrial waste, the cost for their disposal must be borne by the consumer.

自動車は産業廃棄物であるため、廃棄コストは消費者負担が原則。ディーラーに引き取ってもらうシステムがある

Waste Disposal

Waste products can be divided into two main categories: the general type of garbage and trash put out from homes and offices, and the industrial waste matter emitted from factories, etc. While regulations for manufacturers concerning industrial waste matter are getting stricter, at present the only stipulation concerning ordinary garbage is that efforts should be made to divide garbage for collection into different categories. Local governmental authorities everywhere have great difficulty in finding suitable places to take the garbage to dump it, sometimes leading to disputes between neighboring authorities who accuse each other of breaching their borders to dump trash. Recycling of trash is thus a task of some urgency (this is true also from the point of view of making good use of resources), but it's unlikely that the problem will be solved without strong government direction.

Refuse items that have to be taken to specific traders

Fire extinguishers
消火器

Bicycles
自転車

Dealers collect items such as fire extinguishers and used gas tanks, which are difficult for local authorities to deal with with their own resources.
一般廃棄物のうち、自治体が独自で処理することが困難な消火器やガスボンベなどは、業者が回収する

A new system is coming into being, whereby bicycle shops collect bicycles from those people wishing to throw them away.
販売店が廃棄希望者から引き取る制度を、全国的に拡大中である

The recycling process for trash put out for collection
包装ごみのリサイクルのプロセス

Metal
金属

| Steel
スチール |
| Aluminum
アルミ |

Plastic
プラスチック

| "PET bottles" (plastic bottles)
ペットボトル |
| Others
その他 |

Sorting
選別

Glass, bottles
ガラス

| Clear glass
透明ガラス |
| Brown glass
茶ガラス |
| Others
その他 |

Paper
紙類

| Paper bags
紙パック |
| Cardboard boxes
段ボール |
| Others
その他 |

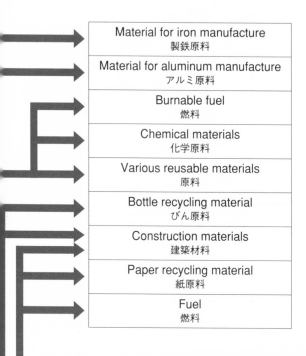

Material for iron manufacture	製鉄原料
Material for aluminum manufacture	アルミ原料
Burnable fuel	燃料
Chemical materials	化学原料
Various reusable materials	原料
Bottle recycling material	びん原料
Construction materials	建築材料
Paper recycling material	紙原料
Fuel	燃料

Reuse 再利用

In May 1995 the Law on the Recycling of Disposable Trash and the Law To Encourage Use of Recycled Goods were effected with the aim of encouraging a change from previous forms of trash disposal (incineration and accumulation in dumps) to recycling. The amount of general trash put out by households has exceeded 50-million tons annually, and at this rate the trash disposal sites will exceed capacity in the 21st century.

95年5月に成立した「包装ごみリサイクル法」「再生資源利用促進法」は、廃棄物処理を従来の焼却・埋立て方式からリサイクル方式へ転換させる目的をもっている。家庭から出される一般廃棄物は年間5000万tを超え、このままでは21世紀には最終処分場がパンクするからだ

第**8**章
この違いが
わかれば……
世の中は2倍おもしろい!

Chapter 8
Knowing the
Difference Goes a
Long Way
A Case of Organizational
Look-alikes

幼稚園と保育園の違い

　就学前の児童を通わせるのに幼稚園か保育園（所）のどちらにすべきか迷った人も多いはず。現実には両者の違いはほとんどない。この両者を分けているのは、それぞれの設置・運営を定める法律と、その法律に基づく行政機関である官庁の違いにある。

　近年の少子化傾向で、幼稚園はいずこも経営難を強いられている。その一方で、保育園は働くお母さんのニーズに応えきれていない。いっそのこと、行政改革で両者を統合・整理してしまったほうがよいという声もある

Nursery schools
保育園

Tuitions are all the same.

保育料は均一的負担となる

Parents choose where they send their children.

利用者が自由に選べるようになる

Nursery schools are under the jurisdiction of the Ministry of Health, Labour and Welfare. Funding is provided for recognized nursery schools, but there are still many problems concerning short-term nursery care.

保育園は厚生労働省の監督下にある。認可保育園に対しては補助金が支給されるが、短時間保育がネックとなり不評である

Ministry of Health, Labour and Welfare
厚生労働省

With the April 1998 revision of the Child Welfare Law, the nature of nursery schools underwent a partial change.

98年4月施行の改正児童福祉法によって、保育園（所）のあり方が一部変更された

Kindergartens and Nursery Schools

Most parents must have wondered about whether to send their preschool children to—kindergarten or nursery school—and wondered what the difference is between them. In reality, there is very little difference. What divides kindergartens from nursery schools are merely the regulations surrounding the facilities and management of such places, and the governmental office that oversees them.

In recent years, with the decrease in the number of children being born, kindergartens all around the country have found it difficult to survive. Nursery schools, on the other hand, find it difficult to meet the needs of working mothers. Many people think that an administrative revolution is necessary that would merge the two types of schools to meet the demands of the times.

Kindergarten
幼稚園

Kindergarten buildings must be single level.
原則は平屋建て

There must be separate washing facilities for hands and feet.
手洗い用と足洗い用の水道は別々に設置

Kindergartens are under the supervision of the Ministry of Education, Culture, Sports, Science and Technology. When new centers are set up, they have to comply with certain regulations under the Kindergarten Center Standards.

幼稚園は文部科学省の監督下にある。新設の際は「幼稚園設置基準」に示される条件をクリアしなければならない

Ministry of Education, Culture, Sports, Science and Technology
文部科学省

The Kindergarten Center Standards were announced in 1956 by the former Ministry of Education, and licenses for kindergartens are given out by local governmental authorities in cities and prefectures according to these standards.

幼稚園設置基準は1956年にかつての文部省によって告示され、都道府県はこれに基づいて許可をする

育児休業と介護休業の違い

　1995年6月に「介護休業法」が国会で成立した。病気の肉親の介護のために一定期間、会社を休むことが法律上で認められることになったのである。介護休業については一部の大企業では制度化も進んでいるが、問題なのは中小企業。すでに先行している育児休業の場合をみても、従業員数30人以下の企業は3年間の猶予期間を経てようやく適用されることになったばかりだ。だが、会社を休んでいる間の所得保障、違反した企業に対する罰則規定がないことなどで実効が危ぶまれている。

Childcare Leave
育児休業

"What a good baby!"

いい子
いい子

It is possible for either one of the parents to take leave from work for childcare until the child reaches 1 year in age. This law applied to all businesses after April 1995. Leave, however, is unpaid, so recourse has to be made to social welfare payments and various other forms of government support. Even so, the system is still far from perfect.

子供が満1歳になるまで両親のどちらかが育児のために会社を休むことができる。1995年4月以降から全企業に適用。休暇中は無給であるため社会保険料保障や国の助成制度などがあるとはいえ、いまのところ万全とはいえない状況である

If an employee applies to his or her company either for childcare or care leave, the company is obligated to accept the application. Further, it cannot fire an employee for the reason that they took such leave.

育児休業、介護休業ともに従業員からの申請があった場合、企業はこれを拒否することはできない。さらに、休業を理由にした従業員の解雇は禁じられている

お願いします

育児休業申請

Office of Labor Standards
労働基準監督署

Supervision
監督

Childcare Leave and Care Leave

In June 1995, the Law for Care Leave was passed in the Diet. It became recognized by law that one could take a certain fixed amount of time off from one's job in a company in order to take care of a sick parent. Systematization of paid care leave has proceeded apace in some of the large corporations, but with small- to medium-size businesses, progress has not been so fast. The same is true for childcare leave, something that was instituted well before care leave; businesses with fewer than 30 employees were given a grace period of 3 years before having to put the system into effect. However, the system is still not exactly watertight since no statutes exist to punish those businesses that fail to guarantee support during the period of leave from work.

Care Leave
介護休業

For company employees who have to take care of a sick family member (spouse, parent, child, or parent of spouse), this system allows one person per family to take 3 months off at a time to do so. The Law for Care Leave came into effect on April 1, 1999, but many problems still exist regarding, for example, guaranteed support during leave from work.

家族(配偶者、父母、子、配偶者の父母)の介護が必要な従業員に対して、対象家族1人について3か月までの休みを1回とることができる制度。1999年4月1日から法律が施行されたが、休業中の所得保障など今後解決しなければならない問題も多い

Application
申請

Corporations
企業

商品券とギフトカードの違い

デパートの商品券は贈答用に重宝されてきたが、ここ数年は景気低迷による法人需要落ち込みもあって販売額が減少の一途をたどっている。そもそもデパートの商品券を利用できるのは、グループ企業や特定の提携先という制約がある。これが不便ということで、消費者は広範な加盟店をもつクレジットカード会社や旅行会社が発行するギフトカードを選ぶようになったことも見逃せない。事実、ギフトカードは年々シェアを拡大中である。デパートでギフトカードで支払いをされた日には、上がったりだ。

Gift certificates
商品券

¥400
¥400
○○市
原田券 ¥10000
○○デパート

Gift certificate
¥10,000

Department stores treat unused gift certificates as non-interest debt capital. In 1993, the 4 percent regional tax on purchases made with gift certificates at department stores in central Tokyo was discontinued, a move which was followed by regional governments.

デパートでは商品券の未回収高を、無利息の借入資本に繰り入れるしくみになっている。大都市のデパートで商品券購入の際に課せられる地方税（4%）については、93年に東京23区で廃止されたのを皮切りに、ほかの自治体でも廃止の方向にある

Department stores
デパート

Fees　手数料

The department store industry is working to make gift certificates usable throughout the country. But since this would leave open the possibility of an imbalance in gift certificates issued and the value recovered, success still seems a long way off.

デパート業界は商品券の全国共通化を図ろうとしているが、その場合は発行額と回収額のバランスが取れないデパートが出る可能性もあり、足並みはなかなか揃いそうもない

Gift Certificates and Gift Cards

Department store gift certificates are known as a convenient way to give something to someone, but sales of gift certificates to companies and individuals have fallen in recent years due to the weak economy. Initially, department store gift certificates could only be used at department stores within the company group and specific affiliated stores. But this was considered inconvenient, and so consumers started buying more gift cards issued by credit card companies and travel agencies. Gift cards are actually increasing their share in the market. Department stores aren't too happy when customers pay with gift cards.

Gift cards
ギフトカード

Gift cards have been popular with consumers not only because they are convenient, but also because of a 3 percent discount offered during the gift-giving season. Since they can be used at department stores around the country, they are now seen as a threat to gift certificates.

利便性の高さに加えて、ギフトシーズン中は額面の3%程度の割引をするなどのサービスがあるため、消費者には好評である。全国どこのデパートでも使えるので、今やデパートの商品券を脅かす存在に成長した

Credit card companies
カード会社

When payment is made with gift cards, department stores have to pay a fee.

ギフトカードによる支払いがあった場合、デパートは手数料を差し引かれる

地震保険と火災保険の違い

　地震保険は30年もの歴史があるのに、加入者は火災保険の7分の1だそうだ。阪神大震災では家が倒壊した被災者に総額1000億円の地震保険金が支払われたという。一件当たりの最高額は96年1月1日契約分から6000万円に拡充された。

　1回の地震で支払われる保険金は、合計が660億円を超え3360億円以下の場合には、660億円を超える部分を民間と政府が半分ずつ負担するしくみである。阪神大震災では初めて「地震再保険特別会計」からの支出が行われた。

Earthquake insurance
地震保険

"This isn't covered!"

こんなものは保険の対象外です
Factory
Office
事務所
Car
車両
地震保険

Housing structures and household goods are covered by the insurance. The premium is set within a range of 30 to 50 percent of the amount of fire insurance with an upper limit of 50 million yen for housing structures and 10 million for household goods. When damage is incurred, the policy pays 50 percent (half loss) or 5 percent (partial loss) according to the extent of damage to the house itself.

保険の対象になるのは居住用の建物と家財である。保険料は火災保険の保険金額の30〜50%の範囲で設定し、建物で5000万円、家財で1000万円を上限とする。被害に遭ったときは、家財自体の損害の程度に応じて50%（半損）または5%（一部損）が支払われる

Insurance company
保険会社

The premiums for earthquake insurance lapse in one year's time, but companies began selling accumulative insurance in February 1995.

地震保険の保険料は1年ごとの掛捨てが原則だったが、95年2月から積立式も発売された

Earthquake and Fire Insurance

Only 1/7 of fire insurance policyholders have earthquake insurance even though it's been around for 30 years. A total of 100 billion yen in earthquake insurance was paid to policyholders who lost their houses in the Hanshin earthquake in 1995. The highest amount per case has been raised to 60 million yen from the amount in the January 1, 1996 policies.

Over 66 billion yen can be paid for one earthquake. If the amount is less than 336 billion yen, then the government and the private sector equally share the burden of the amount in excess of 66 billion yen. The Hanshin earthquake marked the first time payment was made from a "special account for earthquake reinsurance."

Fire insurance
火災保険

「地震火災費用
保険金」
↓
契約金額の5%

火災
保険

This insurance policy covers losses sustained in the event of a fire. Even if earthquake insurance isn't added to this in a supplementary contract, the policy pays "earthquake fire expense insurance" with a limit of five percent (three million yen) of the policy amount if partial loss by fire is sustained due to an earthquake.

火災によって物損をこうむった場合の損害額を査定して契約をする保険。特約として地震保険を付けていない場合でも、地震によって半焼以上の被害を受けると契約金額の5%（300万円）を限度に「地震火災費用保険金」が支払われる

Earthquake insurance cannot be bought separately. It must be purchased as part of a larger fire or householder's comprehensive insurance policy.

地震保険は単独では契約できない。火災保険または住宅総合保険を主契約とするセット契約が必要だ

手形と小切手の違い

　手形は一般の金銭債権にくらべ流通性が高く、約束手形と為替手形の２種類がある。約束手形は振出人が受取人に対し一定期日に一定額の支払いを約束するもので、商品または原材料の仕入代金のために振り出される商業手形、銀行等が借用証書代わりに振り出させる手形貸付という２つの方法がある。為替手形は振出人が第三者（一般に金融機関）に一定額の支払いを委託する証券である。

　小切手は振出人が銀行に対し、あらかじめ当座預金契約をしたうえで、受取人への支払いを委託する有価証券である。手形が信用の手段として用いられることが多いのに対して、小切手は主に現金の代用とされる。

Checks
小切手

Checks are current securities used in the economy in place of cash. When the recipient takes the check to a specified bank to cash, no signature is required. In general, checks must be cashed within ten days of their date of issue.

小切手は現金の代用として流通している有価証券である。支払人は銀行に限定され、譲渡の際には裏書きを必要としない。原則として振出日付後10日以内に支払日が設定される

Check

小切手　｜｜
¥1,000,000

小切手の斜斜線は事故防止のためのもの

The horizontal lines on checks are there to prevent mistakes.

Bank drafts
手形

Bank drafts can be taken to a bank and cashed even before the settlement date. The bank will cash drafts for a fee and a discount that depends on the level of credit and the settlement date. Drafts with a low level of credit are usually only cashed by lending institutions.

商業手形はその決済日以前でも金融機関に持ち込むと現金化できる。その場合は振出人の信用度や決済期間によって、割引手数料を差し引かれる。信用度の低い手形は高利の金融業者しか扱わないことが多い

When transferring to a third party, the back needs to be endorsed.

約束手形
¥1,000,000

第三者に譲渡する場合は手形の裏書きとして記載します

Promissory note

Bank Drafts and Checks

Bank drafts (tegata), used more often than other forms of debit, come in two forms, promissory notes and bills of exchange. The issuer of a promissory note promises the receiver to pay a certain amount of money within a certain period of time. One type of promissory note is called a mercantile note, issued to obtain products and materials, and the other type is for loans on bills when borrowing money from banks or other institutions. Bills of exchange are used when the issuer entrusts a third party (usually a financial institution) to make payment of a set amount.

A check (kogitte) is considered paper money and is issued after a current deposit contract has been formed. While bank drafts are used as a form of credit, checks are generally used in place of cash.

When checks are cashed at the bank, the client's name and address must be written on the back. It generally takes two or three days for banks to process checks.

小切手は銀行に入金する際は裏面に住所・氏名を記入する。小切手が現金化されるまでは、通常2〜3日かかる

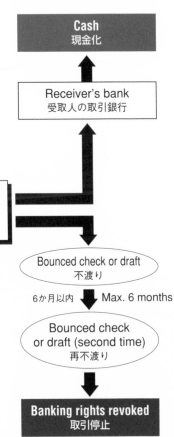

Cash
現金化

Receiver's bank
受取人の取引銀行

Exchange location
手形交換所

Bounced check or draft
不渡り

6か月以内　Max. 6 months

Bounced check
or draft (second time)
再不渡り

Banking rights revoked
取引停止

When a draft or check is not honored before the written settlement date, it is treated as a bounced check or draft. When this happens a second time, the bank will refuse to continue doing business with the company.

手形は記載された決済日に額面通り支払われないと不渡りの扱いになり、2回目の不渡りで振出人は銀行取引停止処分を受ける

上場株と店頭株の違い

株の暴落で株式市場はすっかり意気消沈している。個人投資家が去り、東証に上場していた外国企業が1年間に16社も上場廃止をするなど、市場の空洞化も取り沙汰されている。日本経済は地価下落・円高・株安のトリプルパンチでデフレ症状だ。

Listed stocks
上場株

上場を
目指すぞ！

成長企業

Companies must comply with a set of conditions to be listed on the exchange market. Being listed improves the social status of the company, raises capital, and makes it easier to get financing, and so many growing companies strive to go public.

証券取引所で売買されている株で、一定の基準（上場基準）をクリアすることが条件。上場することで企業の社会的信用が増す、資金調達や増資・起債に有利などのメリットがあるため、成長企業は上場を目標とする

Listing and transactions
上場・売買

Securities exchange
証券取引所

There are security exchanges in Sapporo, Niigata, Tokyo, Nagoya, Kyoto, Osaka, Hiroshima, and Fukuoka. About 90 percent of transactions take place at the Tokyo Securities Exchange.

札幌、新潟、東京、名古屋、京都、大阪、広島、福岡の8証券取引所がある。取引高のシェアの約9割を東京証券取引所が占める

Transactions
売買

Securities companies
証券会社

Japan Securities Dealers Association
日本証券業協会

Listed Stocks and Over-the-Counter Stocks

The fall in stock prices has left a dark shadow. The market is now mostly devoid of individual investors and 16 overseas companies have withdrawn from the Tokyo Stock Exchange within a one-year period, indicative of the poor state of affairs. Japan's economy has taken three deflationary punches from the drop in land prices, the inflated yen, and a collapsed stock market.

Over-the-counter stocks
店頭株

Over-the-counter stocks are unlisted, but recorded with the Japan Securities Dealers Association. They get their name because the shares are bought and sold over-the-counter at securities companies. Getting shares on the over-the-counter market is much easier than getting them listed, but some companies prefer over-the-counter shares. Shares taken off the exchange markets are also recorded on the over-the-counter market as controlled shares.

Listed stocks

Over-the-counter stocks

ちょっと
ハードルが
高いからなぁ

"What a high hurdle!"

非上場で、日本証券業協会に登録している株。取引は証券会社の店頭で行われることからこう呼ばれる。登録基準は上場基準よりはるかに緩いが、あえて上場しない企業もある。上場廃止した銘柄は管理銘柄としてここに登録される

Registration
登録

Secondary over-the-counter market
第二店頭市場

Established in July 1995, the secondary over-the-counter market is for venture companies focused on research and development. There are no requirements for a minimum number of shares and companies in the red can also participate, opening the way for promising companies to raise funds.

1995年7月に発足した研究開発型ベンチャー企業の株取引市場。発行株数に下限がなく、赤字決算でも登録でき、将来性の高い企業の資金調達の途が開かれた

Venture!

将来性
を買って

信用金庫と信用組合の違い

金融不祥事などで何かと話題の信用金庫と信用組合。実は、この2つの金融機関のルーツは同じである。信用協同組合という組織が分かれ、1949年に「中小企業等協同組合法」に基づいて信用組合が発足し、51年に「信用金庫法」に基づいて発足したのが信用金庫だ。

いずれも"地域密着"をその金融業務のバックボーンとしているが、資金量が少ないことと金利自由化の向かい風を受けて経営状態は悪化の一途。取付け騒ぎの火種を抱えている点でも共通している。

Credit associations
信用金庫

Total savings and lending from non-members cannot exceed 20 percent.

会員以外の融資額は総額の2割までです

○○信用金庫

Trust

Credit associations can only lend out 20 percent of their capital to investors who have deposited a certain amount in the association. However, they are able to accept savings from non-members. Executives are not allowed to hold other positions, and they are overseen by the Ministry of Finance, just as with banks.

一定の出資金を出した会員以外には、総額の2割までしか貸し出せないという制限がある。だが、預金については会員以外からも自由に集められる。役員の兼業は認められず、銀行と同じく財務省の監督を受ける

In 1985, there were about 450 credit associations throughout Japan, but this number had dropped by more than 50 by 1990. As of May 2000, the number was 376.

全国の信用金庫の数は85年には約450あったが、90年以降は再編によって50以上も減った。2000年5月現在では376

When business area crosses prefectural borders

複数の都道府県にまたがって営業している場合

Ministry of Finance
財務省

Supervision　監督

Credit Associations and Credit Unions

Scandals in recent years have brought credit associations and credit unions to the public's attention in Japan. These two types of organizations have similar roots. The way was made clear for trust unions to be established when an organization called the Trust Association Union was divided; credit unions were established based on the Small and Medium-sized Business Cooperation Association Law of 1949. Credit associations got their start with the passing of the Credit Association Law of 1951.

Both of these organizations are intended to provide financial services for local communities. But they are now facing difficult times due to their limited capacities and the liberalization of interest. They also face the risk of panicking depositors wanting their money back.

Credit unions
信用組合

〇〇信用組合

預金や融資は
組合員またはその
家族に限ります

窓口

Union

Credit unions are established as mutual-aid organizations for workers and small-and medium-sized businesses. Members need to live, work or conduct business in the area. Savings accounts and lending are mostly limited to members and their immediate family who have made a certain investment in the credit union.

勤労者や中小企業の相互扶助を目的とした協同組合。組合員になるには、その営業地域に居住するか、勤務または事業をしていることが必要。預金や貸し出しは、一定額の出資をした組合員やその家族に限られるのが原則だ

The number of credit unions in 1985 was about 450, but it dropped sharply in the second half of the 1980s. As of May 2000, there were 306 credit unions still in existence.

全国の信用組合の数は85年には約450あったが、80年代後半から激減。2000年5月末現在では306

Prefectural governments
都道府県

本醸造酒と吟醸酒の違い

日本酒の等級表示が廃止されて、品質の基準がわかりにくくなったという声がある。現在は製法による品質表示が行われているが、一つの目安として下表のような5段階に分かれている。もっとも酒好きには日本酒の貴賤など、どうでもよいだろうが。

Sake brewed from the finest rice
吟醸酒

これは芸術だ！

High-grade sake made from rice polished to 60 percent of its original size and fermented at low temperatures is called Ginjōshu. Reducing the rice kernels to 50 to 35 percent of their original size by polishing and grinding produces Daiginjōshu. The rice loses almost all of its nutrients anyway, but the higher the quality of Japanese sake, the lower the nutritional value. Because shipment at Kuramoto is limited to 100 to 150 one-sho bottles, it is prized as a "sake work of art."

精米歩合60%以下で低温発酵させて醸造した高級酒を吟醸酒という。さらに精米歩合を低くして、50〜35%に米粒を削ったのが大吟醸酒である。米の栄養分はほとんどなくなるが、高質の日本酒ほど栄養価が低いのだ。大吟醸酒は、蔵元では一升瓶で100〜150本の限定出荷であるため、"酒の芸術品"として珍重される

Standards for Descriptive Labeling of Japanese Sake 日本酒の品質表示基準
Pure rice sake 純米酒
Authentically brewed sake 本醸造酒
Regular sake 普通酒
Sake brewed from the finest rice (Ginjōshu) 吟醸酒
Grand sake brewed from the finest rice (Daiginjōshu) 大吟醸酒

Authentically Brewed Sake and Quality Sake

Markings that show the grade of Japanese sake have been abolished, giving rise to criticism that grading is not easy to understand. Recently, descriptive labeling based on brewing technique has been used, but as shown above this one standard has been separated into five categories. For people who put quantify before quality, such matters have little meaning.

Authentically Brewed Sake
本醸造酒

Sake brewed with 70% or less polished rice is called pure rice sake. It's a thick sake made only from rice and malted rice. Adding 15 percent brewing alcohol to this pure rice sake makes regular sake, and adding less creates authentically brewed sake. Authentically brewed sake has no added carbohydrates, so it slips down the throat smoothly. Sake labeled as authentically prepared (hon jikomi) and authentically made (hon zukuri) is the same type as authentically brewed sake.

精米歩合70%以下で醸造した酒を純米酒という。米と麹だけでつくられ、濃厚でコクのある酒だ。この純米酒に醸造用アルコールを25%添加したのが普通酒、それ以下のものを本醸造酒として区別している。本醸造酒は糖質も一切添加しないため、のどごしがすっきりしている。本仕込み、本造りと表示されている酒も本醸造酒と同類だ

The brewing and distribution of alcohol, including sake, is subject to the Liquor Tax Law. Those brewing sake without permmission are liable to punishment. FYI, the law defines sake as having a alcohol content of 1 % or more.

日本酒を含め、酒の製造・販売は「酒税法」という法律に基づかなければならない。許可なく造ったり、売ったりすれば罰せられる。ちなみに、法律が定める酒とは、アルコール分が1度以上の飲料のことだ

The Japanese sake-making process
日本酒造りのプロセス

Polished rice　精米

The rice kernels are milled to remove proteins and fatty membranes. The grade of the sake is determined by how much protein and fatty membrane are removed (extent of milling).

米粒を磨いて内部のたんぱく質・脂肪層を削る。この削り具合(精米歩合)で品質が決まる

Soaking polished rice　洗米浸漬

Polished rice is washed and soaked in water so that it absorbs the water content. Sterilized high-quality spring water is used.

精米を水洗いした後に、水に漬けて水分を吸収させる。水は殺菌した良質の地下水を使用する

Steamed rice　蒸米

The rice is sterilized with steam. This process also makes the starch break down easily.

蒸気で蒸して殺菌する。でんぷんを分解しやすくする働きもある

Making a sake culture of rice, malt and yeast　酒母造り

Malted rice is added to steamed rice, then the yeast is cultured in a tank. This is also called, "making the moto."

蒸米に麹を加え、タンクの中で酵母を培養する。酛(もと)づくりともいう。

Authentically Brewed Sake and Quality Sake⋯⋯2

Blending 調合

Alcohol is added to bring the sake up to market specifications.
アルコールを添加して市販の規格に仕上げる

Storage 貯蔵

The sake stored in a tank is approximately 20 percent alcohol.
アルコール分約20％の状態でタンクに貯蔵しておく

Sterilization 殺菌

The sake is heated to approximately 65°C to stop the action of the yeast.
65℃前後に過熱し、酵母の働きをとめる

Filtration ろ過

Compression 圧搾

The unrefined sake is compressed, and the sake and sake lees are separated. The sake becomes cloudy at this stage.
もろみを搾って酒と酒粕に分ける。酒はこの段階では白濁している

Preparation 仕込み

The operation of adding steamed rice, water and malted rice to the yeast mash lasts four days and is repeated three times. Then, 20 to 25 days of saccharification by malted rice and yeast fermentation results in unrefined sake.
酒母に蒸米、水、麹を加える作業を4日間で3回繰り返す。そして20〜25日間、タンク内で麹による糖化と酵母による発酵をさせ、もろみができ上がる

Malt is made implanting malt bacteria into steamed rice and letting it ferment. Water used for preparation is hard water with iron, magnesium, and other impurities removed.
蒸米に麹菌を植え付けて繁殖させたのが麹である。仕込水は鉄分やマンガンなどを除去した硬水が用いられる

第9章
医学の進歩は永遠なり 命にかかわる大事なことです!

Chapter 9
Medicine Marches On *It's a Matter of Life and Death*

医療費のしくみ

　国民皆保険制度を原則とするわが国では、医療を受けるときに保険証を提出すれば保険診療を受けることができる。この場合の医療費を診療報酬といい、医療行為を点数で計算する方法がとられている。診療報酬は、厚生労働大臣が中央社会保険医療協議会（中医協）に諮問したうえで決定される。

　これは出来高によって支払われるため、とにかく医療機関側が請求額を増やそうとして過剰医療を行いがちな点が指摘されてきた。患者側も自己負担分以外の医療費については無関心であるところから、濫診乱療の温床となっていることも見逃せない。また、歯科材料代・差額ベッド代という名目による医療費の差額徴収は、法律上は問題視される。

Paying medical expenses
医療費支払いのプロセス

The fee structure at hospitals and private practices changed in 1992.

92年以降、病院と開業医では料金体系が異なっている

Portion of medical expense to be paid individually

自己負担分支払い

Insured individual
被保険者

Payment of insurance expense
保険料支払い

Insurer	National or Health Insurance Union, etc.
保険者	国や健保組合など

Claim
請求

Payment
支払い

Payment Fund/National Insurance Alliance
支払基金・国保連

Institution entrusted with the investigation and payment from the insurer.

保険者から審査・支払い業務を委託された機関

Medical Expenses

Japan has a policy of universal health care. Health care services are provided through health insurance. In this system, medical expenses are referred to as medical compensation, and a points system is used for calculating the medical treatment. Proof of insurance is submitted when receiving medical care, and the medical compensation is decided after the Minister of Health, Labour and Welfare consults the Central Social Insurance Medical Council (CSIMC).

It has been pointed out that medical institutions tend to provide excessive medical treatment in order to make the amount of medical compensation as high as possible. This is aggravated by the fact that patients only care about individually paid medical expenses, making medical institutions notable hotbeds of over treatment. Also legally problematic is the fact that patients pay the difference on nominal medical expenses such as dental material charges and the amenity bed charge.

Hospitals and other medical service providers
病院などの保険診療医療機関

Claim for medical compensation
診療報酬請求

Rezept
レセプト

A medical institution's bill of particulars that is submitted on a monthly basis. In 1997, the Ministry of Health, Labour and Welfare effected a policy whereby insurers disclose the Rezept to the insured, but compliance has been mixed.

医療機関の請求明細書。1ヵ月単位で提出される。97年に厚生労働省は保険者が被保険者にレセプトを開示する方針を打ち出したが、対応はまちまちだ

Payment of medical compensation
診療報酬支払い

Drug costs are more than 30 percent of medical expenses, and over 50 percent for outpatients over 70 years old.
医療費のうち薬剤費の割合は3割強で、70歳以上の外来患者は5割以上を占める

認定医承認制度のしくみ

　医者が1人しかいない医院の看板に、内科・小児科・外科……といくつもの診療科目が並んでいて不思議に思ったことはないだろうか？　実はたいがいの医師は専門科目が1つにもかかわらず、あれこれ間口を広げているのであって、単なる営業施策の一環にほかならない。

　日本医師会、日本医学会、学会認定医制協議会によって、従来専門学会別に与えていた認定医資格を、医師1人につき1科承認してシールを発行し診察室への表示を義務付けたのは、患者にとっては朗報。何が専門なのかが一目でわかり、医師への信頼感が増すというわけだが、裏を返せば、医師の世界はそれほどまでに不明朗だったということなのだ。

> The doctor specialization system was implemented in September 1994 to let patients know in what fields of medicine their doctor specializes.
>
> 1994年9月から実施された認定医承認制度は、医師の専門分野が何かを患者にもわからせるための制度だ

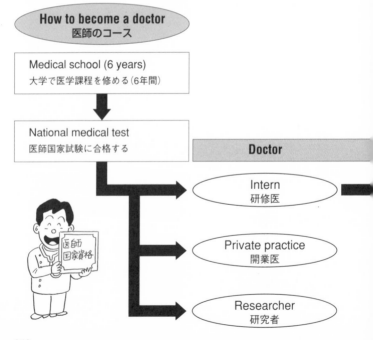

How to become a doctor
医師のコース

Medical school (6 years)
大学で医学課程を修める（6年間）

National medical test
医師国家試験に合格する

Doctor

Intern
研修医

Private practice
開業医

Researcher
研究者

The Doctor Specialization System

Medical clinics in Japan, even those with only one doctor, will put out signs showing their areas of specialization—internal medicine, pediatrics, external medicine, and so forth. It may surprise you to learn that most doctors specialize in only one area—the sign is nothing more than a sales tactic.

The Japan Medical Association, the Japanese Association of Medical Sciences, and the conference of doctor specialization system certify doctors in specialized areas of medicine, and issue seals for each area that doctors are required to display in their examination rooms. This is all a show for the patients—to make them think that their doctor specializes in something and can be trusted. On the other hand, this could be taken as an indicator of how opaque the medical world is.

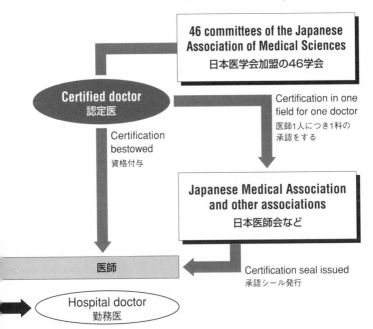

46 committees of the Japanese Association of Medical Sciences
日本医学会加盟の46学会

Certified doctor
認定医

Certification in one field for one doctor
医師1人につき1科の承認をする

Certification bestowed
資格付与

Japanese Medical Association and other associations
日本医師会など

医師

Certification seal issued
承認シール発行

Hospital doctor
勤務医

Hospital doctors work under difficult conditions for little pay. It's the doctors in private practice that make the money. In cities where land prices are high, most doctors on their own simply rent rooms in a building, resulting in a shortage of doctors to treat emergencies at night.

勤務医はハードな勤務条件の割には薄給である。儲けるには開業医だが、都市部では地価高騰でビルの一室で診療する "ビル診" ばやり。だが、医師がいなくなる夜間の急病人はどうなる？

在宅医療のしくみ

医学の進歩は永遠なり

「畳の上で死にたい」という言葉があるように、人生の終章を病院で過ごすことを嫌がる感覚は、日本人には根強くある。身体の一部が不自由になっても、病院や老人ホームに入らず、自宅で治療を受けながら余生を送る「在宅医療」が見直されているのも、そうした日本人の伝統的な考えが底流にあるからだろう。

在宅医療のメリットの1つに医療費の節減があるが、もちろんそれだけが目的ではない。病院では与えられない精神の安らぎが自宅にはあり、それが治療にも大きな効果をもたらすとの考えがあるからである。今後、在宅医療を専門に行う地域医療チームも増えてくるはずだ。

Recent changes in the national insurance system provide care to bedridden elderly, but the system is still lacking in care for other at-home patients.

寝たきり老人については健康保険適用となったが、そのほかの在宅患者の在宅医療システムの充実化は急務の課題だ

Patient's home

患者宅

どうも血圧が……

"Your blood pressure seems to be..."

Digital line
デジタル回線

Visiting nurse services
訪問看護サービス

Home help
ホームヘルパー派遣

Bathing services
入浴巡回サービス

Hospital food delivery services
病院食宅配サービス

Medicine delivery services
薬剤宅配サービス

Home Medical Care

A common Japanese saying is, "I want to die at home on the tatami mat." This indicates the dislike that many Japanese have for spending the last days of their life in hospitals. It is likely that such traditional thinking is behind a review of the medical system to make it possible for patients with disabilities to stay out of hospitals and nursing homes and live out their lives with medical care at home.

One merit of home care is the cost savings, but that of course is not the only purpose. A peace of mind such as is not possible in the hospital is often available at home, and such a feeling is thought to play a key role in the healing process. It is likely that more and more medical teams will be formed to provide localized home care.

Remote medical system
遠隔医療システム

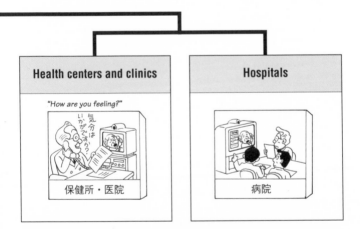

Remote medical treatment using multi-media technology is already happening on a test basis. Using videophones, such procedures as making diagnosis and checking blood pressure, heartbeat and urine will soon be possible.

すでにマルチメディアによる遠隔医療が実験的に行われている。テレビ電話による問診、血圧・心電図・尿などのデータチェックによる診療も可能になるだろう

介護保険のしくみ

寝たきりや痴呆で介護が必要になった場合に備えた公的介護保険制度。介護が必要な高齢者にどの程度のサービスを提供するかを決める「要介護認定」を経て、「介護サービス計画（ケアプラン）」にもとづく公的介護制度が、全国の大半の市町村で始まった。

サービスは、自立・要支援・要介護１～５までの７ランクに分けて判定されるが、自立と判断された場合は給付を受けられない。65歳未満40歳以上の人でも、パーキンソン病や慢性関節リウマチなどの15種類の特定疾病は受給対象となる。公的介護保険の保険料は、市町村によって若干異なるが、国民健康保険の被保険者の場合はおおむね1280円の上乗せになる。

Long-term Care Insurance
公的介護保険制度

Everyone over 40 must make payments into the Long-term Care Insurance System, implemented in April 2000.

40歳以上の人に加入を義務付ける公的介護保険制度は、2000年4月から施行

Revenue
財源

Cities, towns and villages operate the system and have special medical care accounting departments.

市町村が制度運営者となり、介護特別会計を設定する

Typical services
サービス例

Home care, home bathing, home nursing, day care, home treatment advice, medical care equipment, etc.

訪問介護・訪問入浴・訪問看護・デイケア・居宅療養管理指導・福祉用具支給など

Payment to the specified institution providing care
指定機関へ介護保険報酬の支払い

Participants in the insurance scheme are classified into first level (those older than 65), and second level (those between 40 and 65). But the only ones, in principle, to receive the service are 65 or older. After an application is made, an investigation and certification is made based on a home visit and an opinion from a doctor. The payment is then made with 10 percent deductible.

65歳以上（第1号被保険者）、40歳から65歳未満で医療保険の加入者（第2号被保険者）の2区分があるが、実際のサービス対象者は原則65歳以上。申請後の訪問調査と医師の意見書をもとに審査・認定が行われ、サービス利用時に限度額の1割負担をする

Long-term Care Insurance

The Long-term Care Insurance System was initiated for the care of
the bedridden and those with senile dementia. Most cities, towns, and
villages throughout the country started the official care system based
on the Care Plan, which consists of a care certification system under
which a doctor decides how much medical care each elderly person
needs.

The elderly are classified into seven categories: independent,
needy of support, and needy of care (levels 1 to 5), with no allowance
for those classified as independent. Those in the 40- to 65-year-old
age bracket with Parkinson's Disease, rheumatoid arthritis, and 13
other illnesses also qualify to receive payment. The premium for this
new insurance varies slightly by city, town, and village, but for those
with national insurance, the approximate premium is an additional
1,280 yen on top of the current expenditure.

Health insurance that includes home care
介護保障付き保険

National insurance under which the bedridden and those with
senile dementia receive payment after the condition has continued for between three and six months.
寝たきりや痴呆で、要介護状態が3〜6か月続いている被保険者に支給され
る民間の保険

Insurance from property insurance companies 損害保険会社の保険	Insurance provided by life insurance companies, the post office, and the agricultural cooperative 生命保険会社・郵便局・農協の保険
Payment made within maximum limits to cover medical expenses, care equipment expenses, and other costs. 支払い限度額内で、医療費や介護機器購入費などの費用が支給される	Depending on the premium, a maximum of 10 million yen is paid out, along with a fixed payment upon death. 保険料額に応じて、年に最高1000万円ぐらいまで支払われ、死亡時も一定の保険金が出る

When taking out insurance, it is important to check the details. The
conditions for payment are often extremely difficult to meet.
加入する際は、保険契約の内容を細部までチェックしておく必要がある。いざという
時の給付条件はかなり厳しいからだ

脳死判定のしくみ

　脳死とは、事故や病気で脳の機能が不可逆的に失われた状態を指す。従来、心臓が停止し、呼吸が停止し、瞳孔が開くことの3つが満たされることを「死」としてきたが、「臓器移植法案」の成立によって、法的には「脳死」も人の死と認められることになった。

　ただし、脳死の判定についてはいまだ議論が続いており、各大学などが独自の判定基準を打ち出している状態だ。判定のガイドラインは、厚生労働省の脳死研究班が85年に作った「脳死判定基準（竹内基準）」である。だが、「脳細胞の死滅を確認すべきだ」という意見や脳死を人の死とは認めないとする意見もまだまだ根強い。

> For brain death to be declared in Japan, six conditions must be met.
> わが国では、脳死の判定基準としての6つの条件をすべて満たしていなければならないとされる

Judgment standards
判定の基準

1 Deep coma
深い昏睡

2 Dilated pupils
瞳孔の拡大

3 Inability to breathe without support
自分で呼吸ができない

4 No brain stem reflex
脳幹反射の消失

5 Flat brain waves
平坦な脳波

Declaration of Brain Death

Brain death refers to a condition where, due to accident or illness, the brain is no longer able to function with any possibility of recovery. In the past, death was declared when the hearts and lungs stopped, and when the pupils dilated, but with the passing of the Organ Transplant Law, it became possible to declare a person dead based on brain death.

However, the discussion concerning when a person should be declared brain dead continues, with various universities and other institutions issuing their own standards. A research committee under the Ministry of Health, Labour and Welfare prepared a document called the Brain Death Judgment Guidelines (The Takeuchi Standards) in 1985. But there are still deep-rooted opinions that the death of brain cells needs to be verified, and that brain death should not be used as a standard for declaring death.

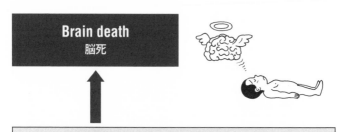

Brain death
脳死

6 The other five conditions must remain unchanged for six hours.
1～5の条件が6時間後の再検査でも変わらない

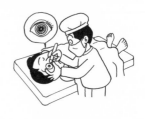

For children aged six and under, more than six hours of observation is required. Japan's standard is based on the concept of total brain death. England and other countries base brain death on the death of the brain stem (all parts of the brain except the cerebral hemisphere and the cerebellum).

6歳以下の小児の場合は、6時間以上の観察時間をとることが求められる。日本の脳死の概念は全脳死であるが、英国などでは脳幹(脳のうち大脳半球と小脳を除いた部分)死を脳死とする立場をとっている

臓器移植のしくみ

臓器移植の問題は医療技術のみならず、極めて倫理的課題をはらんでいる。臓器移植は、提供者（ドナー）の存在があって初めて可能になる。この提供者として脳死者が法的に認められることになったのは、臓器移植を希望する患者にとっては朗報である。

わが国では、1968年の札幌医大の和田教授による心臓移植（殺人罪で告発されたが不起訴処分）などの例外を除き、心臓と肝臓の脳死移植は行われることは皆無だった。

99年2月、日本で初の脳死移植が実施されたが、脳死判定をめぐって難題が山積。15歳以下の子供は対象外とされることも、改めて問題視された。

Advances in technology for heart and other organ transplants have brought the issue of brain death to the forefront.

脳死が問題にされる理由は、心臓移植をはじめ、他の臓器移植の可能性を高めるからだ

Possible organ donors
臓器の提供可能者

Heart 心臓	Brain dead 脳死者

Bone marrow 骨髄	Brain dead 脳死者
	Living 生体

Pancreas 膵臓	Brain dead 脳死者
	Living 生体

心臓移植は脳死者だけ

Heart transplants require a brain-dead donor.

Organ Transplants

Medical technology is not the only issue relevant to organ transplants: there are serious moral implications. An organ transplant becomes possible only when a donor is available. And for those whose survival depends on a transplant, the recent passing of a law that allows a person to be declared dead based on brain death comes as good news.

With a few exceptions—such as when Professor Wada of Sapporo Medical University performed a heart transplant and was charged with murder in 1968 but won acquittal—there had been no heart or liver transplants performed in Japan.

The first brain-death transplant took place in February 1999, but troubles abounded concerning the way in which the donor was declared brain dead. Another problem with the current system is that children under 15 cannot be recipients.

| Liver
肝臓 | | Brain dead
脳死者 |
| | | Living
生体 |

Cornea 角膜		Brain dead 脳死者
		Dead 死体
		Living 生体

Kidney 腎臓		Brain dead 脳死者
		Dead 死体
		Living 生体

Transplants from an animal to a human are called xenotransplantation. In 1992, a patient in the United States survived two months after receiving a liver transplant from a baboon.

人間以外の動物からの移植は異種臓器移植と呼ばれる。米国では92年にヒヒの肝臓を移植された人が、2か月間生きた記録がある

The kidney transplants process
腎臓移植のプロセス

Kidney donor
腎臓提供者

US kidneys
US腎

Since 1993, the United States has made 22 kidneys available to Japan, seven of which were not transplanted. The average cost for a kidney operation was around 1.1 million yen.

米国からは1993年以降、22個の移植用腎臓が提供され、うち7個は移植されなかった。1個当りの患者の経費負担は平均約110万円だった

The Japan Organ Transportation Network was established in October 1997 to serve as a window for receiving organs from abroad.

97年10月に設立された社団法人日本臓器移植ネットワークは、海外からの臓器受入れの窓口になる

Registration
登録

Reception
受入れ

Japan Organ Transportation Network
日本臓器移植ネットワーク

Registration
登録

Patient
患者

Transplant operation
移植手術

District center
地方ブロックセンター

Kidney transplants are possible only with the consent of the family after the donor's heart stops, but transplants conducted in case of brain death need the prior written consent of the donor.
腎臓移植は、脳死移植のようにドナーの書面による意思表示がなくとも、心停止後なら家族の承諾だけで可能

Kidney bank
腎バンク

Donor hospital
腎提供病院

Kidney Transplant Center (National Sakura Hospital)
腎移植センター
（国立佐倉病院）

Hospital where kidney transplant takes place
腎移植病院

Kidney transportation
腎輸送

骨髄バンクのしくみ

　白血病や再生不良性貧血にかかると、健康な血液成分が作れなくなってしまうが、健康な人の骨髄を移植すると、治ることが多い。骨髄とは、白血球や赤血球の成分を作る組織である。しかし、人間にはそれぞれ白血球の血液型ともいうべきHLA（ヒト組織適合性抗原）のタイプがあり、患者と提供者のHLAが一致しないと、移植は成功しない。しかも、HLAの適合率はきわめて低い。

　そこで、適合する骨髄提供者（ドナー）を効率的に探すため、提供者の登録を募っているのが、骨髄バンク（骨髄移植推進財団）だ。なお、日本に骨髄バンクが設立されたのは1991年末のことである。

When the number of registered marrow donors reaches 100,000, there will be enough donors to meet the needs of all recipients.

骨髄提供者が10万人になると、当面移植が必要とされる白血病患者のほとんどに適合するといわれている

At the end of November 2000, there were about 133,000 registered donors. There have been 3,043 marrow transplant operations since the first operation in January 1993.

2000年11月末現在のドナー登録者数は、約13万3000人。移植例は、93年1月の第1号以来3043例

Donor
骨髄提供者（ドナー）

Marrow collection
骨髄採取

There's a one in four chance that the marrow HLA (Human Leukocyte Antigen) of a brother or sister donor will match that of the recipient. It takes between 500 and 10,000 donors to find a match for a non-relative recipient.

移植の前提となるHLA（白血球の型）が一致するのは兄弟で4分の1、非血縁者では500～1万人に1人の割合

Donor registration　ドナー登録

Bone Marrow Banks

People suffering from leukemia and aplastic anemia lose the ability to create healthy blood. Such illnesses can often be effectively treated by transplanting healthy bone marrow where white and red blood cells are created. However, the type of HLA (human leukocyte antigen) differs with different people. In order for a transplant to succeed, both the donor and the recipient must have the same type of HLA. But the range of matching HLA types is very low.

In order to effectively find appropriate donors of marrow, the Marrow Bank (Japan Marrow Donor Program) registers potential donors. The Marrow Bank in Japan was established at the end of 1991.

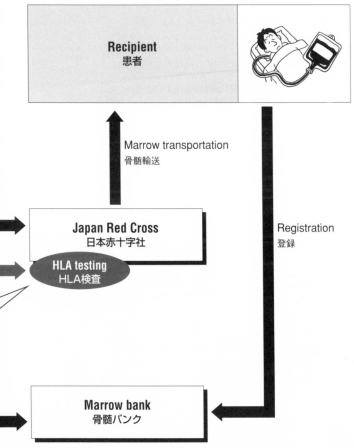

Recipient
患者

Marrow transportation
骨髄輸送

Registration
登録

Japan Red Cross
日本赤十字社

HLA testing
HLA検査

Marrow bank
骨髄バンク

予防接種のしくみ

　1994年10月、「予防接種法」などの法律改正によって、予防接種のやり方が変わった。インフルエンザの予防接種の後遺症をめぐる判決で、国側が敗訴したことが引き金になって制度の見直しが行われたものだ。子供の予防接種は従来、集団接種を原則としてきたが、1人の医師が1時間ほどで100人前後の子供に接種をしなければならないため、予診がおろそかになり、それが副作用事故につながるおそれのあることが指摘されていた。今後、予防接種は家庭の判断で行う努力義務とされた。

Children are now vaccinated individually at the discretion of the parent or guardian.

子供の予防接種は、原則として保護者の判断で選択し、個別に医師から受ける

Local government office
市町村役所（場）

Notice
お知らせ
○○市役所

Notification
通知

Payment
費用支払い

Each resident 家庭	Hospital or clinic 医院
Parents take the child to the hospital or clinic for vaccinations on a day when the child is feeling well. A pre-vaccination form is filled out before the shots are given. 親は子供の体調の良い日を選んで、内科・小児科医院へ連れて行き、予診票を提出して接種を受ける	

Vaccinations

In October 1994, various laws were revised to change the way that vaccinations in Japan are carried out. This change in the system was triggered by a suit brought against the government concerning the aftereffects of influenza vaccinations. Childhood vaccinations were typically carried out in groups, but in circumstances where one doctor would give around a hundred shots in an hour, it was almost impossible to make a pre-diagnosis, and this led to harmful aftereffects. Under the new system, parents are encouraged to have their children vaccinated.

Illness 対象疾病	
Diphtheria	ジフテリア
Whooping cough	百日ぜき
Polio	ポリオ
Measles	はしか
German measles	風疹
Japanese encephalitis	日本脳炎
Tuberculosis	結核
Tetanus	破傷風

From 1995, the government started paying for all vaccinations, except for tuberculosis, for children up to 7 1/2-years old.
95年度から、公費負担の予防接種の年齢範囲が7歳6か月まで（結核を除く）に延長された

- German measles vaccinations can only be given 12 months after birth.
- Japanese encephalitis vaccinations can only be given 6 months after birth.
・風疹は、生後12か月から
・日本脳炎ワクチンは、生後6か月から

This excludes vaccinations for cholera, smallpox, Weil's disease, and influenza (partly paid at public expense for people over 65), which were obligatory before the law was revised.
法改正前に予防接種が義務付けられていたコレラ、天然痘、ワイル病、インフルエンザ（65歳以上は一部公費負担）は除外された

医薬分業のしくみ

　医院で診療を受けると、帰りにはどっさり薬が渡されるという経験は多くの人がもっているはず。数多くの病気をかかえて通院している人は、いわゆる薬づけという状態を余儀なくされている。このような人ほど、薬物の相互作用による薬害の危険性が高いのである。それを防止する意味で、医薬分業化が厚生労働省によって推進されつつある。この言葉にみられるように、医師は診療及び処方せんを書くまでを担当し、その処方せんにもとづいて薬剤師が調剤した薬を患者に渡すというしくみである。実は、医薬分業は明治以来からの課題で、これまで実現に至らなかった。この古くて新しいテーマがこれからどう具体化してゆくかを、監視する必要があろう。

This is how medical care and medicine should be.
これが本来の医薬分業のあり方だ！

Under-the-counter medicine can only be purchased with a prescription or instructions from a doctor.
医師の処方せんか指示がなければ購入できない薬を要指示医薬品という

The Separation of Pharmacy and Clinic

Most Japanese have had the experience of going to a clinic and coming home with all kinds of medicine. Patients with multiple illnesses often become "pickled" in medicine. The more medicine a person takes, the higher chance they face of suffering from side effects. To prevent this from happening, the Ministry of Health, Labour and Welfare is promoting the division between medical care and medicine. The purpose is to have the doctor diagnose patients and write prescriptions and have a pharmacist fill the prescription. This approach has been discussed since the Meiji era, but never implemented. The country will be focusing closely on how this very old and also very new policy changes medicine in the near future.

Clinics provide medicine in anticipation of profit gained from the margin they add to costs. Doctors are legally not supposed to be involved in issuing medicine except in special cases, but many doctors abuse this loophole.

医院が薬を出すのは、利ざやとしての薬価差益が入るからだ。本来、医師は特別なケース以外は薬を調剤してはならないことになっているが、この例外規定を悪用する医師もいる

Special cases
〈例外〉

When the patient or guardian makes a special request

患者または看護者が特に希望した場合

When the diagnosis requires it

診療上必要な場合

In areas where medicine is not readily available

薬品が十分普及していない地域

新薬許可のしくみ

現在、製造されている医薬品は医療用と一般用を合わせると4万品目を超えるといわれている。さらに、毎年30品目前後の新薬が登場しているのである。人間の生命に関わることなので、医薬品については厚生労働省による厳重な監視体制がとられている。特に、新薬の承認申請にあたっては、製造者側に対して各種の試験データの提出が求められ、半年から1年半程度の審査・審議を経て認可の判断が下される。厚生労働大臣による承認許可が出た新薬は、国民皆保険体制のわが国では健康保険に適用される必要があるため、適正価格基準となる薬価基準への収載を義務づけられ、販売価格が決定する。これで初めて販売が可能になるのだが、開発費は厖大な金額になる。

Pharmaceutical manufacturers
医薬品メーカー

Basic study 基礎調査	Collection of scientific information 科学情報収集 Legal matters　法律関係
Study of effectiveness 薬効検定	Decisions concerning substance 物質決定
Primary clinical tests 前臨床試験 (Animal testing) （動物実験）	Effectiveness research　効力研究 Toxicity research　毒性研究 Preparation research　製剤研究

Clinical testing
臨床試験（治験）

(Human testing)
（人体実験）

Phase 1 フェーズⅠ	Phase 2 フェーズⅡ	Phase 3 フェーズⅢ
Testing on a small number of healthy bodies 少数の健康人に投与	Testing on a small number of patients 少数の患者を対象に投与	Testing on a large number of patients 多数の患者を対象に投与

This is called an Independent New Drug (IND).
これを治験薬（IND）という

Approval of New Medicine

Counting both medical and general items, there are said to be over 40,000 medical products on the market. And 30 new products are added every year. As this is a life- and- death matter, new medicines are under the strict supervision of the Ministry of Health, Labour and Welfare. When a new medicine is introduced, the manufacturer must submit a wide range of test documentation to the Ministry of Health, Labour and Welfare, which takes between 6 and 18 months to make a decision about approval. Medicine that receives the approval of the Minister of Health, Labour and Welfare must also be covered by the national insurance system, and so new medicines must conform to drug pricing standards for new prices to be set. After this long process, which boosts the price, the drug is finally ready for the market.

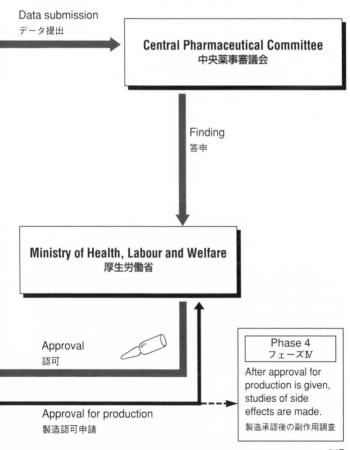

Data submission
データ提出

Central Pharmaceutical Committee
中央薬事審議会

Finding
答申

Ministry of Health, Labour and Welfare
厚生労働省

Approval
認可

Approval for production
製造認可申請

Phase 4
フェーズⅣ

After approval for production is given, studies of side effects are made.
製造承認後の副作用調査

薬価差益のしくみ

　昔から"薬九層倍"といわれてきたように、薬は儲かるのである。日本国民の1年間の医療費は約30兆円で、そのうちの約3割の9兆円を薬剤費が占めている。もっとも医療保険で使う薬には、あらかじめ差益を考慮した基準があるため、ボロもうけはできないことになっている。そこで薬の仕入価格を低くさせ、こちらで利幅を大きくする抜け道が登場する。医療機関の多くはバッタ屋よろしくせっせと薬を買いたたくことになる。差益の総額は推定1兆円ともいわれる。安く仕入れて高く売る、まさに"医は算術"だ。

Under the current insurance system, the more medicine medical institutions use, the more money they make.

医療保険は薬を多く使うほど、医療機関の収入が多くなるしくみになっている

Ministry of Health, Labour and Welfare
厚生労働省

Central Social Insurance Medical Council
中央社会保険医療協議会

Advisory body of the Minister of Health, Labour and Welfare that discusses how to set prices

厚生労働大臣の諮問機関で薬価の決め方を話し合う

Notification
告知

Medicine price standards
薬価基準

Based on a chart that gives the name and official price of medicine approved for medical coverage, the average price for medicine includes a 13 percent profit margin.

医療保険で使える薬の品目名と支払いの際の公定価格を定めた表で、薬価は取引価格に平均13%の差益を上乗せしてある

A price calculation method was introduced in 1992 to lower profit margins once every two years. The margin in 1998 was 11 percent.

薬価差益を小さくするため92年から薬価算定方式が定められ、2年ごとに差益の幅が縮小される方向だ。98年からは11%になった

Differences in Medicine Prices

From ancient times, medicine has been known as a profitable business. Japanese spend about 30 trillion yen a year on medical care, about one-third or 9 trillion yen of which is spent on medicine. The profit margin on medicines that are covered by medical insurance is regulated to keep profits from getting out of hand. But this leaves open a loophole where companies can lower their delivery prices to boost their profits. Most medical institutions do seem like black markets of medicine. The gap is estimated to be as much as one trillion yen. Buying cheap and selling high has made medicine an enormously profitable business in Japan.

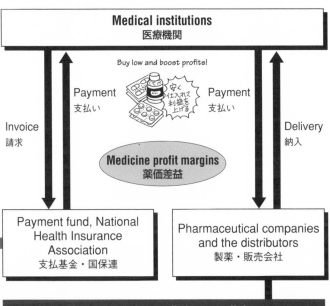

Medical institutions
医療機関

Buy low and boost profits!

安く仕入れて利益を上げる

Payment 支払い | Payment 支払い

Invoice 請求 | Delivery 納入

Medicine profit margins
薬価差益

Payment fund, National Health Insurance Association
支払基金・国保連

Pharmaceutical companies and the distributors
製薬・販売会社

How companies profit from medicine
薬で儲けるこんな手口

Hospital | Bulk transactions | New and improved

病院 | 総価山買い取引 | ゾロ新

Companies copy new medicines on the market and make similar products.

先に発売された新薬のコピーをつくって販売

Dumping transactions of bulk orders for various products

多品種、大量仕入れによるダンピング取引

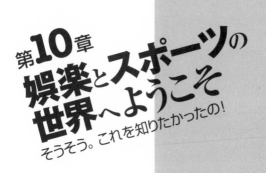

第**10**章
娯楽とスポーツの世界へようこそ
そうそう。これを知りたかったの!

Chapter 10
Sports and Entertainment
Some Facts You Never Knew

祇園のしくみ

　祇園は一種独特の世界である。特に舞妓の髪型は、日本文化の一断面を覗かせていて興味深い。髪型は、型から入ることを伝統とする日本文化のなかにあっては、ある面では一人の人間の成長過程を表すものであった。舞妓の場合でも、髪型はその娘時代の微妙な移り変わりを物語る。この明治以前からの伝統が、祇園では今なお生き続けているのである。

　古き時代の女性と同様、現代女性にとっても髪は女の命である。朝シャンに励む彼女たちにも、その血は流れているのかも知れない。

The rules of the teahouse
お茶屋遊びのしくみ

You can't just turn up at an o-chaya (teahouse) and expect to be served. You must first be introduced by a longtime customer, a first-class ryokan, or a traditional inn.

お茶屋へは、飛び込みでは入れない。なじみ客や一流旅館などの紹介が必要

Popular among women are the Kyoto shops that transform tourists into maiko. Don't be fooled by these fake maiko parading around the streets!

京都市内には、観光客向けに舞妓に変身させてくれる店がたくさんあって、女性に大人気。くれぐれも街を練り歩く舞妓姿に騙されないように！

すんません。もうご予約が入ってますんで…。

Sorry, we are fully booked.

O-kami (proprietress of the teahouse) 女将

Even though there are empty rooms, first-time customers are gently turned down.

店が空いていても、やんわりと断られる

The o-kami (proprietress) is the one who arranges for maiko and geisha to come to the teahouse.

舞妓や芸妓は、お茶屋の女将が手配してくれる

The Rules of Gion

Gion is a special world with its own particular set-up and rules. The hairstyles of maiko (apprentice geisha) are particularly interesting, and reflect an aspect of Japanese culture. In Japanese culture, which has long put special emphasis on the prerequisite of kata (form), a person's hairstyle can express the particular stage he or she is in during life. The hairstyles of a maiko tell a story about the subtle developments and changes that occur as a young girl grows to womanhood. This is a tradition dating from before the Meiji period that is alive and well in Gion.

A woman's hair has always been considered a vital part of her femininity. Perhaps this lies behind the thinking of those contemporary women and girls who assiduously carry out asa-shan, daily morning shampoos.

正式な紹介のされ方

Get a long-time patron of the o-chaya to introduce you
一度紹介してもらう

O-kami, you remember the fellow I brought along last month...

女将、この前のな・・・・・

Long-time patron
なじみ客

おいでやす

Welcome!

You need an introduction to be accepted as a regular customer.
なじみ客になるまでは、口添えが必要

花奴どす

None of the food items are prepared on the premises: they are instead specially ordered from caterers.
お茶屋では料理はつくらず仕出し屋から取り寄せる

273

祇園のしくみ……2

How a maiko becomes a geisha
舞妓から芸妓へのプロセス

Ochobo-san
お小女さん

Before a girl formally becomes a maiko, while she's still learning the basics by observation, she is called ochobo-san or oshikomi-san ("little learner").

お仕込さんともいい舞妓になる前の見習い期間

Debut
初出し

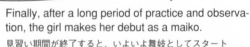

Finally, after a long period of practice and observation, the girl makes her debut as a maiko.

見習い期間が終了すると、いよいよ舞妓としてスタート

> The amount of time she spends as a maiko does not last all that long. You can tell what stage a maiko is in her apprenticeship by the style in which she wears her hair.
>
> 舞妓としての期間はさほど長くはない。舞妓のキャリアは、髪型の変化でわかる

Warishinobu
割りしのぶ

Warishinobu, "divided chignon," worn for about year after her debut

初出しから1年目くらい

Girls who have decided that they want to become maiko take up residence in an o-chaya from middle-school age. After graduating from middle-school, they enter the special school to learn traditional performing arts, where they pursue training in dancing the Dances of the Old Capital and playing the shamisen.

舞妓をめざす少女は中学生の頃から、お茶屋に住み込む。中学を卒業後は八坂女紅場学園（やさかにょこうばがくえん）に入って、京舞や三味線などの修業を積む

The Rules of Gion……2

Turns her collar
襟替え

I guess this means I'm finally qualified!

これで一人前になれるのね！

Once a maiko has finished her apprenticeship, she can become a full-fledged geisha. Instead of styling her own hair, she will now wear an ornamental wig. Her obi (sash), which previously would have been tied to hang down voluminously in front, will be tied in a much neater knot (called a taiko, or "drum") at the back. Her collar, previously red, will now be white.

舞妓の時代を終え芸妓になること。自前の髪はかつらになり、だらりの帯はお太鼓に、赤い襟が白い襟に変わる

Sakkō
さっこう髪

Sakkō-gami, worn for a few days before the maiko "turns her collar"

襟替えの数日前から

Yakko
奴

Yakko, worn from about one month before the maiko "turns her collar"

襟替えの1か月前から

O-fuku
おふく

O-fuku, the usual hairstyle for a maiko who is well on her way in her apprenticeship

キャリアを積んだ舞妓の一般的髪型

宝塚歌劇団のしくみ

　宝塚歌劇団は不思議な存在である。そもそも、今の時代に"清く正しく美しく"というモットーを掲げ、良妻賢母の養成が目的と言ってはばからないのが、何とも凄い。

　団員は生徒と呼ばれ、入団年次や試験の席次によって名簿順位が決められる。この順位は全生徒が対象で、退団後も効力をもち、宝塚出身者が集まる会合では座る順番にも影響を及ぼす。現役の団員は約400人前後で、その1割ほどが毎年入退団する。トップスターは入団6～10年の生徒がなるケースが多い。"生徒"の定年は57歳だ。

Entrance test
入学試験

Prospective applicants include middle-school graduates, high-school students, and high-school graduates. A person may try up to 4 times to pass the entrance exams. On average, around 40 people join every year. Since there are 20 to 30 times the number of applicants for openings, entry is difficult indeed.

受験資格者は中卒、高1、高2、高卒者で、1人4回まで受験できる。例年40人ほどが入学を許可され、競争率20～30倍の超難関だ

Takarazuka Music School (2-years)
宝塚音楽学校（2年制）

Preparatory courses—1 year
予科　1年間

Regular courses—-1 year
本科　1年間

At this stage, a member receives a professional stage name. She is also permitted to wear make-up.

芸名が決まり、化粧が許される

Graduation　卒業

The successful graduate enters the Takarazuka All Women's Opera Company. Her formal title will now be Takarazuka Research Center Female Artistic Apprentice.

宝塚歌劇団に入団をする。研究科所属の女子技芸員という身分が正式な呼称である

The Takarazuka All Women's Opera Company

The Takarazuka All Women's Opera Company is a truly bizarre entity. What on earth, one may wonder, is an organization that openly declares its motto to be "Purity, Sincerity and Beauty," and its mission to be the fostering of "Good Wives and Wise Mothers" (a slogan dating from the Meiji period, 1868–1912) doing in the modern world?

All the performers in the company punctiliously refer to themselves as "students," and their lives are ordered by hierarchy: their names are all entered onto a class list and ranked according to year of entry and place in the exams. This hierarchy has an influence even after retirement, making itself felt, for example, in the seating arrangements in gatherings of Takarazuka alumnae. There are at present about 400 members in the company, and 40 new members enter annually. Top stars usually spend from 6 to 10 years as junior students. The age of retirement for these students is 57.

Groups 組

Once she enters the company, she will belong to 1 of 5 classes (gumi), known as the "Flower Class," the "Moon Class," the "Snow Class," the "Star Class," and the "Sky Class." Each class has a head and a vice-head, and these positions are acceded to members according to strict seniority. There are more or less 70 members in each class.

入団後の団員は花組、月組、雪組、星組、宙（そら）組の5つの組のいずれかに所属する。組には組長、副組長が1人ずついて、入団年次の古い団員が任命される。1組の生徒数は70人前後

Performances 公演

Takarazuka Theater

The Takarazuka Opera Company has two permanent theaters: one is the Takarazuka Grand Theater (in Takarazuka City, Hyogo Prefecture; 8 runs of roughly 45 days) and the other is Tokyo Takarazuka Theater (a new theater, opened in Hibiya in January 2001). But aside from the shows here, the group also goes on tour to various regions throughout the country and the world, with each of the classes taking turns putting on productions.

常設の舞台は宝塚大劇場（兵庫県宝塚市・年8回各45日前後の公演）と、東京宝塚劇場（2001年1月から東京日比谷に新劇場オープン）の2か所。その他に地方公演や海外公演を、組単位のローテーションでこなしている

> **How a student becomes a star.**
> スターへのプロセス

1 Debut
デビュー

New students make their appearance in the special chorus line at the Takarazuka Theater in April. Names are listed in the program in the order of graduation results.

4月の宝塚大劇場公演に出演し、ラインダンスを披露する。卒業成績順にプログラムに名前が載る

2 Level tests
実技試験

Tests are held at the end of the 1st, 3rd and 5th year to determine class-ranking.

入団後1年目、3年目、5年目に行われ、試験のたびに席次が変わる

3 Reshuffles
組替え

Annual promotions and re-arrangements necessitate changes in the composition of the classes, inevitable every time a Takarazuka star retires. Such changes are opportunities for rising stars to come to prominence.

スターの退団に伴う補強や人材登用のために、各組間での人事異動を原則として年1回行う。昇進のチャンスでもある

The Takarazuka All Women's Opera Company⋯⋯2

Players of male roles are accorded the higher status in the Takarazuka All Women's Opera Company. Though quite a few stars have switched from male to female roles switching in the opposite direction is rare.

宝塚歌劇団は、男役上位の世界である。これまで男役から娘役に転向した例は多いが、その逆のケースはほとんどない

4

Making it to the top
トップ昇進

トップ男役　　トップ女役

In every class, there's a designated top player of male roles, and a top player of women roles. The women who get to hold these positions have reached the highest pinnacle of success for a Takarazuka star.

各組にはそれぞれトップ男役、トップ娘役がいる。文字通り宝塚スターの頂点である

Fan Clubs
後援会

"We only serve fans of the stars!"

契茶メルサイユ

ここはトップスターのファンクラブしか入れないのよ！

Women who have been in the Takarazuka for more than two years are permitted the pleasure of setting up their own personal unofficial fan clubs known as "kai." These clubs are actually an important source of moral and material support to the would-be stars, and play a vital role as they climb the ladder to success.

入団3年目以上の団員には、歌劇団は未公認だが"会"と呼ばれる私設後援会をつくってもらえる楽しみがある。物心両面にわたる後援会のバックアップもまた、スター街道を駆け上がるための条件だ

歌舞伎界のしくみ

　歌舞伎役者は原則的に世襲制である。原則的に、というのは役者の家に生まれなくとも、その道に入ることはできるからだ。23歳未満で役者を志す人は、国立劇場の歌舞伎俳優研修生試験のコースがある。合格すると2年間の基礎課程を経て、修了後は現役の役者のところに入門し、大部屋生活からスタートする。だが、研修生出身者の出世は望めず、親の七光り組がチャンスに恵まれるというのが梨園の伝統でもある。

　その伝統を打破して新しい歌舞伎の世界を創ろうと意欲を燃やしているのが、市川猿之助。猿之助のもとでは、研修生出身者が大きな役を与えられるチャンスが多いだけに、新たな潮流が歌舞伎界のしくみを変える可能性も高い。

How kabuki actors succeed to their names
主な襲名のプロセス

Ichikawa Danjūro
市川団十郎

The Ichikawa family is the most important family of the kabuki world. The present Ichikawa Danjūro is Ichikawa Danjūro XII. His acting house name is Narita-ya.

歌舞伎界の宗家。現在は
第12代。屋号は成田屋

- Shinnosuke 新之助
- Ebi-zō 海老蔵
- **Danjūro** 団十郎

Nakamura Utaemon
中村歌右衛門

The present Nakamura Utaemon is Nakamura Utaemon VI. His acting house name is Narikoma-ya.

現在は第6代。屋号は成駒屋

- Kotarō 児太郎
- Fukusuke 福助
- Shikan 芝翫
- **Utaemon** 歌右衛門

The Kabuki World

One becomes a kabuki actor generally only through hereditary succession. We say generally because even if one is not born into a kabuki family, it is still possible to take up training to become a kabuki actor. There is a special course of Kabuki Actor Training and Apprenticeship available at the National Theater for people under 23 years of age who decide that this is the career for them. If they are accepted, they study the basics for two years, and upon completion become the disciple of a professional kabuki actor, and make their start as actors who play less important roles (and all share one, large, communal dressing room). However, such actors can☐t hope to become great kabuki stars, for it is still very much the tradition of this world of the theater for only a very select few, the offspring of the most illustrious families, to be given opportunities.

The only actor who has broken with such traditions in his passionate enthusiasm to fashion a kabuki that has contemporary appeal is Ichikawa Ennosuke. Apprentices who study under this actor are given many more opportunities than they would have otherwise to play major roles in plays, and for this alone the kabuki world is bound gradually to be affected and changed by new currents and trends.

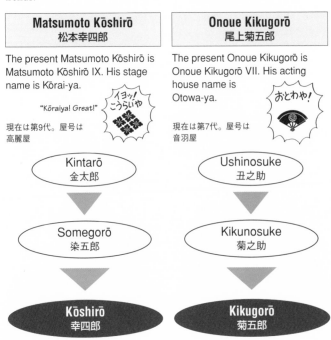

Matsumoto Kōshirō 松本幸四郎	**Onoue Kikugorō** 尾上菊五郎
The present Matsumoto Kōshirō is Matsumoto Kōshirō IX. His stage name is Kōrai-ya.	The present Onoue Kikugorō is Onoue Kikugorō VII. His acting house name is Otowa-ya.
"Kōraiya! Great!" イヨッ！こうらいや	おとわや！
現在は第9代。屋号は 高麗屋	現在は第7代。屋号は 音羽屋
Kintarō 金太郎	Ushinosuke 丑之助
Somegorō 染五郎	Kikunosuke 菊之助
Kōshirō 幸四郎	**Kikugorō** 菊五郎

娯楽とスポーツの世界へようこそ

Tricks of the kabuki stage
歌舞伎舞台のしくみ

Sometimes the stage has a round section that revolves, powered by electricity. The diameter of this section is 18 meters.

Black curtain (the musicians who provide accompaniment sit behind this.)
黒御簾（くろみす）

The large and small seri in the floor are contraptions (lifts, really) that allow objects and people to appear on stage—in the case of the large seri, stage props such as buildings, and in the case of the small seri, people. The suppon (literally, "snapping turtle") in the hanamichi (raised dais coming through the audience on which actors may make exits or entries) is a trapdoor that allows ghosts and the like to suddenly loom up onto the hanamichi, seemingly out of nowhere.

Kumadori
くまどり

goody
善人

villain
悪人

Suppon (trapdoor)
すっぽん

Hanamichi
花道

Audience seats
客席

Curtain (through which actors make their entry and exit)
揚幕

The Kabuki World······2

Revolving stage
廻り舞台

Large seri (lift)
大ぜり

Floor-plan of stage
舞台平面図

Small seri
小ぜり

円の部分が廻り舞台で、電動で回転する。直径は約18m

舞台の大ぜりは建物など、小ぜりは人物、花道のすっぽんは妖怪などがせり上がって登場するしかけだ

おとわゃ
!!

こうらいや
!!

Audience seats
客席

落語界のしくみ

落語界の系譜は江戸時代にさかのぼることができるが、江戸落語と寄席の開祖は天保年間に活躍した初代三笑亭可楽である。三笑亭の流れをくむ亭号が、柳亭・柳家・春風亭などで"柳派"と称されている。一方、柳派に並ぶ門閥として"三遊派"がある。これには、三遊亭・橘家・林家・古今亭・桂などの各亭号が連なっている。現在の柳派の看板は、人間国宝の五代目柳家小さんであるが、三遊派の家元名ともいえる三遊亭円生は七代目の襲名者なしという状態。大阪には、上方落語協会がある。

Rakugo Organizations 落語団体
Tokyo　東京
Rakugo Association 落語協会
Rakugo Arts Association 落語芸術協会
Enraku School 円楽党
Tatekawa Rakugo School 立川流落語会
Osaka　大阪
Kamigata (Kyoto-Osaka region) **Rakugo Association** 上方落語協会

There are 4 rakugo organizations in Tokyo: the largest is the Rakugo Kyōkai, with about 200 members. Sanyūtei Enraku and Tatekawa Danshi broke away from this organization to form their own groups, the Enraku Tō and the Tatekawa-ryū Rakugo Kai.

東京には4つの落語団体があるが、最大のものは落語協会（約200名）。ここから三遊亭円楽と立川談志が脱会して独立し、円楽党と立川流落語会をつくった

The World of Rakugo (Traditional Comic Monologues)

The roots of rakugo, an art in which a professional raconteur entertains an audience with a story, often a humorous one, go back as far as the Edo period (1600–1868). The originator of Edo rakugo and the related art of yose was Sanshōtei Karaku I, who was active during the years of the Tempo period (1830–1844). Famous names handed down from artist to artist in this group, called the Yanagi school, are Ryūtei, Yanagi-ya, and Shunpūtei. The other main lineage of comparable stature is the Sanyū school, to which belong such names as Sanyūtei, Tachibana-ya, Hayashi-ya as well as Kokontei, and Katsura. At present Yanagi Kosan V, who has been officially listed as a Living National Treasure, is the most prominent performer in the Yanagi school. Sanyūtei Enshō VII, the equivalent of the head of the Sanyū school, is at present without a successor to his name. There is the Kamigata Rakugo Association in Osaka.

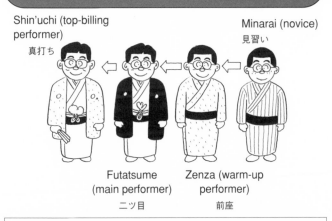

Grades of rakugo performers
(Note the important differences in clothing)
落語家の階級

Shin'uchi (top-billing performer)
真打ち

Minarai (novice)
見習い

Futatsume (main performer)
二ツ目

Zenza (warm-up performer)
前座

It takes about 5 or 6 years after becoming a novice in rakugo to become a futatsume. One perfects one's art as a futatsume for 10 years, and may then become a top performer. Such is the case, at least, in the Tokyo region.

入門（見習い）から5、6年目で二ツ目。二ツ目修業10年で真打ち昇進が一般的ケース（関東のみ）

落語界のしくみ……2

How things work backstage
楽屋のしくみ

Gakuya-chō
楽屋帳

The first thing every rakugo artist will do on arriving backstage is to check the gakuya-chō, the list of stories other rakugo artists have recounted that day, to decide which stories he is going to tell during his performance. It is essential that the rakugo artist avoid telling any story that another person may have told.

楽屋入りするとまず楽屋帳（ネタ帳）を見て、その日の演題を決める。前の人と同種の演題は話せないきまりになっている

For performers of the futatsume rank and upwards, the order of appearance is fixed.

二ツ目以上になると、それぞれの演目が決まっている

Debayashi
出ばやし

Before each rakugo artist goes out on stage, performers will play a short musical piece, which differs according to each artist.

The drum is played by a zenza.
太鼓は前座がたたく

Takings are split 50–50 between the owner of the hall in which the performance is held and the performers. Each performance runs for 10 days, and payments are made on a daily rate every 2 days. The income a rakugo performer earns often amounts to little more than a pittance.

入場料は寄席と出演者で折半する。10日間興行で、2日目ごとに日割り計算で支払われるが、収入としてはさほど多くない

Wari ("takings")
わり（給金）

Props used in the performance
高座の小道具

The rakugo artist uses these to mime objects
such as a purse, a letter, or a tobacco pouch.
財布・手紙・煙草入れなどにみたてる

Tenugui handcloth
まんだら（手拭い）

Fan　かぜ（扇子）

The rakugo artist uses this to mime or evoke
items such as a writing brush, or chopsticks
in the course of his monologue.
箸・筆などにみたてる

Haori coat (worn by futatsume and above)
だるま（羽織）

After his introductory remarks, when he enters his story proper, the rakugo artist will take off his coat and toss it behind him. At a certain point, a
zenza will come on and remove the coat to let him know that the person
due to follow him is ready and waiting. The rakugo artist on stage will then
bring his monologue to a suitable end.

噺し家が途中で羽織を後に投げるのは、次の人の出の準備を確認するためで、羽織が引か
れると準備OKの合図だ

Props used on stage by rakugo artists vary
according to whether the rakugo is from the
Tokyo region or Osaka-Kyoto region. In the
Tokyo region the artist will simply sit on a
cushion on stage, whereas in the Kyoto-
Osaka region he will sit behind a small desk
with a low screen in front of it to hide his lap.

screen　desk

Implements used to punctuate the course of the talk are a
leather-wrapped folding fan and wooden blocks, which are occasionally rapped on the desk.

上方落語の高座は関東とは異なり噺し家の前に見台・膝かくしが置かれる。
小道具としては張り扇や小拍子木が使われる

将棋界のしくみ

　一般的になじみが薄いが、11月17日は「将棋の日」。これは、江戸時代に八代将軍徳川吉宗がこの日、江戸城内に棋士を集めて対局させた故事に由来する。将棋界最高のタイトルは「名人」で、これも江戸時代以来の伝統的な終身制の名称であるが、現在は実力名人制に移行している。名人位を5期以上保持した棋士には「永世名人」が与えられる。

　1996年には、当時25歳の羽生善治名人が王将位を獲得して、史上初の七冠（00頁のタイトル）を達成した。プロ棋士の世界では、20代の若手の台頭がめざましい。

Promotion of professional Shogi players
棋士の昇段のしくみ

"I'm going for the pros!"

目指すはプロ!

Amateur Master

People who want professional status must pass a test given by the Promotional Association.

プロを目指す人は、奨励会の試験に合格しなければならない

Japan Shogi Association
日本将棋連盟

Main amateur title competitions
主なアマチュアタイトル戦

Amateur Masters　アマチュア名人戦

Amateur Championship　アマチュア王座戦

Amateur Women's Masters　アマ女流名人戦

University League　大学リーグ戦

High School Players　高校選手権

Junior High School Masters　中学生名人戦

Elementary School masters　小学生名人戦

Others include the Occupational Association Competition and the Kansai Labor Organization Competition.

その他、職域団体対抗戦、関西勤労者団体戦などがある

Shogi

November 17 is commonly known as "Shogi Day." This originated in the Edo period when the eighth Tokugawa Shogun, Yoshimune, assembled all of the Shogi players in Edo Castle on this day and held a big gaming event. The highest title in Shogi is "Meijin" (Master), which has traditionally been granted for life since the Edo period, but this is currently changing to a merit system. Shogi players who hold the title of Meijin for five or more periods are granted the title of "Eisei Meijin" (Permanent Master).

In 1996, 25-year-old Master Yoshiharu Habu gathered Osho titles, and attained the first Seven Crowns title in history (see titles on P. 291). It was truly remarkable for such a young man to rise so fast in the world of professional Shogi.

Promotional association
奨励会

This is the organization that fosters professional shogi players. All classes and levels of players are members, but this gateway to professional success is governed by a strict seniority system.

プロ棋士の養成機関で、六級から三段までが奨励会員とされる。ただし、厳しい年齢制限があるプロへの登竜門だ

First-dan level
初段

As a general rule, players start here when they are 22 years old. Players who haven't reached the fourth-dan level by the time they are 25 drop out.

22歳で初段、原則として25歳で四段にならないと脱落だ

Second level
二段

Third level
三段

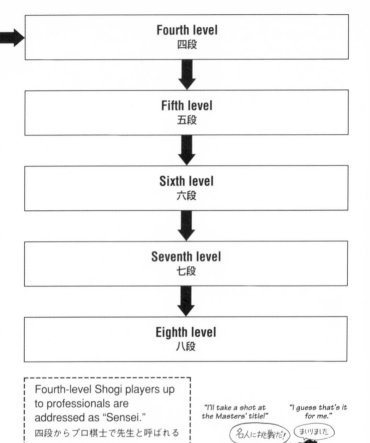

Fourth level 四段

↓

Fifth level 五段

↓

Sixth level 六段

↓

Seventh level 七段

↓

Eighth level 八段

Fourth-level Shogi players up to professionals are addressed as "Sensei."
四段からプロ棋士で先生と呼ばれる

"I'll take a shot at the Masters' title!"

"I guess that's it for me."

名人にお挑戦だ！

まいりました

Players must either have 250 wins in official competitions or meet any of the following conditions to reach the ninth and highest level in Shogi: 1. Hold the title of Mejin for one period. 2. Hold the title of "Ryuo" for two periods. 3. Hold another title for three periods.

最高位の九段になるには（1）名人1期（2）竜王2期（3）他のタイトル3期のいずれかを取るか、公式戦で250勝することが条件

Players move up or down in class based on the results of league competitions.

プロ棋士は、クラスごとにリーグ戦を行い、その成績でクラスが昇降する

Ranking match 順位戦	
C Class, second team	C級2組
C Class, first team	C級1組
B Class, second team	B級2組
B Class, first team	B級1組
A Class	A級

Grand titles and sponsors of title matches ビッグタイトルとタイトル戦主催者	
Meijin 名人	Mainichi Newspapers Co., Ltd. 毎日新聞社
Ryuō 竜王	Yumiuri Newspapers Co., Ltd. 読売新聞社
Kisei 棋聖	Sankei Newspapers Co., Ltd. サンケイ新聞社
Ōi 王位	Sansha Rengo Bureau 三社連合事務局
Ōza 王座	Nihon Keizai Newspaper Co., Ltd. 日本経済新聞社
Kiō 棋王	Kyodo News Service 共同通信社
Ōshō 王将	Sports Nippon, Mainichi Newspapers Co., Ltd. スポーツニッポン・毎日新聞社

囲碁界のしくみ

　囲碁の入段試験は、東大入試並みの難関といわれる。日本棋院の院生と一般応募者が、総当たりのリーグ戦を行い、例年60人前後の受験者から3人ほどが晴れて入段（初段）できる。初段になるとプロ棋士の資格が得られ、八段までは昇格試験によって昇段してゆく。プロ棋士は、日本棋院（本部・東京）所属棋士と日本棋院から分離独立した関西棋院所属の棋士がいる。7大タイトルを制覇したのは趙治勲棋士ただ1人。最高位は「棋聖」で、「名人」と「本因坊」は江戸時代から続く位である。

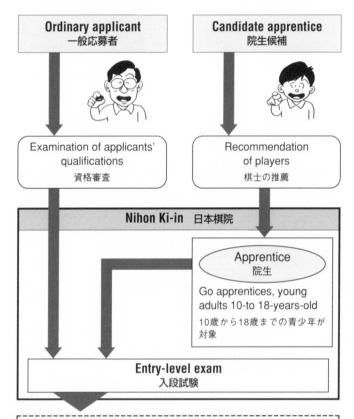

Ordinary applicant
一般応募者

Candidate apprentice
院生候補

Examination of applicants' qualifications
資格審査

Recommendation of players
棋士の推薦

Nihon Ki-in 日本棋院

Apprentice
院生

Go apprentices, young adults 10-to 18-years-old
10歳から18歳までの青少年が対象

Entry-level exam
入段試験

Players who pass the entry-level examination enter the first level and have professional status.

入段試験に合格すると初段になり、プロ棋士の資格を持つことになる。初段から八段までは、昇格試験がある

Go

The entry-level test for Go is said to be as challenging as the Tokyo University entrance examination. Apprentice Go professionals of the Nihon Ki-in and everyday applicants participate in round-robin league competitions. In a typical year, two or three players out of approximately 60 examinees are elevated to the entry level (first level). Players elevated to the entry level have pro status, and rise through the levels to the eighth level through tests for advancement. Professional players belong to either the Nihon Ki-in (headquartered in Tokyo), or the separate and independent Kansai Go Institution. Chō Chihun is the only player to have won the seven grand titles. The highest title is "Kisei," while "Honinbo" and "Meijin" are titles passed down from the Edo period.

Rules of the game
対局のしくみ

In Go, black has the advantage of moving first, so a handicap for black is accepted practice. A handicap is called a "komi," and when the game is between two players of equal skill the "komi" for black is five and a half "me." Also, if the two players are not of equal skill, another way to level the playing field is to allow the player of lesser skill to pre-place two to nine pieces on the board before the game begins.

"Thank you."　"Here, have a handicap."

いただきます　ハンデをあげましょう

Beginner

囲碁は先番（黒）が有利なため、対局のときには黒にハンデをつけるのが慣例になっている。これを「コミ」というが、両者の実力が対等な場合は五目半の「コミ」を採用する。また、上級者が下級者と対局するときは、二子～九子をハンデとして先に置かせるのが通例になっている

There are also plenty of international professional competitions, including the World Go Players' Competition and the Japan China Super Go (Team Knockout Tournament). In May 1997, the Nihon Ki-in, together with the Japan Pair Go Association, announced efforts to make Go an official Olympic event for 2008.

プロの国際棋戦も盛んで、世界囲碁選手権戦や日中スーパー囲碁（団体勝ち抜き戦）などがある。97年5月には日本棋院が日本ペア囲碁協会と共に、囲碁をオリンピックの正式競技にする運動を発表し、2008年の実現をめざしている

囲碁界のしくみ……2

Seven grand title competitions
7大タイトル戦

Meijin
名人戦

Hon-in-bō
本因坊戦

Small league competition
少人数のリーグ戦

Kisei
棋聖戦

Small tournaments
少人数のトーナメント戦

Ōza
王座戦

Tengen (Center Point)
天元戦

All-player tournaments
全棋士によるトーナメント戦

Tenth level
十段戦

Gosei
碁聖戦

Tournaments for the fifth level and above
五段以上のトーナメント戦

Meijin is basically the ninth level. It is used to designate players with the highest level of achievement, but now the title can be taken regardless of level.

名人位は本来は九段のことで、棋士の最高の地位と実力を示すものだったが、現在は段位に関係なく名人位がとれる

Main International Go Competitions
主な国際棋戦

Professional
プロ

The World Go Players' Competition, Fujitsu Cup
世界囲碁選手権戦・富士通杯

Ing Cup/World Professional Go Players' Competition
応昌期氏杯・世界プロ囲碁選手権戦

Japan China Center Point Competition
日中天元戦

Japan China Meijin Competition
日中名人戦

Japan China Super Go
日中スーパー囲碁

Japan China Television Play offs
日中テレビ決戦

Amateur
アマ

World Amateur Players' Competition
世界アマ選手権戦

プロ野球界のしくみ

　わが国のプロ野球は1936年に1リーグ制でスタートしたが、50年から2リーグ制となり、今日に至っている。現在、このリーグ制の見直しをはじめ、選手枠の拡大や処遇などの面での改革論議が巻き起こっている。だが、これらはプロ野球界の憲法ともいうべき「野球協約」の改正に通ずる問題であり、プロ野球実行委員会が議決するところである。同委員会の議決には、4分の3以上の賛成が必要とされているが、リーグ間や球団間さらには承認権を持つオーナー会議の利害が入り乱れて、議案採決に至らない場合が多い。

Organization of Professional Japanese Baseball
日本プロフェッショナル野球機構

Commissioner コミッショナー	Professional Baseball Executive Committee プロ野球実行委員会
	Comprised of 14 members: 12 team representatives and 2 league chairmen. This is the administrative organ for all professional baseball.
Appoints 選任	両リーグ会長・12球団代表の14名で構成。プロ野球界全体の運営機関
The highest authority in professional baseball. His decisions are final. プロ野球界の最高権威者で、決定には従わなければならない	
Bureau of the Commissioner コミッショナー事務局	Approval 承認
	Owners Association オーナー会議
	Owners of the 12 teams. 12球団のオーナー

Professional Baseball

Professional baseball in Japan began with a one-league system in 1936, and in 1950 it adopted a two-league system that has lasted until today. Recent re-thinking of the leagues has triggered discussion on broadening limitations on player compensation. However, doing so would mean amending the baseball charter, or the "Professional Baseball Agreement." Passing such a resolution would require a three-quarters majority in the Professional Baseball Executive Committee, and the approval of the Owners Association, which also has an interest in inter-league and inter-team decisions. As a result, such proposals do not often reach a vote.

Central Baseball League (se riigu)
セントラル野球連盟（セ・リーグ）

6 teams
6球団

Pacific Baseball League (pa riigu)
パシフィック野球連盟（パ・リーグ）

6 teams
6球団

Professional Baseball Players' Union
プロ野球選手会労組

Authorized in 1985, the union has the right to bargain collectively and to strike.

1985年認可の労働組合。団体交渉権・スト権を持つ

Team
球団

Eligible players
支配下選手

A team has up to 70 players who may take the field of play in games involving first or second teams.

1軍・2軍の試合に出場できる選手で、1球団70人以内

Active list
現役選手登録

Players who take to the field in an official game must be registered beforehand. There is a 28-player limit per team. Up to four foreign nationals may register (two pitchers and two fielders). The first and second teams may be changed up to once a month.

公式戦に出場できる選手を登録しておく。定員は28人で、1軍登録ともいう。登録できる外国人選手は4人以内（投手、野手各2人以内）で、1か月に1度、1・2軍の入れ替えができる

Leaving a team
退団

There are two ways to leave a team: voluntary retirement and free agency. When a player leaves a team voluntarily then subsequently wants to re-enter professional baseball, he must sign a new contract with the team to which he had originally belonged since the team has the right to retain a player even after retirement.

選手の退団には、任意引退と自由契約の2種類がある。任意引退は退団後も球団に選手の保留権が残るため、球界へ復帰する場合は前の所属球団と新たな選手契約を結ぶ必要がある

Removal from the active list
現役登録抹消

Player registration may be changed several times during a season, but a player removed from the active list may not play in a game for 11 days.

選手の登録変更は1シーズン中に何度でもできるが、1度登録を抹消された選手が試合に出られるのは11日目から

On the roster
ベンチ入り

Twenty-five of the registered players on the bench may take to the field in a game. The manager must submit a list of their names to the umpire for each game.

登録選手の中からベンチ入りして試合に出られる選手は25人。試合のたびに監督がその名簿を審判に提出する

FA制度のしくみ

1993年から導入されたプロ野球のFA（フリーエージェント）制度は、超一流選手の年俸高騰をもたらした。FA宣言をさせないために所属球団は年俸を上げ、獲得したい他球団はそれを上回る年俸を提示したからだ。だが、95年のシーズンに入るとFA選手は軒並み大不振に見舞われ、年俸の大幅ダウンや解雇通知を受ける者も出て情勢は一変した。資格を得るまでの期間が長すぎて選手が峠を越してしまうのが原因とか。このままでは、せっかくのFA制度も"無用の長物"になりかねない。

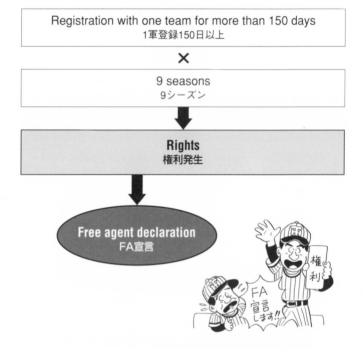

Registration with one team for more than 150 days
1軍登録150日以上

✕

9 seasons
9シーズン

Rights
権利発生

Free agent declaration
FA宣言

In 1996, Kazuhiro Kiyohara of the Seibu Lions declared himself a free agent, and both the Giants and Hanshin Tigers showed interest. After negotiations, Kiyohara decided to go with the Giants. This fulfilled his 11-year dream of joining the Giants after being passed up in the draft.

96年秋、西武の清原和博選手がFA宣言をし、巨人と阪神が獲得の意思を表明。交渉の結果、巨人移籍が決定した。清原選手は、ドラフト会議で断念した巨人入りの夢を11年後にかなえた

The Free Agent System

The free-agent system was introduced to Japanese pro baseball in 1993, resulting in skyrocketing salaries for the best players. To keep players from becoming free agents, clubs paid their players more, while other teams enticed the free agents with higher offers. However, the situation changed with the 1995 season when the offers to free agents declined sharply and many found themselves out of work. The reason was that by the time players had been around long enough to become free agents, they were past their peak. The current system is likely to give free agents a reputation as "white elephants."

By declaring free agency, players are exercising their right to move to a different baseball team.

FA宣言をすることで、他球団へ移籍する権利を行使したことになる

Team negotiations
球団との交渉

Affiliated team
所属球団

When free agents remain on the same team, they are entitled to once again receive a contract fee for renewal.

所属球団にとどまった場合、選手は再契約金を手にすることができる

Other teams
他球団

One team can only contract up to two FA players.

FA宣言をした選手を獲得できるのは1チーム2人まで

When no team accepts the free agent, the player is forced to retire.
どの球団も相手にしてくれない場合は、
選手廃業を覚悟しなければならない

Free agent rights can be carried over for one year. If rights are used, they can be exercised again after three years.

FAの権利は翌年にもち越せる。また、権利を行使しても、3年後には再び権利が生じる

ドラフト制度のしくみ

　抽選によってプロ野球選手の入団交渉権を決定するドラフト制度がスタートをしたのが1965年。93年には、この制度の見直しが行われ、高校生を除く大学・社会人選手への事前交渉、有力選手による球団の逆指名が可能になった。さらに、契約金が最高1億6000万円（入団時に支払う第1次契約金の上限は1億円）にアップされ、プロ野球界の"金力主義"が危惧されている。

　指名選手の資格は従来と変わらず、学生の場合はドラフト会議の翌年3月卒業見込者、社会人の場合は大卒者が入社後2年目、高卒者が同3年目のシーズン終了後に指名（1球団8人まで）を受けられることになっている。

Pre-negotiations between college students and company players are no longer forbidden. Players can choose teams they would like to join.

大学・社会人選手と球団との事前交渉が解禁、意中の球団の逆指名も可能に

Professional teams
プロ球団

Before the draft conference, teams submit a list of players, 24 at the most, that they wish to recruit.
ドラフト会議前に「獲得希望選手リスト」（最大24人）を提出する

Reverse selection
逆指名

Commissioner's office
コミッショナー事務局

Verification of choice
意思確認

High school students are not allowed to participate in pre-negotiations, reverse selection, and verification of choice by the commissioners.

高校生については、球団との事前交渉、逆指名、コミッショナー事務局による意思確認の対象外とされる

The Draft System

The current draft system by which teams gain authority to negotiate with players was established in 1965. In 1993, the system was reviewed and changes were made to allow promising college and other players, high school students excluded, to hold pre-negotiations and choose the team they want to join. Later, the maximum was raised on contracts to 160 million yen (100 million for first-time contracts when joining a team), raising the fear of money politics in baseball.

Clubs can draft up to eight players a year, those eligible being (1) college students who plan to graduate in March of the year following the draft conference, (2) company employees who have worked for two years after graduating from college, and (3) high school graduates three years after graduation.

Draft conference process
ドラフト会議の進行

Rights to negotiate with players receive first-and second-level negotiations
交渉権決定1位・2位選手

Each team simultaneously makes their number 1 and 2 picks.
各球団が、それぞれの1位・2位の選手を同時指名する

When only one team chooses a player, the team's choice is final.
選手が希望しない球団でも単独指名の場合は決定

When multiple teams choose a player, the player goes to the team that made the player their number 1 choice.
指名球団が重複した場合は1位指名球団が優先

When multiple teams make a player their number 1 or number 2 pick, the player's destination is decided by lottery.
同順位で指名した場合は抽選によって決定する

Repeated until all teams have made their choices.
全球団が決定するまで繰り返す

Third-level nominations　3位以下

Lowest-ranking teams have choice of players with an odd number of nominations (no lottery).
奇数指名回は、最下位球団から決める（抽選なし）

Highest-ranking teams have choice of players with an even number of nominations (no lottery).
偶数指名回は、上位球団から決める（抽選なし）

Jリーグのしくみ

1993年にスタートしたJリーグは、日本中にサッカー・ブームを巻き起こした。海外の有名選手の加入によって、レベルは急激にアップ、ついに初のワールドカップ出場（フランス）を果たした。ワールドカップは4年に1度、オリンピックの中間年に開催され、参加選手はプロ、アマを問わない。予選は世界各地で2年がかりで行われ、32か国の代表チームが本大会に出場できる栄誉に輝く。日本は韓国と共にアメリカ大陸とヨーロッパ大陸以外で初めて2002年大会の開催国になった。

Japanese Professional Soccer League, Incorporated Association
社団法人　日本プロサッカーリーグ

J1 (16 Teams) (January 2001)
J1（16チーム）（2001年1月現在）

Jubilo Iwata	ジュビロ磐田
Nagoya Grampus Eight	名古屋グランパスエイト
FC Tokyo	FC東京
Gamba Osaka	ガンバ大阪
Cerezo Osaka	セレッソ大阪
Vissel Kobe	ヴィッセル神戸
Sanfrecce Hiroshima	サンフレッチェ広島
Avispa Fukuoka	アビスパ福岡
Kashima Antlers	鹿島アントラーズ
JEF United Ichihara	ジェフユナイテッド市原
Kashiwa Reysol	柏レイソル
Urawa Red Diamonds	浦和レッドダイヤモンズ
Tokyo Verdy 1969	東京ヴェルディ1969
Yokohama F. Marinos	横浜F・マリノス
Consadole Sapporo	コンサドーレ札幌
Shimizu S Pulse	清水エスパルス

The J. League

The J. League was started in 1993 and triggered a soccer boom throughout Japan. The participation of famous players from overseas drastically raised the level of Japanese soccer, and Japan finally appeared in the World Cup (in France) for the first time. The World Cup is held every four years between the Olympics, and participating players can have either professional or amateur status. After the preliminaries, which are held all over the world and last two years, teams representing 32 countries are granted the honor of appearing in the actual competition. Japan and Korea are hosting the World Cup in 2002. This is the first time it will be held outside of the American or European continents.

Japanese Soccer Team
日本代表チーム

Comprised of the elite, selected from the ranks of the Japanese players.

日本人選手の中から選抜された精鋭で編成

J2 (10 Teams)
J2（10チーム）

All teams are members of the J club. There are four round-robin competitions. Each team has 36 games from March to November to try and get into J1.

全チームがJクラブの会員。4回戦総当たりで、3月から11月まで各チーム36試合を行い、J1入りを目指す

Referee
審判

Class/Level

1級 ◀ 2級 ◀ 3級 ◀ 4級

Referees also dream of getting international qualifications and being selected to referee the World Cup.

審判の夢も国際審判員の資格を得てワールドカップのレフェリーに選ばれることだ

Game regimen (for the J. League)
ゲームの方式（Jリーグの場合）

Two round-robin seasons were adopted in 1997.
97年からは総当たりの2シーズン制をとっている

First half (45 minutes)
前半戦（45分間）

Second half (45 minutes)
後半戦（45分間）

If the contest hasn't been decided…
ここで勝負がつかない時は

The game is extended (two 15-minute halves), and the game ends if either team scores a point (V-goal rule).

延長戦（前後半戦各15分間）を行い、どちらかのチームが1点入れた時点でゲーム終了（Vゴール方式）

If the game isn't decided in extended play…
それでも勝負がつかない時は

The game is called a draw.
引き分け

Points are granted as follows: (1) three points for winning the game within 90 minutes, (2) two points by V-Goal in an extended game, and (3) one point for a draw.

勝ち点は、（1）前後半90分以内の勝利で「3」、（2）延長Vゴールで「2」、（3）引き分けで「1」、（4）敗戦で「0」が、それぞれ与えられる

Reshuffle 入れ替え制

The top two teams and the bottom two teams are automatically reshuffled.
J1の下位2チームとJ2の上位2チームが自動的に入れ替わる

Schedule 年間スケジュール	
March to July 3月～7月 **J. League First Stage** Jリーグ1stステージ	March 3月 **Xerox Super Cup** ゼロックス・スーパーカップ
August 8月 **All Star Soccer** オールスター	**Nabisco Cup** ナビスコカップ J1 teams are matched in tournament games from April to October. 4月～10月にかけて、J1チームがトーナメント方式で対戦し、優勝チームを決める
August to November 8月～11月 **J. League Second Stage** Jリーグ2ndステージ	
December 12月 **The Championship** チャンピオンシップ	January 1月 **The Emperor's Cup** 天皇杯

J. Leaguers' yearly salary
選手の年俸

There are three parts to a J-Leaguer's yearly salary. There's the base salary, money for appearing in a game, and fringe benefits (victory bonus). Of course, players have to appear in games and win to earn a living.

Jリーガーの年俸は、基本給＋出場給＋特別給（勝利ボーナス）の3本立て。当然のことながら、ゲームに出て勝たなければ稼げないのである

プロゴルフ界のしくみ

　プロゴルファーは、プロゴルフ協会（PGA）が認定する資格である。わが国には、日本プロゴルフ協会と日本女子プロゴルフ協会があり、それぞれ厳しい認定基準がある。プロゴルファーには、プロショップを経営するクラブ・プロ、ゴルフ場や練習場でアマチュアに指導をして収入を得るレッスン・プロ、ツアー・トーナメントに出場して賞金を稼ぐツアー・プロの3種がある。1999年からトーナメント部門が、日本ゴルフツアー機構として独立した。

Qualifying for the elimination rounds authorized by JPGA
JPGA認定プロテスト出場資格

The competitions

Qualified trainees
ゴルフ研修生として受験資格を獲得した人

Amateurs who performed well in the amateur competitions.
アマチュア競技大会で優秀な実績をあげた人

Players, including Japanese, who are granted licenses from other countries.
他国のPGAライセンスを取得した人（日本人を含む）

People with a handicap of three or less as officially recognized by the JGA, R&A and USGA.
JGA・R&A・USGAのハンディキャップ3までの人

Others approved by the JGA.
その他、JGAが承認した人

Professional Golf

A professional golfer is authorized by the Professional Golfers' Association (PGA). In Japan there are two associations: the Japan Professional Golfers' Association (JPGA) and the Japan Ladies Professional Golf Association (JLPGA). Each association has strict standards for authorization. There are three types of professional golfers; 1) club pros, who run pro-shops; 2) teaching pros, teaching amateurs on the course or at driving ranges; and 3) tour pros, who compete for prizes on the circuit. The tour pro category, as the Japan Golf Tour Organization, has been independent since 1999.

The path to becoming a professional golfer
プロゴルファーになるまで

Pre-elimination round
プレ予選

First elimination round
第1次予選

Second elimination round
第2次予選

Final elimination round
最終テスト

Training seminar for the qualifiers
合格者研修セミナー

At each stage special consideration is given to a players' performance as an amateur, training competition record, and whether the player has a overseas tour license or not.

各段階には、アマチュア時代の実績や研修会の成績、海外ツアーライセンスの有無によって予選免除制度がある

プロゴルフ界のしくみ……2

JPGA tour
JPGAツアー

First stage
第1次ステージ

⬇ 72 holes　　72 ホール

Second stage
第2次ステージ

⬇ 72 holes　　72 ホール

Final stage
最終ステージ

108 holes　　108 ホール

Japan Golf Tour tournament
ジャパンゴルフツアートーナメント

Tour tournament
ツアートーナメント

Total amount of the prizes is more than 50 million yen, 72 holes in 4 days
賞金総額5000万円以上、4日間制72ホール

Challenge tournament
チャレンジトーナメント

10 million yen prize, 36-hole stroke play
賞金1000万円、36ホールストロークプレイ

Pro-amateur tournament
プロアマ大会

Seed players
シード権

Seed players have priority in tournament appearances. Ordinarily, this right is granted to players ranked in the top 60 for prize money the previous year.

トーナメントに優先的に出場できる権利で、通常は前年の賞金ランキングの上位60位（JPGAの場合）までの選手に与えられる

"I did it! I can appear in the regular tours for one year!"

やったーっ 1年間、常時 ツアーに出場 できるぞ!!

Prize money ranking
賞金ランキング

1位

60位
61位

"I gotta climb out of the elimination rounds."

予選会から はい上がって こなくっちゃ!!

Seed plays are limited to the top 50 for the JLPGA.

女子プロの場合は上位50位まで

The Japan Series ゴルフ日本シリーズ

This is the annual year-end climax of professional golf. Winners of official competitions and players ranked in the top 20 for prize money compete with each other.

毎年、年末に開催される日本ゴルフ界のトップ・イベント。公式戦の優勝者と賞金ランク20位までの選手が日本一を争う

ゴルフ日本シリーズ

ツアー 優勝者

賞金ランク 20位以上

競馬界のしくみ

　中央の騎手は原則として地方競馬には騎乗できない。その逆も同様である。最近は若い女性で賑わう競馬界だが、女性騎手は中央競馬では1996年春にようやく3名がデビューしたところだ。一方、馬のトレードは盛んに行われているが、地方から中央には移籍できても、中央競馬の馬が一度地方に移籍すると、もう二度と中央競馬には戻れないことになっている。

　勝ち馬投票券の購入に関しては、八枠連複制に加えて1頭1枠制（いわゆる馬連）がすっかり定着している。

National racing
中央競馬

Special corporation
Japan Racing Association
特殊法人　日本中央競馬会

10 locations throughout the country
全国に10か所の競馬場

Shared locations in Sapporo and Niigata
札幌・新潟（併用）

Regional public racing
地方競馬

Local government
地方自治体

30 locations throughout the country
全国30か所で開催

Horseracing

Jockeys belonging to the Japan Racing Association cannot, in principle, participate in regional races, and neither can regional jockeys participate in central races. With the popularity of horseracing among women in recent years, the first three female jockeys made their appearance in the spring of 1996. While horses are actively traded, regional horses can be registered for central races, but once horses have entered a central event, they cannot return to the regional races.

The two most common types of winning ticket are the eight-frame type and a one-horse one-frame type.

Grade races 中央競馬のグレード（G）制

From 2001 horses' ages are given according to international standards.

2001年から馬齢表記が国際基準になった

G I 21 races
G I　21レース

G II 33 races
G II　33レース

G III 64 races
G III　64レース

February Stakes	フェブラリーステークス	4-year-old or older 4歳以上
Prince Takamatsu Cup	高松宮記念	3-year-old or older 3歳以上
Oka Sho (Japanese 1,000 Guineas)	桜花賞	3-year-old filly 3歳牝
Satsuki Sho (Japanese 2,000 Guineas)	皐月賞	3-year-old 3歳
Emperor's Cup (spring)	天皇賞(春)	4-year-old or older 4歳以上
NHK Mile Cup	NHKマイルカップ	3-year-old 3歳
Oaks	オークス	3-year-old filly 3歳牝
Derby	日本ダービー	3-year-old 3歳
Yasuda Memorial	安田記念	3-year-old or older 3歳以上
Takarazuka Memorial	宝塚記念	3-year-old or older 3歳以上
Sprinter Stakes	スプリンターズステークス	3-year-old or older 3歳以上
Shuka Sho	秋華賞	3-year-old filly 3歳牝
Kikka Sho (Japanese St. Leger)	菊花賞	3-year-old 3歳
Emperor's Cup (fall)	天皇賞(秋)	3-year-old or older 3歳以上
Queen Elizabeth Cup (mares only)	エリザベス女王杯	3-year-old or older filly 3歳牝上
Mile Championship	マイルチャンピオンシップ	3-year-old or older 3歳以上
Japan Cup Dirt	ジャパンカップダート	3-year-old or older 3歳以上
Japan Cup	ジャパンカップ	3-year-old or older 3歳以上
Hanshin Juvenile Fillies	阪神ジュベナイルフィリーズ	2-year-old filly 2歳牝
Asahi Cup Futurity Stakes	朝日杯フューチュリティーステークス	2-year-old filly 2歳牝
Arima Memorial	有馬記念	3-year-old or older 3歳以上

競馬界のしくみ……2

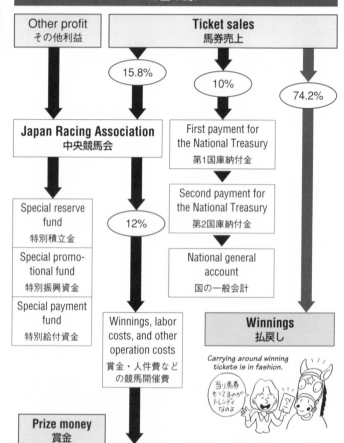

Flow of money
お金の流れ

| Other profit その他利益 | Ticket sales 馬券売上 |

15.8% · 10% · 74.2%

Japan Racing Association
中央競馬会

First payment for the National Treasury
第1国庫納付金

↓

Second payment for the National Treasury
第2国庫納付金

↓

National general account
国の一般会計

Special reserve fund
特別積立金

Special promotional fund
特別振興資金

Special payment fund
特別給付資金

12%

Winnings, labor costs, and other operation costs
賞金・人件費などの競馬開催費

Winnings
払戻し

Carrying around winning tickets is in fashion.

当り馬券もってるのがトレンディなのよ

Prize money
賞金

1st place (100), 2nd place(40), 3rd place (25), 4th place (15), 5th place (10)

6th,7th,and 8th place finishers receive participation payments.
Figures based on 1st-place finish with ratio of 100.

1着(100)・2着(40)・3着(25)・4着(15)・5着(10)

以下6・7・8着には出走奨励金が出る
（　）内は1着賞金を100とした場合の比率

How the return is calculated
払戻額算出のしかた

(1) Single win or continuous wins

Number of tickets sold × 73.8% / number of winning tickets sold +
10 = 100 yen return

(2) Place betting (1st − 2nd)

(Number of tickets sold − No. of winning tickets sold) × 36.9% /
Number of tickets on each winning horse + 83.8 = 100 yen return

(3) Place betting (1st − 3rd)

Using formula (2), 36.9% is replaced by 24.6%.

①単勝式および連勝複式

販売総枚数×73.8%÷勝ち馬に投票された枚数+10=100円当りの払戻金

②複勝式で2着まで支払う場合

（販売総枚数－勝ち馬に投票された枚数）×36.9%÷それぞれの勝ち馬に
投票された枚数+83.8=100円当りの払戻金

③複勝式で3着まで支払う場合

上記②の36.9%を24.6%にして算出する

Special payment
特別給付金

(5% of revenue / No. of tickets on each winning horse) / No. of winning horses

（売得金の5%÷各勝ち馬の的中票数）÷勝ち馬の頭数

The number of winning horses for single-wins is one and two or three
(except when there are dead heats), depending on the number of
horses in the race, for place betting.

勝ち馬頭数は単勝式は1頭、複勝式は出走頭数により2頭～3頭（同着馬のある場合は除く）

Stabler
厩務員 5%

Jockey
騎手 5%

Trainer
調教師 10%

Owner
馬主 80%

Distribution
配分

相撲界のしくみ

　力士をめざす若者たちは、なんと年間100人を超えるという。この背景には、50近くを数える相撲部屋がその興亡を賭けて行う新人発掘の戦いがある。外国人力士の増加も、部屋の乱立と決して無縁ではない。部屋には力士のランクに応じて、相撲協会から養成費や奨励金が入る。それが部屋の経営をうるおす財源になるというしくみなのだ。

　現在、力士総数は約1000人といわれている。このうち関取へ出世できるのは1割程度、最高位の横綱へ昇りつめられるのはせいぜい1人か2人という厳しい世界である。

Grand Sumo Wrestling Official Tournaments 大相撲本場所
Hatsu-basho (First Tournament of the Year) January, Tokyo 初場所　1月　東京
Haru-basho (Spring Tournament) March, Osaka 春場所　3月　大阪
Natsu-basho (Summer Tournament) May, Tokyo 夏場所　5月　東京
Nagoya-basho (Nagoya Tournament) July, Aichi Prefecture 名古屋場所　7月　愛知
Aki-basho (Autumn Tournament) September, Tokyo 秋場所　9月　東京
Kyūshū basho (Kyūshū Tournament) November, Fukuoka 九州場所　11月　福岡

The ranking of sumo wrestlers in a particular tournament will have been decided by a special committee within 3 days of the end of the previous tournament. In the case of ranking sumo wrestlers, it's the rule that they move up or down one rank, gaining or losing a rank with successions of victories or defeats.

番付は、本場所終了3日以内に番付編成会議が開かれ決定する。関取の場合は、勝ち越し、負け越し1点につき1枚上下するのが原則となっている

The World of Sumo Wrestling

The number of youths who join up to train to become sumo wrestlers has apparently topped 100 annually. There are nearly 50 sumo wrestling "stables," where the wrestlers live and train; and there's fierce competition between such places to discover new talent, something upon which their very existence depends. The increase in the number of non-Japanese wrestlers has also definitely affected the way the stables have become inundated with candidates. Each of the stables receive training fees and subsidies in accordance with the ranking of its wrestlers from the Japan Sumo Wrestling Association, and this funding becomes the financial source that enables the management of each stable to prosper.

At present, the total number of sumo wrestlers is said to be around 1000. Only about 100 can actually make it to the level of sekitori, or ranking wrestler, and of these the number of wrestlers who make it to the supreme rank of yokozuna is 1 or 2 at the most—such is the fierce competition in the world of sumo.

The new apprentice undergoes a check-up to see if he meets the standards.
新弟子検査

According to a new standard inaugurated in February 2001, he must be more than 167 cms in height, weigh more than 67 kilos, and pass eight kinds of physical tests.

相撲取りになるには、新弟子検査（身体検査）に合格しなければならない。2001年2月から身長167cm以上、体重が67kg以上、8つの運動能力テストが新基準に

Sumo training school
The new apprentice attends for six months.
相撲教習所（6か月間通う）

Jonokuchi: lowest rank
序ノ口

Jonidan: second-to-lowest rank
序2段

Sandanme: third rank
3段目

Makushita: lower junior grade sumo wrestler
幕下

317

相撲界のしくみ……2

Wrestlers above the rank of jūryō, or junior sumo wrestler, are all referred to as sekitori. They have attendants, and are paid a monthly salary by the Japan Sumo Wrestling Association, as well as receiving remuneration with every tournament they appear in, and a retirement benefit.

十両以上は関取と呼ばれ、付け人がつき、協会から月給が出るほか、場所ごとの褒賞金や退職金がもらえる

Jūryō junior sumo wrestler (has 2 attendants)
十両　付け人2人

Makuuchi (as many as 3)
幕内（前頭）　3人まで

Komusubi (as many as 4)
小結　4人まで

Sekiwake second junior champion sumo wrestler (as many as 5)
関脇　5人まで

Ōzeki champion (as many as 6)
大関　6人まで

Yokozuna grand champion sumo wrestler (as many as 8)
横綱　8人まで

Wrestlers who become yokozuna must win two grand tournaments in a row as an ozeki, or else have shown equivalent results. They will first be recommended, and the matter will be deliberated by the Yokozuna Deliberation Council, after which a decision will be made.

横綱は、大関で2場所連続優勝かそれに準ずる成績をあげた力士が推挙され、横綱審議委員会の審議を経て、決定する

Sumo wrestlers
平均

Their average height is 185 cm;
average weight is 154 kilos.
(September, 1998)

身長185cm
体重154kg（98年9月現在）

But the average size is getting bigger
every year.

年々、力士の大型化がすすんでいる

A sekitori's monthly salary varies from 957,000 yen for the lower
jūryō grade to 2,606,000 yen for the yokozuna grand champion.
A special fee is given to sanyaku and above. The tournaments
are of course shown on TV, and the prize money given by sponsors amounts to 60,000 yen per Kenshō banner, from which the
amount that is given to each wrestler is 30,000 yen.

関取の月給は、十両95.7万円〜横綱260.6万円（98年時点）。三役以上は場所
ごとの特別手当がつく。取組ごとにスポンサーが出す懸賞金は1本当たり6
万円で、力士の手取り額は3万円（引退時に残分支給）

The wrestler who wins a tournament receives prize money of
ten million yen, as well as many prizes which vary from region
to region.

優勝力士には賞金1,000万円のほかに、場所によってさまざまな商品がある

**The tournament
championship
優勝**

打ち上げ花火のしくみ

　夏の風物詩・花火は、打ち上げ花火、仕掛け花火、玩具花火の3種に大別される。なかでも打ち上げ花火は、そのスケールの大きさから花火の王様とも呼ばれている。花火の玉は、今も変わらず手作りで、打ち上げの方法も古くからの伝統に基づいている。

　手間と費用がかかるわりに、あっという間に終わってしまう花火大会は、ぜいたく極まりないイベントと批判され、近ごろは自粛する自治体も多いようだが、"ドーン、パッ"でせめてものうさ晴らしをする庶民感情も考えてほしいものだ。

How fireworks are made
花火玉の構造

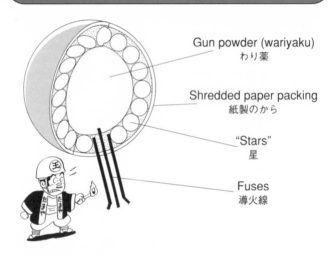

Gun powder (wariyaku)
わり薬

Shredded paper packing
紙製のから

"Stars"
星

Fuses
導火線

The stars are balls that emit the colors of the firework. The color varies and changes according to the particular composition and arrangement of chemicals.
星は花火の色を出すための玉で、薬品の配合で色が変化する

red　赤	strontium　ストロンチウム
yellow　黄	sodium　ナトリウム
blue　青	copper　銅
green　緑	barium　バリウム

Fireworks

The typical summer firework shows can be divided into three categories: uchi-age fireworks, which shoot up into the sky; shi-kake fireworks, which are attached to something, for example, to a post in the ground; and the smaller gangu firework toys (like sparklers), which can be held in the hand. Of the three types, the first is the most majestic because of the grand scale. The balls used for these fireworks are made by hand, just as in the past; and the way in which they are sent shooting up into the sky is based on traditional methods handed down from hundreds of years ago.

Firework shows involve so much effort to arrange and are so costly, that in recent years they have been criticized as the ultimate in extravagance and waste; many local governments trying to cut down on expenditures have discontinued them. These local authorities would do well to remember, however, that such displays bring a much needed sense of grand spectacle to the average citizen's rather less-than-thrilling life.

The size of the firework ball is measured using the traditional measurements of shaku and sun (1 shaku is 30.3 cm, 1 sun is a 1/10 of that). Some local authorities do not permit firework balls of shaku size, because of fire and safety regulations. Since the ball is made of paper, there is a limit to how much a single ball can hold: the 3-shaku 3-sun ball, which weighs around 380 kilos, is said to be the limit.

花火の玉の大きさは尺寸 (30.3cmが1尺で、1寸はその10分の1) で表される。防災上の規制で、尺玉が認められない自治体もある。玉は紙製であるため、重さが約380kgになる3尺3寸玉が、打ち上げられる限界と言われる

3-shaku
3-sun ball
3尺3寸玉

直径約1m
重さ約380kg

打ち上げ花火のしくみ……2

How an uchi-age firework is sent shooting up into the sky
単発打ち上げのプロセス

1 A cylindrical container is placed securely in the ground.
筒を土中に固定する

2 The end of the fuse is shaved down.
導火線の先端をけずる

3 Gunpowder is placed in the cylinder.
火薬を筒の中に入れる

4 The ball is lowered into the bottom using a cord.
玉をひもで吊りおろす

5 Gunpowder is sprinkled over the firework ball.
火薬を玉の上にふりかける

6 An ignited splint is thrown into the cylinder.
着火薬に火をつけ放り込む

7 The gunpowder under the firework ball explodes!
玉の下の火薬が爆発する

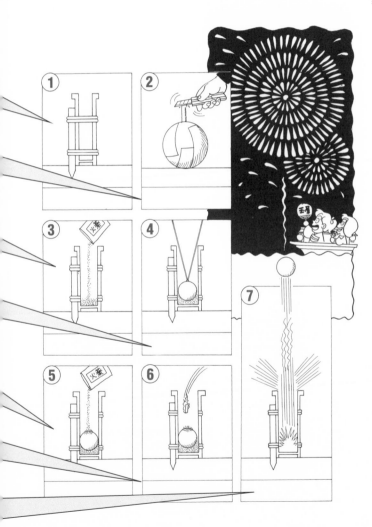

日本のしくみ[生活文化・社会・医療・娯楽・スポーツ編]
The 100% Complete Illustrated Guide to Japanese Systems:
Society, Customs, Health Care, Recreation, and Sports

2001年4月27日　第1刷発行
2003年2月26日　第2刷発行

著　者　　安部　直文

　　　　　テッド・高橋

発行者　　畑野文夫

発行所　　講談社インターナショナル株式会社
　　　　　〒112-8652　東京都文京区音羽1-17-14
　　　　　電話　03-3944-6493（編集部）
　　　　　　　　03-3944-6492（業務部・営業部）
　　　　　ホームページ　http://www.kodansha-intl.co.jp

印刷所　　大日本印刷株式会社

製本所　　大日本印刷株式会社

落丁本、乱丁本は購入書店名を明記のうえ、講談社インターナショナル業務部宛に
お送りください。送料小社負担にてお取替えいたします。なお、この本についての
お問い合わせは、編集部宛にお願いいたします。本書の無断複写（コピー）は著作
権法上での例外を除き、禁じられています。

定価はカバーに表示してあります。

Copyright © 2001 by Abe Naobumi and Ted Takahashi.
ISBN4-7700-2727-3

1 増補改訂第2版 英語で話す「日本」Q&A

Talking About Japan *Updated* Q&A

講談社インターナショナル 編　　　　　　　　352ページ　ISBN 4-7700-2568-8

外国の人と話すとき、必ず出てくる話題は「日本」のこと。でも英語力よりも前に困るのは、日本について知らないことがいっぱいという事実です。政治、経済から文化までモヤモヤの知識をスッキリさせてくれる「日本再発見」の書。

3 英語で折り紙 Origami in English

山口 真 著　　　　　　　　　　　　　　　168ページ　ISBN 4-7700-2027-9

たった一枚の紙から無数の造形が生まれ出る……外国の人たちは、その面白さに目を見張ります。折るとき、英語で説明できるようにバイリンガルにしました。ホームステイ、留学、海外駐在に必携の一冊です。

4 英語で読む日本史 Japanese History: 11 Experts Reflect on the Past

英文日本大事典 編　　　　　　　　　　　　232ページ　ISBN 4-7700-2024-4

11人の超一流ジャパノロジストたちが英語で書き下ろした日本全史。外国人の目から見た日本史はどういうものか、また日本の歴史事項を英語で何と表現するのか。新しい視点が想像力をかき立てます。

5 ベスト・オブ 宮沢賢治短編集 The Tales of Miyazawa Kenji

宮沢賢治 著　ジョン・ベスター 訳　　　　　216ページ　ISBN 4-7700-2081-3

「注文の多い料理店」「どんぐりと山猫」「祭の晩」「鹿踊りのはじまり」「土神ときつね」「オツベルと象」「毒もみの好きな署長さん」「セロ弾きのゴーシュ」の代表作8編を精選。ジョン・ベスターの名訳でどうぞ。

7 マザー・グース 愛される唄70選 Mother Goose: 70 Nursery Rhymes

谷川俊太郎 訳　渡辺 茂 解説　　　　　　　184ページ　ISBN 4-7700-2078-4

「マイ・フェア・レディー」や「お熱いのがお好き」という題名も、マザー・グースからの引用だったってこと、ご存じでしたか? 英米人にとって必須教養であるこの童謡集を、詩人・谷川俊太郎の名訳と共にお楽しみください。

9 ベスト・オブ 窓ぎわのトットちゃん

Best of Totto-chan: The Little Girl at the Window

黒柳徹子 著　ドロシー・ブリトン 訳　　　　240ページ　ISBN 4-7700-2127-5

小学校一年生にして「退学」になったトットちゃんは、転校先の校長先生に「君は本当にいい子なんだよ」と温かい言葉のシャワーで励まされます……バイリンガル版で、あの空前の大ベストセラーの感動をもう一度!

11 英語で話す「日本の謎」Q&A 外国人が聞きたがる100のWHY
100 Tough Questions for Japan

板坂 元 監修　　　　　　　　　　　　248ページ　ISBN 4-7700-2091-0

なぜ、結婚式は教会で、葬式はお寺でなんてことができるの？　なぜ、大人までがマンガを読むの？　なぜ、時間とお金をかけてお茶を飲む練習をするの？──こんな外国人の問いをつきつめてゆくと、日本文化の核心が見えてきます。

12 英語で話す「日本の心」 和英辞典では引けないキーワード197
Keys to the Japanese Heart and Soul

英文日本大事典 編　　　　　　　　　　328ページ　ISBN 4-7700-2082-1

一流のジャパノロジスト53人が解説した「日本の心」を知るためのキーワード集。「わび」「さび」「義理人情」「甘え」「根回し」「談合」「みそぎ」など、日本人特有な「心の動き」を外国人に説明するための強力なツールです。

13 アメリカ日常生活のマナーQ&A Do As Americans Do

ジェームス・M・バーダマン、倫子・バーダマン 著　　264ページ　ISBN 4-7700-2128-3

"How do you do?" に "How do you do?" と答えてはいけないということ、ご存じでしたか？　日本では当たり前と思われていたことがマナー違反だったのです。旅行で、駐在で、留学でアメリカに行く人必携のマナー集。

15 英語で日本料理 100 Recipes from Japanese Cooking

辻調理師専門学校　畑耕一郎、近藤一樹　272ページ（カラー口絵16ページ）　ISBN 4-7700-2079-1

外国の人と親しくなる最高の手段は、日本料理を作ってあげること、そしてその作り方を教えてあげることです。代表的な日本料理100品の作り方を、外国の計量法も入れながら、バイリンガルで分かりやすく説明します。

16 まんが 日本昔ばなし Once Upon a Time in Japan

川内彩友美 編　ラルフ・マッカーシー 訳　　　160ページ　ISBN 4-7700-2173-9

人気テレビシリーズ「まんが日本昔ばなし」から、「桃太郎」「金太郎」「一寸法師」など、より抜きの名作8話をラルフ・マッカーシーの名訳でお届けします。ホームステイなどでも役に立つ一冊です。

17 イラスト 日本まるごと事典 Japan at a Glance

インターナショナル・インターンシップ・プログラムス 著　256ページ（2色刷）　ISBN 4-7700-2080-5

1000点以上のイラストを使って日本のすべてを紹介──自然、文化、社会はもちろんのこと、折り紙の折り方、着物の着方から、ナベで米を炊く方法や「あっちむいてホイ」の遊び方まで国際交流に必要な知識とノウハウを満載。

19 英語で話す「世界」Q&A Talking About the World Q&A

講談社インターナショナル 編　　　　　　　320ページ　ISBN 4-7700-2006-6

今、世界にはいくつの国家があるか、ご存じですか？　対立をはらみながらも、急速に1つの運命共同体になっていく「世界」──外国の人と話すとき知らなければならない「世界」に関する国際人必携の「常識集」です。

20 誤解される日本人 外国人がとまどう41の疑問 The Inscrutable Japanese

メリディアン・リソーシス・アソシエイツ 編　賀川 洋 著　232ページ　ISBN 4-7700-2129-1

あなたのちょっとした仕草や表情が大きな誤解を招いているかもしれません。「日本人はどんなときに誤解を受けるのか？」そのメカニズムを解説し、「どのように外国人に説明すればよいか」最善の解決策を披露します。

21 英語で話す「アメリカ」Q&A Talking About the USA Q&A

賀川 洋 著　　　　　　　　　　　　　312ページ　ISBN 4-7700-2005-8

仕事でも留学でも遊びでも、アメリカ人と交際するとき、知っておくと役に立つ「アメリカ小事典」。アメリカ人の精神と社会システムにポイントをおいた解説により、自然、歴史、政治、文化、そして人をバイリンガルで紹介します。

22 英語で話す「日本の文化」 Japan as I See It

NHK国際放送局文化プロジェクト 編　ダン・ケニー 訳　　208ページ　ISBN 4-7700-2197-6

金田一春彦、遠藤周作、梅原猛、平川祐弘、西堀栄三郎、鯖田豊之、野村万作、井上靖、小松左京、中根千枝の10人が、日本文化の「謎」を解く。NHKの国際放送で21の言語で放送され、分かりやすいと世界中で大好評。

23 ベスト・オブ・天声人語 VOX POPULI, VOX DEI

朝日新聞論説委員室 著　朝日イブニングニュース 訳　　288ページ　ISBN 4-7700-2166-6

「天声人語」は「朝日新聞」の名コラムというよりも、日本を代表するコラムです。香港返還、アムラー現象、たまごっち、マザー・テレサの死など、現代を読み解く傑作56編を、社会・世相、政治、スポーツなどのジャンル別に収録しました。

24 英語で話す「仏教」Q&A Talking About Buddhism Q&A

高田佳人 著　ジェームス・M・バーダマン 訳　　240ページ　ISBN 4-7700-2161-5

四十九日までに7回も法事をするのは、「亡くなった人が7回受ける裁判をこの世から応援するため」だということ、ご存じでしたか？　これだけは知っておきたい「仏教」に関することがらを、やさしい英語で説明できるようにした入門書です。

28 茶の本 The Book of Tea

岡倉天心 著　千 宗室 序と跋　浅野 晃 訳　　264ページ　ISBN 4-7700-2379-0

一碗の茶をすする、そのささやかで簡潔な行為の中に、偉大な精神が宿っている——茶道によせて、日本と東洋の精神文化の素晴らしさを明かし、アジアの理想が回復されることを英文で呼びかけた本書は、日本の心を英語で明かす不朽の名著。

29 まんが 日本昔ばなし 妖しのお話 Once Upon a Time in *Ghostly* Japan

川内彩友美 編　ラルフ・マッカーシー 訳　　152ページ　ISBN 4-7700-2347-2

妖しく、怖く、心に響く昔ばなしの名作を英語で読む。人気テレビシリーズ「まんが日本昔ばなし」から、「鶴の恩返し」「雪女」「舌切り雀」「耳なし芳一」「分福茶釜」など8話を収録しました。

30 武士道 BUSHIDO

新渡戸稲造 著　須知徳平 訳　　312ページ　ISBN 4-7700-2402-9

「日本が生んだ最大の国際人」新渡戸博士が英語で著した世界的名著。「日本の精神文化を知る最良の書」として世界17ヵ国語に翻訳され、1世紀にわたって読みつがれてきた不滅の日本人論。国際人必読の1冊。

35 英語で話す「雑学ニッポン」Q&A Japan Trivia

素朴な疑問探究会 編　　272ページ　ISBN 4-7700-2361-8

日本にいる外国人と飲んでいて、一番盛りあがる話はなんといっても、「ニッポンの謎」についての雑学です。「日本の女性は、なぜ下唇から口紅を塗るの？」「なぜ“鈴木”という名字が多いの？」など、外国人が疑問に思う「なぜ？」に答えます。

36 英語で話す日本ビジネスQ&A ここが知りたい、日本のカイシャ
Frequently Asked Questions on Corporate Japan

米山司理、リチャード・ネイサン 著　　320ページ　ISBN 4-7700-2165-8

「世界市場で高いシャアを誇る日本の会社は？」「日本で最も古い会社」「日本の企業の世界での実力」「世界に通用する名経営者は誰？」「郵便局は世界最大の銀行？」など、日本の会社の人と組織について日本人も詳しく知りたい情報満載！

37 英語で話す国際経済Q&A 一目で分かるキーワード図解付き
A Bilingual Guide to the World Economy

日興リサーチセンター 著　マーク・ショルツ 訳　　320ページ　ISBN 4-7700-2164-X

不安定な要素をかかえて流動する国際経済の複雑なメカニズムを、日本最良のシンクタンクのひとつ、日興リサーチセンターが、最新の情報をおりこみながら初心者にも分かるようにやさしく解説。

40 英語で比べる「世界の常識」 Everyday Customs Around the World

足立恵子 著　　　　　　　　　　　　　304ページ　ISBN 4-7700-2346-4

海外の情報が簡単に手に入るようになった現在でも、日常生活での文化や風習の違いは意外に知られていないもの。世界各国の独特の文化や風習に対する理解を深め比べることで日本の独自性を再確認する本書から、国際交流の本質が見えてきます。

43 「英国」おもしろ雑学事典 All You Wanted to Know About the U.K.

ジャイルズ・マリー 著　　　　　　　　240ページ　ISBN 4-7700-2487-8

「英国人とアメリカ人はどう違うの?」「英国料理はなぜあんなにマズいの?」など、英国のナゾから大英帝国の盛栄、産業革命についての文化的考察、政治や王室のシステムまで、英国のすべてに迫ります。

45 バイリンガル日本史年表 Chronology of Japanese History

英文日本大事典 編　　　　　　　160ページ(2色刷)　ISBN 4-7700-2453-3

日本の歴史を英語で語る。意外に難しいこの問題を解く鍵は年表です。歴史的事項が簡単に引けてまわりに対する英語が一目でわかります。さらにそれぞれの時代の解説や、天皇表・年号表なども収録。日本の歴史を語るキーワード集として活用できます。

47 英語で「ちょっといい話」 スピーチにも使える222のエピソード
Bits & Pieces of Happiness

アーサー・F・レネハン 編　足立恵子 訳　　　208ページ　ISBN 4-7700-2596-3

「逆境」「年齢」「感謝」「ビジネス」「希望」「笑い」「知恵」など47項目のテーマを、短く機知に富んだエッセイ・逸話・ジョーク・ことわざの形式で鋭く描写。意味のある話をしたいときに、スピーチ原稿のヒントに、一日を明るくするために、実用的なアイデアが満載!

49 英語で話す「医療ハンドブック」 Getting Medical Aid in English

東京海上記念診療所 監修　黒田基子 著　　　336ページ　ISBN 4-7700-2345-6

海外で病気になったらどうしよう?──本書では、小児科・内科・婦人科などの科目別に、さまざまな症状を想定した「会話」と「文章」を対訳形式で展開することによって、英語で話さなくても指で指すだけで医者や看護婦とコミュニケーションできるようになっています。

51 「人を動かす」英語の名言 Inspiring Quotations from Around the World

大内 博、ジャネット大内 著　　　　　256ページ　ISBN 4-7700-2518-1

世界中の人々の心に焼きついている名言を、ジョン・F・ケネディ、プリンセス・ダイアナ、マザー・テレサ、アガサ・クリスティ、ウォルト・ディズニー、新渡戸稲造、手塚治虫ら、世界的に有名な現代人を中心に集め、その背景や意義を解説していきます。

52 英語で「いけばな」 The Book of Ikebana

川瀬敏郎 著　　　　240ページ(カラー口絵16ページ)　ISBN 4-7700-2529-7

本書では、いけばなの基本技術、基礎知識を中心にした花レッスンで、だれでも花がいけられるようになります。また日常の生活に役立つ花の愉しみ方と贈り方をビジュアルに提案しています。気品に満ちた川瀬敏郎氏の花とともに、「いけばな」がやさしく解説されています。

53 英語で話す「日本の伝統芸能」
The Complete Guide to Traditional Japanese Performing Arts

小玉祥子 著　　　　　　　　　　　288ページ　ISBN 4-7700-2607-2

外国人に日本の文化を語るときに、避けて通れないのが「伝統芸能」です。「歌舞伎」「文楽」「能・狂言」をメインに、「日本舞踊」「落語」「講談」「浪曲」「漫才」といった「日本の伝統芸能」についての必要不可欠な基礎知識と、会話を盛りあげるための面白雑学を満載しました。

57 「日本らしさ」を英語にできますか? Japanese Nuance in Plain English!

松本道弘、ボイエ・デ・メンテ 著　　　　256ページ　ISBN 4-7700-2595-5

多くの日本語には、表面的な意味ではうかがい知れないニュアンスや文化的な陰影がたくさん秘められています。外国の人が、それに気づかなければ、言葉を誤解し、ビジネスや生活で、大きな行違いを生み出しかねません。「ウソも方便」「けじめ」「水に流す」といった日本語を英語にできますか? そして外国の人たちに、英語でわかりやすく説明できますか?

58-1 全図解 日本のしくみ [政治・経済・司法編]
The Complete Illustrated Guide to Japanese Systems:
Politics, Economics, Law and Order

安部直文 著　テッド・高橋 イラスト　　　　　256ページ　ISBN 4-7700-2726-5

日本の社会システムがどんどん複雑化し、不透明になればなるほど、ものごとをすっきり、はっきりさせたいとは思いませんか？「いったいこれは、どうなっているの？」と思っている、日本に関する身の回りの素朴な疑問から、気になる仕事の意外な実体、わけのわからない政治・行政・経済・司法のシステムなどを"絵解き"でズバリ解説。学生からビジネスパースンまで必携の小事典！

58-2 全図解 日本のしくみ [生活文化・社会・医療・娯楽・スポーツ編]
The 100% Complete Illustrated Guide to Japanese Systems:
Society, Customs, Health Care, Recreation, and Sports

安部直文 著　テッド・高橋 イラスト　　　　　336ページ　ISBN 4-7700-2727-3

日本で生活するときに誰もが必ず経験する「身近なものごと」のしくみについて"絵解き"でズバリ解説します。家庭の中を見回しても、「確定申告」や「国勢調査」から「米の流通」「ゴミ処理」に至るまで、知らないと困ってしまうことが多々あります。そのような「日本のしくみ」について、簡潔な文章とイラストで、すべてにお答えする小事典です。

60 英語で話す「キリスト教」Q&A Talking About Christianity Q&A

足立恵子 著　ジョン・ベスター 訳　　　　　288ページ　ISBN 4-7700-2350-2

外国の映画を観ても、本を読んでも、外国の人と話をしても、キリスト教に関することがらや聖書の言葉が頻出します。たとえあなたが信者ではないにしても、キリスト教の基礎知識を身につけておくことは決して損にはならないはず。英語学習者にとっては、異文化理解のためにも必要で不可欠な知識かもしれません。本書は、これだけは知っておきたいキリスト教に関することがらを、やさしい英語で解き明かした入門書です。

62 まんが 日本昔ばなし 愉快なお話 Once Upon a Time in JOLLY Japan

川内彩友美 編　ラルフ・マッカーシー 訳　　　　144ページ　ISBN 4-7700-2881-4

「このはしわたるべからず」のとんちでも有名な「一休さん」をはじめ、「こぶとり爺さん」、「古屋のもり」、「屁ひり女房」、「たぬきと彦市」など、愉快で楽しいお話ばかり8編、集めました。

63 数字で読む日本人 A Statistical Look at Japan

溝江昌吾 著　ジャイルズ・マリー 訳　　　　　288ページ　ISBN 4-7700-2900-4

いま日本人はどんな状態にあるのか？どこにいるのか？どこに行こうとしているのか？最新のデータ・資料を駆使して、現代の日本人像を探ってみようというのが本書のテーマです。「仕事」から「食事」、「お金」から「心」の問題まで、さまざまな角度から現代日本人の実像を数字が浮き彫りにします。ビジネスに雑学知識に役立つ情報源の決定版！

64 英語で占う「あなたの運勢」 The Future Revealed: The Japanese Way

田中四海 編著　デービッド・F・ノーブル 訳　　　208ページ　ISBN 4-7700-2926-8

「手相占い」あなたの運命線はどこに伸びてますか？太陽線は見えますか？一番人気の占いです。「十二支占い」海外の友人の干支を教えてあげましょう。「風水占い」鬼門はどの方角？裏鬼門はどこで御存知ですか？「アルファベット画数占い」英語の名前も占えます。「九星気学占い」五行（ごぎょう）九星（きゅうせい）を使った中国古来の占いです。

65 英語で贈るグリーティング・カード Sweet Cards

講談社インターナショナル編　　　　　176ページ　ISBN 4-7700-2906-3

海外の友だちや仕事相手とのコミュニケーションの潤滑油として、グリーティング・カードは大きな役割を果たしてくれます。本書では、単なる米英のカードの決まり文句だけでなく、日本人だったら添えてみたい言葉、自分らしさを出す表現などを、豊富な実例と共に紹介します。

66 英語で楽しむ日本の家庭料理 Japanese Family-Style Recipes

浦上裕子 著　　　　　268ページ（カラー口絵 8ページ）　ISBN 4-7700-2962-4

日本の「家庭料理」が、近年世界的に人気を集めています。カロリーが低く、しかも栄養的なバランスのとれた、日本の「家庭料理」は、健康指向の現代人にとって、まさに理想的な食事といえましょう。本書では、日本人なら誰でも味わったことのある家庭料理を、海外や国内で外国の人に教えてあげられるように、また日本に滞在中の外国の人たちが楽しくつくれるように、バイリンガルで70のレシピを紹介しています。

実用英語の総合シリーズ

- 旅行・留学からビジネスまで、コミュニケーションの現場で役立つ「実用性」
- ニューヨーク、ロンドンの各拠点での、ネイティブ チェックにより保証される「信頼性」
- 英語の主要ジャンルを網羅し、目的に応じた本選びができる「総合性」

46判変型、仮製

1-1 これを英語で言えますか？　　学校で教えてくれない身近な英単語

講談社インターナショナル 編　　　　　　　232ページ　ISBN 4-7700-2132-1

「腕立てふせ」、「○×式テスト」、「短縮ダイヤル」、「$a^2+b^3=c^4$」……あなたはこのうちいくつを英語で言えますか？　日本人英語の盲点になっている英単語に、本書は70強のジャンルから迫ります。読んでみれば、「なーんだ、こんなやさしい単語だったのか」、「そうか、こう言えば良かったのか」と思いあたる単語や表現がいっぱいです。雑学も満載しましたので、忘れていた単語が生き返ってくるだけでなく、覚えたことが記憶に残ります。弱点克服のボキャビルに最適です。

1-2 続・これを英語で言えますか？　　面白くって止まらない英文＆英単語

講談社インターナショナル 編　　　　　　　240ページ　ISBN 4-7700-2833-4

「英語」って、こんなに楽しいものだった！「知らなかったけど、知りたかった…」、「言ってみたかったけど、言えなかった…」、本書は、そんな日本人英語の盲点に、70もの分野から迫ります。「自然現象」「動・植物名」から「コンピュータ用語」や「経済・IT用語」、さらには「犬のしつけ」「赤ちゃんとの英会話」まで…、雑学も満載しましたので、眠っていた単語が生き返ってきます。ついでに「アメリカの50の州名が全部言えるようになっちゃった」、「般若心経って英語の方が分かりやすいわネ」…となれば、あなたはもう英語から離れられなくなることでしょう。英語の楽しさを再発見して下さい。

---

4 ダメ！ その英語［ビジネス編］　日本人英語NG集

連東孝子 著　　　　　　　　　　　　　176ページ　ISBN 4-7700-2469-X

社長賞をもらった同僚に "You are lucky!" と言ってはダメ！　本書では、ビジネスの場面を中心に、日本人が「誤解した例」、「誤解された例」を110のエピソードを通してご紹介します。本書の随所で、「えっ、この英語なぜいけないの？」「この英語がどうして通じないの？」と気付く自分を発見することでしょう。日本人英語のウイークポイントが克服できます。

---

5 米語イディオム600　ELTで学ぶ使い分け＆言い替え

バーバラ・ゲインズ 著　　　　　　　　　208ページ　ISBN 4-7700-2461-4

堅苦しくない自然な英語で話したい。これは英語を勉強している人にとって永遠のテーマと言えるのではないでしょうか。そのひとつの答えは英会話でイディオムを自然に使うことです。なかなかイディオムを使いこなすことは難しいことですが、効果的なイディオムを使うことで、より会話はずむこともまた事実です。80のレッスンで600以上のイディオムの使い方が自然に身につきます。へそくり(a nest egg)、言い訳(a song and dance)など日常生活でよく使われる表現が満載です。

---

8 マナー違反の英会話　英語にだって「敬語」があります

ジェームス・M・バーダマン、森本豊富 共著　　208ページ　ISBN 4-7700-2520-3

英語にだって「敬語」はあります。文法的には何の誤りもない「正しい英語」表現ですが、"I want you to write a letter of recommendation." （推薦状を書いてくれ）なんてぶっきらぼうな英語で依頼されたら、教授だってムッとしてしまうでしょう。「アメリカ人はフランクで開放的」と言われますが、お互いを傷つけないように非常に気配りをしています。逆に、親しい仲間うちで丁寧な英語表現ばかりを使っていては、打ち解けられません。英語にだってTPOがあります。場に応じた英語表現を使い分けましょう。

10 「英語モード」で英会話　これがネイティブの発想法

脇山怜、佐野キム・マリー 共著　　　　　　　224ページ　ISBN 4-7700-2522-X

英語でコミュニケーションをするときには、日本語から英語へ、「モード」のスイッチを切り替えましょう。タテ社会の日本では、へりくだって相手を持ち上げることが、人間関係の処世術とされています。ところが、「未経験で何もわかりませんがよろしく」のつもりで "I am inexperienced and I don't know anything." なんて英語で言えば、それはマイナスの自己イメージを投影することになるでしょう。「日本語モード」の英語は誤解のもとです。

11 英語で読む「科学ニュース」　話題の知識を英語でGet!

松野守峰 著　　　　　　　　　　　208ページ　ISBN 4-7700-2456-8

科学に関する知識とことばが同時に身につく、画期的な英語実用書。「ネット恐怖症候群」「スマート・マウスパッド」から「デザイナー・ドラッグ」「DNAによる全人類の祖先解明」まで、いま話題の科学情報が英語でスラスラ読めるようになります。ていねいな語句解説と豊富な用語リストにより、ボキャブラリーも大幅アップ！

12-1 CDブック 英会話・ぜったい・音読［入門編］　英語の基礎回路を作る本

國弘正雄 編　久保野雅史 トレーニング指導　千田潤一 レッスン選択
160ページ CD (25分)付　ISBN 4-7700-2746-X

「勉強」するだけでは、使える英語は身につきません。スポーツと同じで「練習」が必要です。使える英語を身につけるには、読んで内容がわかる英文を、自分の身体が覚え込むまで、繰り返し声を出して読んでみることです。音読、そして筆写という、いわば英語の筋肉トレーニングを自分自身でやっていて、初めて英語の基礎回路が自分のなかに構築出来るのです。中学1、2生用の英語教科書から選び抜いた12レッスンで、「読める英語」を「使える英語」に変えてしまいましょう。まずは3カ月、だまされたと思って練習してみると、確かな身体の変化にきっと驚くことでしょう。

12-2 CDブック 英会話・ぜったい・音読　頭の中に英語回路を作る本

國弘正雄 編　千田潤一 トレーニング指導　144ページ CD (40分)付　ISBN 4-7700-2459-2

英語を身につけるには、英語の基礎回路を作ることが先決です。家を建てる際、基礎工事をすることなしに、柱を立てたり、屋根を作るなんてことはしないはずです。英語もこれと同じです。基礎回路が出来ていない段階で、雑多な新しい知識を吸収しようとしても、ざるで水をすくうようなものです。単語や構文などをいくら覚えたとしても、実際の場面では自由には使えません。英語を身体で覚える…、それは、何と言っても音読です。本書には、中学3年生用の文部省認定済み英語教科書7冊から、成人の英語トレーニングに適した12レッスンを厳選して収録しました。だまされたと思って、まずは3ヵ月続けてみてください。確かな身体の変化にきっと驚かれることでしょう。

12-3 CDブック 英会話・ぜったい・音読［挑戦編］　英語の上級回路を作る本

國弘正雄 編　千田潤一 トレーニング指導　160ページ CD (45分)付　ISBN 4-7700-2784-2

「使える英語」を身につけるには、徹底的に足腰を鍛える必要があります。「分かる」と「使える」は大違いです。「分かる」だけでは使える英語はぜったいに身につきません。「分かる英語」を「使える英語」にするには、スポーツと同じで、「練習」が欠かせません。そのためには、何と言っても音読です。日常会話はできるけど、交渉や説得はなかなか…、そんな方のため、高校1年生用の文部省検定済み英語教科書から10レッスンを厳選しました。まずは3カ月、本書でトレーニングしてみると、確かな身体の変化にきっと驚かれることでしょう。

15-1 AorB？ ネイティブ英語　日本人の勘違い150パターン

ジェームス・M・バーダマン著　　　　　　　192ページ　ISBN 4-7700-2708-7

日本人英語には共通の「アキレス腱」があります。アメリカ人の筆者が、身近でもっとも頻繁に見聞きする、日本人英語の間違い・勘違いを約150例、一挙にまとめて解説しました。間違いを指摘し、背景を解説するだけでなく、実践的な例文、関連表現も盛り込みましたので、日本人共通の弱点を克服できます。これらの150パターンさえ気をつければ、あなたの英語がグンと通じるようになることでしょう。

15-2 AorB？ ネイティブ英語 II　どっちが正しい、この英語？

ジェームス・M・バーダマン 著　　　　　　　　　　192ページ　ISBN 4-7700-2921-7

初心者・上級者にかかわらず、日本人英語には特有の間違いがあります。第Ⅰ巻に引き続き、そんな日本人英語特有の間違い例を、さらに140パターン紹介しました。間違いを紹介するだけでなく、その間違いや勘違いがどうして生じたのかを、ネイティブの観点から、日本人向けに解説してあります。これら日本人共通の弱点を克服すれば、英語の間違いを格段に減らすことができます。

16　英語でEメールを書く　ビジネス＆パーソナル「世界基準」の文例集

田中宏昌、ブライアン・アズビョンソン 共著　　　224ページ　ISBN 4-7700-2566-1

Eメールはこんなに便利。英文Eメールは、他の英文ライティングとどう違う？　気を付けなければならないポイントは？　など、Eメールのマナーからビジネスでの使いこなし方、さらには個人的な仲間の増やし方やショッピングの仕方まで、様々な場面に使える実例を豊富に掲載しました。例文には考え方をも解説してありますので、応用が簡単に出来ます。また英文には対訳が付いています。

19　CDブック 英会話・つなぎの一言　質問すれば会話がはずむ！

浦島 久、クライド・ダブンポート 共著　　240ページ CD（62分）付　ISBN 4-7700-2728-1

質問は相手の答えを聞き取るための最大のヒント！　初級者（TOEIC350〜530点　英検3級〜準2級）向けの質問例文集。英会話にチャレンジしたものの、相手の英語がまったく理解できなかった、あるいは、会話がつながらなかった、という経験はありませんか？　そんなときは、積極的に質問してみましょう。自分の質問に対する相手の答えは理解できるはずです。つまり、質問さえできれば相手の英語はある程度わかるようになるのです。ドンドン質問すれば、会話もつながり、それはまた、リスニング強化にもつながります。本書では、質問しやすい99のテーマに1800の質問例文を用意しました。

20　似ていて違う英単語　コリンズコービルド英語表現使い分け辞典

エドウィン・カーペンター 著　斎藤早苗 訳　　　256ページ　ISBN 4-7700-2484-3

SayとTellはどう違う？　最新の生きている英語　使い分け辞典　英語には英和辞書を引いても、違いがわからない単語がいくつもあります。そんな一見同じに見える表現にはどんな違いがあるのだろうか。どう使い分ければ良いのだろう。そんな疑問に答えるのが本書です。Collins COBUILDの誇る3億語以上の英語のデータベースの分析から生まれた辞典です。例文も豊富に掲載しました。

22　チャートでわかるaとanとthe　ネイティブが作った冠詞ナビ

アラン・ブレンダー 著　　　　　　　　　　　　288ページ　ISBN 4-7700-2643-9

最も基本的でありながら最も理解されていない単語aとanとthe。冠詞は最も頻繁に使われる英単語トップ10にランクされ、日本人が決してスペリングの間違いをしない単語でありながら、日本人の中で正確に理解している人がほとんどいないという不思議な単語です。本書では、冠詞の機能を単独にではなく、主語や動詞との一致、語順、文脈、話者の心理などから多面的に説明することで十分な理解と応用力が得られるよう工夫しています。

24　こんな英語がわからない！？ 日本人が知らないネイティブの日常フレーズ386

ジェームス・M・バーダマン 著　岸本幸枝 編訳　　272ページ　ISBN 4-7700-2830-X

とっても簡単な単語、数語の組み合わせなのに、どんな意味かわからない。ネイティブの日常会話では、こんなフレーズが飛び交います。難しい単語を覚える前に、実際に使われるこれらの表現の補強をしましょう。本書では、教科書やテキストだけでは知ることのできない日常的なフレーズの中から、とくに日本人の盲点となっているものを厳選して、詳しい解説と会話例をつけて紹介しました。これがわかれば気分はネイティブです。

25　英語で電話をかける　これだけは必要これだけで十分

ブライアン・アズビョンソン、田中宏昌 共著　　224ページ　ISBN 4-7700-2835-0

言葉だけで意志を伝えるのは難しい。それが英語ならなおさらです。電話でのコミュニケーションが難しいのは、表情などが伝わらないからです。しかし、電話の会話にもそれなりのコミュニケーションのストラテジーがあるのです。それさえ理解すれば、それほど苦労せずに電話を使いこなすことができます。効果的なフレーズが豊富に掲載されていますので、ビジネスにプライベートに、様々な場面ですぐに活用ができます。

27 謎の英単語230　日本人にはわからない「裏」の意味

ボイエ・デ・メンテ、松本道弘 共著　　　　　256ページ　ISBN 4-7700-2883-0

一見とても簡単そうなのに、どうにも意味がわからない、そんな単語や熟語が、現代英語にはたくさんあります。それがLoaded English（多彩な意味をもつ、含みのある英語）です。これらは、欧米の英語では日常的に使われているものの、日本にはない文化や発想のために、たいていの日本人には理解しづらいのです。でも、そうしたパワフルで、人気が高く、そして味のある、230のLoaded Englishを厳選し、その背景と本当の意味と、実際の使われ方を説明してあります。現代英語のキーワードが使いこなせるようになる本書は、英文雑誌や英字紙や、さまざまなペーパーバックを読む上でも不可欠のものです。

28 CDブック「プロ英語」入門　通訳者が実践している英語練習法

鳥飼玖美子 著　　　　　176ページ CD (23分)付　ISBN 4-7700-2836-9

「シャドーイング」「サイト・トランスレーション」「ボキャビル」……。本書では、通訳者養成課程で採り入れられている訓練方法の中から、一般の英語学習者が応用できる練習方法を、レッスン付きでご紹介します。「ビジネスで使える英語を身につけたい」「ボランティア通訳くらいは出来るようになりたい」……。それなら、自分の習熟度や目的を考慮しながら、プロがすすめるこんな方法で練習してみませんか。今まで苦手だった「長文読解」「リスニング」「要約」なども、この方法でなら克服できることでしょう。

29 「英語モード」でライティング　ネイティブ式発想で英語を書く

大井恭子 著　　　　　192ページ　ISBN 4-7700-2834-2

「英語で書く」時には、英語式発想の書き方をすることです。日本人の書いた英語の文章は、「文法的には正しいが、何を言いたいのかがさっぱり分からない！」としばしば指摘されます。文法的に正しいことは、もちろん望ましいことですが、英語で書く時には英語式考え方で書かなければ、せっかく書いた企画書やレポートも読んでもらえません。英語を書くためには、「英語式書き方」の基本をまず身につけましょう。「英語で書く」を通じて、英語式発想の方法を身につけたら、英会話やプレゼンテーションだって、後はその応用です。

30 ビジネスに出る英単語　テーマ別重要度順キーワード2500

松野守峰、松林博文、鶴岡公幸 共著　　　　　656ページ　ISBN 4-7700-2718-4

「実践ですぐに役立つ」、「知らないと致命的」、そんな最重要ビジネス英単語2500を厳選！ 本書の特徴：●キーコンセプト（用語の基本概念）を徹底解説●最新キーワードを含む2500語を分野別・重要度順に配列●同義語・反義後・関連語・頻出イディオムを併記●現場に密着した"生きた"表現を学べる用例を豊富に収録●MBA取得、TOEIC対策に最適

31 語源で覚える最頻出イディオム　意味がわかればこんなにカンタン！

マーヴィン・ターバン 著　松野守峰、宮原知子 共訳　352ページ　ISBN 4-7700-2723-0

英語を聞いたり読んだりしていると日常的に出てくる600以上の最頻出イディオムの意味と由来についてわかりやすく解説！ イディオムがややこしいのは、イディオムの意味と、そのイディオムを構成する１つ１つの単語の意味がほとんど関係ないからです。でも、その由来がわかれば頭にスラスラ入ってきます。例えば、**"let the cat out of the bag"** は「秘密を漏らす」という意味になります。今では、このイディオムはcat「猫」やbag「袋」と何ら関係がありませんが、何百年もの昔には関係がありました。猫を袋に入れて豚だと偽って高く売ろうとしたら猫が出てきてしまったことに由来しているからです。どうですか？ イディオムの隠された由来がわかれば、覚えるのに便利でしょ?!

32 ダメ！ その英語 ［日常生活編］　暮らしの英語NG集

連東孝子 著　　　　　192ページ　ISBN 4-7700-2922-5

帰宅した同僚あての電話を受けて、"He left the company." と言ったら、「えっ、彼は退職したの！」と相手を驚かせてしまった立野さん……。日本人が「誤解した例」、「誤解された例」、「日々の生活と交流の中で気持ちがうまく伝わらなかった例」を、アメリカ滞在歴30余年になる著者が、約110のエピソードを通してご紹介します。アメリカ生活を疑似体験しながら、日本人英語のウイークポイントが克服できます。

ビジネスに出る英単語

テーマ別重要度順
キーワード2500

"生き残る"ビジネスマンの
ための英単語集

ビジ単。™

松野守峰、松林博文、鶴岡公幸 [共著]

四六判変型　仮製　656ページ
ISBN 4-7700-2718-4

- ●MBAと実務経験をあわせ持つ著者が収録語彙を厳選
- ●ジャンル別（マーケティング、生産管理、財務・経理など）に分類、重要度順に配列
- ●見出し語：2,500/総収録語彙：10,000（類義語・反義語・派生語等含む）
- ●訳語を提示するのみならず、日本語の語彙そのものを平明な表現で十分に解説
- ●解説部分では国名・都市名・企業名を具体的に挙げ、ビジネス界のナマ情報を提供
- ●辞書的な解釈では誤訳となりやすい語は、ビジネス的見地から特に解説・用例を付記
- ●米語・英語間の定義の差異を明示
- ●重要略語は見出し語として採用
- ●検索が容易な英和＆和英インデックスつき
- ●見やすく、暗記にも便利な2色刷り